EVERY DAY IS DIFFERENT

Absorbing, the story of a full life and more, Ian McGill sheds light on service in the British Army over a notably complex period: from the Cold War's relative stability through to its unsettled aftermath, including operations at home, the Middle East and beyond. A deeply moral, decent man, he personifies all that is good about Britain's Armed Forces; no coincidence that towards the end of his long and distinguished service he was commissioned to produce a study into the Army's 'Spiritual Needs'. This is a fascinating account of his time, its ups, its downs, its richness: no two days the same!

Lieutenant General Sir Cedric Delves, KBE, DSO.
Former Commander Field Army.

A wonderfully vivid picture of the life of a distinguished and much respected Royal Engineer. Ian McGill's plain speaking insights, told with a human touch, provide an absorbing account of his childhood and subsequent military career, enriched with tales of family life. From the antics of maize-stealing baboons, the horrors of the conflict in Northern Ireland to the complexities of more recent military deployments, the book's title says it all. It is a most engaging read.

Lieutenant General Sir Mark Mans, KCB, CBE.
Former Adjutant General and Chief Royal Engineer.

This is a fabulous, engaging and heart-warming book, a soldier's story of a full life extending from a childhood in rural Rhodesia to retirement from the British Army as a Brigadier. Ian's story is beautifully written, full of fascinating detail about the family and colleagues who have enriched his life over a career that encompassed a number of the British Army's major operations during his service. I heartily recommend it.

Dr Robert Lyman, FRHistS. Writer and military historian.

I much enjoyed reading about Ian McGill's career and his fascinating experiences. His range of responsibilities was remarkable; from addressing arduous military, engineering and logistical challenges to dealing with difficult human issues. Above all, his respect for people shines through.

Professor Denise Bower, OBE. Professor of Engineering
Project Management at the University of Leeds and
an Executive Board Member of Mott MacDonald.

EVERY DAY IS DIFFERENT

IAN McGILL

Chalk Stream Books

ISBN (Paperback): 978-1-913012-30-4
ISBN (ePub): 978-1-913012-31-1

The moral right of the author has been asserted.
A full CIP record for this book is available from the British Library.

Published by Chalk Stream Books,
an imprint of Riverside Publishing Solutions Ltd
riversidepublishingsolutions.com

Designed and typeset by Chalk Stream Books, Salisbury, UK
www.riversidepublishingsolutions.com

Printed and bound in the UK.

CONTENTS

To Mary, David and Anna

PROLOGUE

"All we have of freedom
All we use or know
This our fathers bought for us
Long and long ago"
(Rudyard Kipling)

June 1972. I am in the Ballymacarret area of Belfast, close to the Short Strand bus station. A few nights earlier on the 28th May the IRA had attempted to plant a home-made bomb to destroy the Willowfield Police Station but found it too well guarded so drove away, intending to conceal the device in a house in Anderson Street ready for use somewhere else at another time. However, it exploded while being transferred from the car, killing the bombers and resulting in serious damage to most houses in the small street, adjacent to the bus station. Body parts were spread over a wide area. It took some days before the numbers and identities of the eight dead, four from the IRA and four local Catholics, were confirmed. A funeral cortege of hearses with some of the bodies is about to depart for the Milltown Cemetery on the other side of Belfast across the river. As the cortege departs and turns on to the Albert Bridge Road a crowd of jeering Protestant women lined one side of the road and sing 'Bits and Pieces' when the hearses passed them, highlighting the deep-seated hatred, fear and contempt between the two communities living in the same city.

June 1991. The detritus from the Gulf War in and around Kuwait City four months after Saddam Hussain's rout by American-led Coalition Forces is strewn everywhere. Minefields more than 50 kilometres long stretch towards the desert horizons; narrower belts of mines and wire obstacles clutter parts of the coastline. Destroyed tanks, guns, vehicles and randomly scattered dumps of unexploded ordnance and munitions, add a touch of menace to the devastation. Dark smoke plumes and the pervasive stench of oil from the hundreds of oil wells set on fire by the Iraqis, once they realised they had lost and before they fled north back over the border, extend over much of the city. The midday temperature is well above 45 degrees Centigrade. Lying among scores of densely laid anti-personnel mines are two seriously injured Kuwaiti boys who had taken a short cut through a minefield towards a beach where they had planned to go fishing. Both had stepped on PMN mines; each had lost a leg and suffered multiple lacerations plus other injuries. A sergeant and a corporal from the UK Explosive Ordnance Disposal Cell deploy as fast as they can to the site. The boys are conscious but in danger of bleeding to death. The sergeant immediately orders all onlookers behind cover. Fastened by a secure line back to the corporal at the minefield's edge, he crawls towards the first boy, breaching a safe passage through the mines. He recovers the boy along the approach route to safety before re-entering the minefield. He is now suffering from dehydration because of the high temperature but carefully breaches through more mines to reach the second boy whom he painstakingly retrieves back along the breached route, between other unexploded mines. He delivers the boy to a Kuwaiti medical team (now on site) and both boys are rushed to hospital. The sergeant later visited the boys in the hospital. While thanking him, one of them cheerfully exclaimed, "You mustn't worry about me; I'm fine. Thanks to you I'm alive and I still have my other leg!"

May 1998. I am standing by a mass grave in Eastern Bosnia, south west of Zvornick by the Cancari Road. The site is being painstakingly excavated by a group of people collecting evidence for the International Criminal Tribunal for the former Yugoslavia (ICTY). It is one of a number of secondary graves containing bodies and bits of bodies previously buried elsewhere and subsequently dug up by mechanised shovels and transported as mangled corpses and body parts in trucks in an attempt to conceal the bodies of victims murdered in the 1995 Sebrenica massacre carried out by the Republika Srpska Army under the command of General Mladić. The surrounding countryside is peaceful, but there is a stench of putrefaction and decay at the grave. The investigators carefully uncover, sift and collect body parts, bits of clothing, shoes and other items which will all be taken to a morgue in Tusla at the end of each day for subsequent analysis in order to identify the victims and trace where they were originally killed. They return each evening to Tusla, under armed escort for their protection, and soldiers from the NATO-led Stabilisation Force (SFOR) maintain a 24-hour presence at the grave in order to prevent any interference, so that continuity of evidence is maintained for subsequent prosecutions for war crimes. I struggle to comprehend the hatred and motivation of the killers who refuse to share their beautiful country with their neighbours, amongst whom they had lived alongside for many generations.

1

EARLY DAYS

I was born in 1946 in the British Military Hospital in Quetta, then in India, a year before it became part of Pakistan. It was a turbulent period and my father was commanding the 2nd/8th Gurkha Rifles having recently returned from Italy after the end of the Second World War. He soon became involved in attempting to keep an uneasy peace between the Sikhs, Hindus and Muslims in the Punjab during the very violent and bloody partition of India into India and Pakistan, after first moving my mother, brother Richard and me to safety in the Nilgiri Hills in Southern India. In October 1947 he helped rescue my mother's parents in Kashmir, isolated by the turmoil. They abandoned their home in Srinagar where they had lived for 57 years, leaving with just a suitcase each. My grandfather, Cecil Tyndale-Biscoe, had moved there in 1890 as a missionary and subsequently ran the school all that time. The Tyndale Biscoe School, named after him, continues to thrive at the time of writing this book.

In November 1947, my father left the Army after 15 years spent mostly on active service in Waziristan, Burma, Africa and Italy and the family were all united in Bombay. From there we sailed on the

SS Tairea to Beira via Mombassa and then travelled by train to
Salisbury, Rhodesia, (now Harare, Zimbabwe), arriving in our new
country just before Christmas. Sadly, my grandmother, Blanche,
died within a few days of arrival, having found the tension of her
last few months in Kashmir and the strain of the journey too much
for her. Grandfather Cecil died 18 months later.

A major influence for moving to Rhodesia was one of my
mother's uncles, Commander Teddy Tyndale-Biscoe RN, who as
a young man had joined Rhodes' pioneer column and who had raised
the Union Jack at Fort Salisbury soon after the pioneers' arrival.
After some years gold digging and fighting in both the Matabele
and Mashona wars he had returned to England with wonderful
stories about the country, which enticed not only my parents but
other Tyndale-Biscoe cousins to settle in this developing country.
Additionally, my father had served with Major Richard Fleming
from Rhodesia and a Black Watch officer during the War, who
had warmly encouraged him to move there and who subsequently
became one of his greatest friends.

I was of course blissfully unaware of all this. Neither can
I remember much about where we lived in Salisbury for our first two
years in Rhodesia nor the arrival of my sister Julia in 1948. My story
begins once my father started farming in 1950.

We moved into a small cottage on Four Winds Farm in Norton
where he worked as an assistant for a year, in order to learn just
enough about tobacco farming before starting on his own. He had
previously undertaken an evening course in Chinyanja, spoken
by African farm workers from Nyasaland (now Malawi), soon
after arriving in Salisbury and had become fairly fluent in the
language, which was a great help. He commuted his army pension
and borrowed money from the bank to buy a 400-acre plot nearby

which my parents called Swallowfield. While learning the ropes as an assistant he somehow found time to supervise the building of a house and rudimentary farm buildings on Swallowfield and we moved into a very basic new home on our own farm in time for the New Year 1951; my parents, Richard aged 8, me 4 and Julia 2. My father's mother (Grandmother Emily) stayed with us periodically during our first two years. She had been stranded in Jersey during the Second World War, with her four sons away fighting and her husband dying a month after the Germans occupied the island and had not seen my father since before the war. She moved to Salisbury shortly before we moved to the farm but sadly never adjusted to Rhodesia and returned to England in 1953 where she died a year later. I barely remember her but recall her once admonishing Julia (then aged about 4) for talking too loudly one morning at breakfast, saying "You seem to have rather a lot to say for yourself for such a little girl" and us all being amused by Julia's immediate retort "I've got a big mouth that's why"!

Before any land could be ploughed and crops planted the bush had to be cleared of trees and the tree stumps dug out. My father also had to borrow money in order to build the barns and sheds, buy machinery, purchase seeds, fertilizer, pesticides and pay the African workers' wages. For the first few years the lifestyle was pretty primitive; no running water or power, the loo a grass shack sheltering a wooden seat over a deep hole in the ground, bath water heated in a forty-gallon drum over a fire and carried by hand into the bathroom, lighting provided by paraffin lamps, water provided from a well. Two of the first essentials were a borehole and generator. In addition to the 50 acres of tobacco planted in the first year, my father planted 10 acres each of maize, beans, and monkey nuts, plus a number of fruit trees and eucalyptus (gum) trees. All the bricks used for the buildings were made on the farm. We had no tractor, so all the ploughing and hauling was done by cattle. When a telephone line was eventually connected to the house, we shared a party line with about a dozen of our neighbouring farmers. Our call was one short, followed by one long ring – repeated until we picked up the phone but we often rushed to answer the phone to find that the ring might be two shorts and a long or some other combination and therefore for another farm. Making a phone call could be a tortuous business as the line was nearly always busy with another user; one had to wait for the conversation to end before then quickly ringing the exchange and asking the operator for the required number. Anyone on the same party line could listen to others' conversations and there were sometimes amusing interruptions if an eavesdropper did not agree with the conversation he or she was monitoring while waiting for the line to become free.

At the start of the season around late August, the tobacco seedbeds had to be prepared and all traces of parasites and bugs were destroyed to a depth of 18 inches by enclosing the beds in plastic sheeting and then projecting methyl bromide gas under the sheeting for a couple of days. The now 'sterile' beds were ready for the tobacco seeds, which were mixed with water and sown on to the beds using watering cans. Some 6 weeks later the resulting plants were transplanted by hand into the fields; each plant was given a generous portion of water, a dose of fertilizer and a dose of DDT insecticide injected close to every plant to neutralize cutworms and other pests. We then all prayed for the appropriate rain, hopefully at regular intervals. As the plants grew the flowers at the top of each plant were picked off (a process known as topping) together with the small suckers on the stems, so that the leaves absorbed the nutrients from the soil rather than the flowers or suckers.

The leaves were picked (reaped) starting from the bottom of each plant and gradually working upwards over the ensuing weeks from early January until around mid-February. During the reaping season Julia and I spent many hours riding on the trailers bringing the tobacco leaves to an open shed, where they were tied onto sticks and stacked on horizontal wooden poles inside the barns to be cured. Throughout such periods the whole farm would be a hive of activity with the workers' wives also lending a hand and there was a constant hum of chatter, often laughter and lots of shouting of instructions or advice between the workers.

While curing, the tobacco leaves were dried out turning from green to a brownish, golden colour. Each barn had metal flues close to the floor, which were heated by a coal fire outside; separate fireplaces and chimneys for every barn. Damp sacks were hung on the bottom layer of poles to adjust the humidity. The temperature and humidity had to be regularly monitored to ensure that the leaves did not cure too quickly or too slowly, and each curing cycle took about 4 or 5 days. On removal from the barns, the leaves were graded into different grades in the grading shed; the lower heavier leaves were darker while the higher leaves were lighter. There were well over 50 different grades of leaf sold at different prices according to the market. Having been graded, each batch of tobacco was then pressed into bales by hand before then being sold at auction in the tobacco sales in Salisbury. These auctions which ran from around May to July were always stressful as it was impossible to predict the prices, but they were also very sociable and my father much enjoyed meeting up with other farmers to compare notes and swap stories.

The farm workers were nearly all from Nyasaland (now Malawi). Around a dozen remained with us right from the start and some of their sons also joined the workforce later. Numbers fluctuated between 20 and 30 throughout the years, depending on the seasons and they all lived on the farm. Some had left their families back in Malawi, but most had their wives and children living with them. They all had a small plot within a communal area where they built their thatched houses, kept some chickens, and grew their own maize and vegetables. As a child I was welcomed into the compound, about a mile from the farmhouse, and enjoyed playing with the African children, but we gradually grew apart after I started at boarding school. The farm workers were paid monthly in cash by my father and provided with a weekly food ration of mealie-meal (ground maize), meat, salt, sugar, beans and monkey nuts, all divided into individual portions and carefully handed out by Basatala, his most trusted worker. Those with families received a larger share than the single men. The Africans enjoyed drinking a local beer brewed by the longer-serving workers entrusted in turns to concoct the brew which they would then sell during a weekly party starting every Saturday afternoon and ending once all the beer was drunk, often not until the next morning. The success of the party was normally judged by the size of the hangovers and the redness of the eyes amongst those turning up for work on the Monday morning!

My father ran sick parades and treated the minor ailments such as cuts, upset or blocked-up stomachs, headaches etc., as best he could. He ferried the workers (and their wives or children) to the nearest doctor or local African clinic in his car – often in the middle of the night. He built and funded a junior school for their children, including paying the teacher's salary. The farm was run very much on paternal lines with my father providing his workers with everything they needed in return for their labour.

Often one or more of the farm workers would ask for credit, usually for something like a bicycle, or to pay for one of their elder children to attend a senior school, or in order to pay the bride price for a wife. There was a particularly quiet and gentle man, called Douglas, who was often beaten up by his wife, usually during a beer-drinking weekend. One day she went too far and almost severed his foot with a badza (an implement used for cultivating her patch of mealies), so Douglas kicked her out of his home and offered her to the highest bidder. Mrs Douglas was reckoned to be a pretty good cook and a month or two later one of the workers called Chingasama approached my father for some credit. When asked why, he rather shyly said he had decided to take Mrs Douglas on as his wife and needed the money to pay Douglas. When my father then asked how much he wanted, he replied, "Twelve pounds."

"Twelve pounds!" my father exclaimed. "For Mrs Douglas! Do you know that you can buy a brand-new bicycle for that?" Whereupon Chingasama thought for a while and then said, "OK, twelve pounds is much too expensive; just give me two pounds, please!!" My father was heartened by his farm workers' sense of humour but sometimes exasperated by their lack of responsibility. When he could eventually afford to pay for tractors, his tractor drivers would sometimes continue ploughing, despite symptoms of the engine overheating, until the engine would seize. They were always reluctant to check the oil or water, as they did not consider simple maintenance to be part of their 'driver's job'. Hence, he would have to supervise them every morning, ensuring that they personally carried out a 'First Parade' maintenance check of the tractors. He also personally had to check the temperature and humidity of every tobacco barn every few hours by night during the curing season, as the man he put in charge of the barns at night would often fall asleep. In order to make ends meet he took on an extra job for about three months each winter as the local agent for the Grain Marketing Board, responsible for loading and dispatching all the maize grown in the Norton area (destined for the Grain Marketing Board) at the local railway station.

My mother ran a small store my father had built on the farm that stocked basic essentials for local Africans and where a local tailor, made clothes that they could buy. She also helped supplement the farm income with selling eggs from around 200 chickens and fattening some 70 turkeys each year in time for Christmas. We also had a few cows for milk, a few ducks, a couple of geese, dogs, cats and, later, horses. Julia and I helped to collect the eggs each morning and afternoon and I well remember being attacked by a very-large cockerel jealously guarding his hens. As a small boy it was quite frightening because he would attempt to rake my legs with his talons. I soon learned that the only way to keep him at bay was to arm myself with a big stick and hit him as hard as I could whenever he came near me. After a few days he kept his distance, but I have since had a sneaking respect for cockerels.

The farmhouse was built very close to a large anthill, which also provided an ideal spot for snake holes. When it rained, the snakes often slithered into the house for a bit of shelter and we sometimes came across one under a table or bed, or in a tree or shrub in the garden. Many, including puff adders, boomslangs, mambas and cobras, were extremely venomous and we steered well clear of these, but had to kill them if we felt threatened. Surprisingly, one of our cats often attacked snakes when they were in or close to the house and dispatched them after a series of feints by suddenly seizing its neck in its jaws from behind, close to the head, and gnawing it to death while vigorously shaking the snake. This cat lived to the ripe old age of 17 and regularly produced between 2 and 3 litters of kittens every year until near her end. We had no idea who the various toms were, and my father had the unenviable task of drowning most of the kittens at birth, allowing the mother only to keep a couple of kittens each time. Somehow, we always managed to find homes for these once they could fend for themselves.

Our dogs were very faithful companions, doubling up as both pets and guard-dogs. My mother liked cocker spaniels, but we also had larger dogs. I was particularly fond of Carla, a great dane/ridgeback cross who we acquired almost as soon as we arrived at Swallowfield. She was incredibly gentle and astonished us with her first litter of pups, numbering sixteen! When she died, her place was taken by Joe, a labrador/collie cross and Winston, a bull mastiff/ridgeback cross. Joe was intelligent and knew exactly what was happening whereas Winston was stupid and boisterous. The spaniels were cunning at their evening meals and would bark loudly as soon as their food was placed before them. Joe and Winston would immediately rush off to frighten off the supposed intruder and, on returning some 10 minutes later very pleased with themselves, were always puzzled to see that the tastier parts of their share had vanished, eaten by the spaniels who by then had returned to their own bowls! When walking or riding on the farm with the dogs they would sometimes flush out a deer, usually a small duiker or steenbok but occasionally a larger animal such as a waterbuck. There would be frenzied barking from the spaniels but Jo and Winston would set off in hot pursuit, with Jo tracking the spoor with his nose close to the ground and Winston bounding off in the direction where he thought the deer was headed. We might catch a glimpse of the chase some minutes later; Jo would be falling behind but still on the right course, tracking the scent, whereas Winston would usually be running randomly completely in the wrong direction!

My father loved horses and soon acquired a chestnut pony called Gingerpop for Richard, Julia and me to share and a grey horse called

Flash who he rode with us whenever he could spare the time during our school holidays, usually early in the mornings just after sunrise. We would all set off together, my father on Flash and one of us on Gingerpop with the other two on bicycles, riding on the farm tracks and along bush paths with those on the bikes struggling to keep up when the horses broke into a canter. After every 20 minutes or so we took turns to change from bikes to ride on Gingerpop and would eventually return home some 2 or 3 hours later ravenously hungry and very ready for our breakfast. I gradually progressed and was then trusted with Flash but always found him a handful, although exciting to ride. He had a mean streak and would sometimes kick out and bite, so my father sold him and found a wonderful old horse, also grey, called Sigi. He was 19 years old and was much loved by a young woman who had ridden him since she was a child and wanted a good home for him. Sigi was a remarkable animal and soon had the run of the farm so that he could find the best grazing, because his teeth were deteriorating, and he was getting thin. One of his ears had suffered a previous screwworm infection and was deformed, so he appeared to be always slightly puzzled with one ear pricked forward and the damaged one folded over. He was very trusting and could be ridden without a saddle or even a bridle by just pulling gently on his mane. He looked forward to his early morning rides, and more than once tried to wander into the house to check who was up! He often joined the family at afternoon tea on the lawn where he would be given titbits and he once stole the show at a wedding held on the farm where he eagerly joined in the toasts by drinking Castle Lager poured into a large bucket by one of the wedding guests!

Richard was severely handicapped and away from home for much of the time, but Julia and I spent a lot of time riding together on

Gingerpop and Sigi. We occasionally entered a local gymkhana on another local farm by riding to the venue the day before, staying the night either in the farmhouse or one of the sheds and riding home after the event arriving home after nightfall. Very sadly Sigi eventually became so thin and weak that he had to be put down, when he was aged 26. The local vet was away and so my father had to shoot him while I held his head with him standing in a pit recently dug for him. Sigi seemed to know that something was up but he did not struggle and just looked at me with a quizzical gaze while I comforted him, struggling not to weep. As soon as he was shot, he crumpled on to his front knees and fell sideways. My father asked Rabson, the herdsman and gardener, and Basatala to finish burying Sigi and gently led me back to the farmhouse.

We had other horses after Sigi but none touched our hearts as much except Amber who was a chestnut mare, with some Arab and thoroughbred breeding in her. She was spirited, fast and exhilarating to ride. The railway line from Salisbury to Bulawayo ran along one of the borders of our farm, with a dirt track alongside the line, and we often used to race passing steam trains. Amber easily outpaced the heavily laden goods trains, especially when they were steaming up the slight incline towards Salisbury and seemed to relish the whistles from the train and the friendly shouts from the drivers and stokers. I also remember winning a bareback race with her at one of the gymkhanas, hoping that I would not fall off and be trampled by the following horses, but her silky smooth gait made it easy to cling on. Tragically she ate some grass contaminated by the insecticide used in the cattle-dip when a gate into the enclosure around the dip was inadvertently left open one day after the cattle had been dipped. She was poisoned by the infected grass, soon developed severe colic and became very distressed. I was away at boarding school at the time but my father waited until I returned home at the end of term to break the news that he could not save her and had called the vet to put her down. She was sorely missed, not only by all the family, but also by Gingerpop who was lonely without her.

Most of the time the weather was wonderful, with hot, sunny days and cool nights at an altitude of 4,000 feet but rainfall was never predictable. The rains normally started in November and ended in April and we seldom saw any rain between April and October. October was very hot whereas the winter months in June and July could be surprisingly cold at night with a few degrees of frost in the early mornings. We often experienced drought during the growing season as well as some tremendous storms when up to 7 inches of rain could be dumped overnight with accompanying high winds ripping off barn roofs and damaging the crops. Through hard work, a bit of luck and a friendly work force, Swallowfield became a successful farm and a very happy family home. My father later managed to buy another 400-acre plot 8 miles away, which he called Thornbury, for growing maize (with a richer soil – reddish in colour – compared to the more sandy-coloured soil at Swallowfield) and gradually switched from growing tobacco to concentrating on growing maize (some 200–250 acres each year) and raising around 100 head of beef cattle.

Maize was far less labour-intensive and simpler to grow than tobacco and my father was also much happier producing a nourishing food product rather than tobacco, especially when the evidence linking tobacco and illness became ever stronger. Our maize fields were each between 50 to 100 acres and the maize plants grew most years to a healthy height of over 12 feet unless there was a drought when they would all be shriveled up. Bushpigs were a nuisance and would uproot an area of maize and trample down the stems.

Baboons were also a menace and loved eating the fresh maize cobs. It was amusing watching them run away whenever we disturbed them; in their rush to escape they would steal a cob and place it under an arm, repeating this every few yards. Each time they raised an arm to stow another cob, the earlier cob would drop to the ground so that they would only have one cob stashed under their arm when they reached the end of the crop. Their bemused behavior as they loped off with only one cob, constantly looking back to check where the rest had gone always made me laugh. Fortunately, they did not trespass on our land very often, as there were other farms between us and the low hills where they lived some distance away.

The risk of bush fires in the dry season was ever present and we ploughed firebreaks around the edges of all our fields. Fires were easily started by someone carelessly throwing away a cigarette stub or by a piece of broken glass focusing the heat of the sun on to a patch of dry grass or leaves. My father also used to burn back the grass between the ploughed strips to increase the width of the breaks to fifty yards. Fires could move surprisingly quickly and sometimes burning embers would even be blown across the main tarmac road from Salisbury to Bulawayo bordering our maize fields. Fortunately, our firebreaks were never breached but there were some close calls most years, with our farm workers beating back approaching flames using cut down branches from trees and my father burning back more grass in the threatened area. My father and I were once nearly trapped by a large fire in some thick-bush and trees when returning from visiting a neighbour. We should not have set off and did not appreciate just how quickly the fire was spreading. We could not turn back as the fire had jumped across the dirt farm road behind us so had to keep driving with the fire roaring beside us along one side for perhaps only five or ten seconds until we broke free of the intense heat, dense smoke, noise and smell. It was terrifying, not just for us but for the wildlife also fleeing to safety.

Life on the farm as children was idyllic. There was always something happening, and we were treated warmly by the farm workers, who were remarkably patient with us. Apart from the farm animals we quite often came across a variety of different antelopes, mostly small duikers and steenboks but occasionally the odd waterbuck, kudu and even an eland once. We sometimes imagined seeing a lion but could never verify this. Rabson, the gardener, was convinced he heard an elephant, but it was only the water tank being blown off the water tower during a huge storm in the middle of the night. He had run from his house to take refuge on our veranda where we found him early the next morning, he was very sheepish when we went looking for the elephant only to find the damaged water tank on the ground. We were blessed with a large variety of beautiful, very colourful birds, butterflies and an interesting array of lizards, chameleons, beetles, scorpions, spiders, ants, crickets, centipedes, grasshoppers and stick insects. A large bougainvillea plant at the front of the verandah was festooned with weaver bird nests and we marveled at the patience of the male weaver birds who would toil away building nest after nest until, at last, a female would choose the one she approved of. We had guinea fowl and partridge on the farm too. I had an air rifle and Rabson was always delighted whenever I shot a pigeon or a crow, as he would take the bird home to eat. We had rabbits which would suddenly break cover when disturbed, sometimes running close to the workers who would all immediately stop whatever they were doing and give chase, shouting and whooping with excitement. Surprisingly they did sometimes catch a rabbit, confused by the hullabaloo and rushing straight into the eager arms of a pursuer who would quickly kill it and take it home at the end of the day for a welcome supplement to his weekly rations.

As a small boy I was fascinated by shongololos (a millipede which rolls itself up when threatened) and by lion ants – and spent many hours catching large matabele ants, especially any that had bitten me, to see if they could escape the lion ant traps. After rain, we sometimes were inundated for a short time with flying ants, which provided a feast for the birds, diving in and out amongst them and also picking up those that had shed their wings and were on the ground. I have already mentioned snakes and was once very startled when I accidentally stood on a puff adder in some long grass while walking from the house to the store, aged five. Fortunately, I was wearing wellington boots, after a recent rainstorm and the snake struck one of my boots and not a bare leg. I ran as fast as I could to the store, but no one believed me when I excitedly recounted the encounter – until my mother saw the small puncture holes in the boot with traces of the venom. There were also pythons about and one of our very young heifer calves was swallowed whole by an enormous python which we found lying very still, digesting the calf close to a track leading from the barns. A couple of the Africans quickly killed the snake by chopping off its head with axes amongst great excitement and then sliced open its underside to reveal the calf, still fully formed. I was amazed how the python managed to swallow something so much larger than its mouth and was forever wary of meeting another python!

As with all farms in Rhodesia, we had our share of pests; white ants, ticks, grubs and slugs, which were all, kept in check with various insecticides. White ants were lethal for any wooden building and would soon eat their way through wooden poles, unless they were first immersed in creosote. Ticks were endemic and we often found a few on our bodies after walking through long grass. We checked the dogs daily for ticks, especially around their ears, and also the horses. The cattle were dipped regularly in a cattle-dip each week.

Late one afternoon Rabson, while bringing in the horses to their stables, shouted an alarm having seen an enormous column of army ants marching steadily towards the farm buildings devouring every living thing in their path. All the workers rushed to intercept the approaching column and my father immediately instructed them to dig trenches, which were filled with a mixture of petrol, old engine oil, diesel, and straw and then ignited. The head of the column marched steadily into the first trench, but the following ants branched around it before being trapped by the fires in the other successive trenches. There were millions of the ants, and it was vital to halt them before they reached the chickens or any of the livestock. By digging furiously and lighting more fires, the enormous column was eventually destroyed just before nightfall.

In addition to riding the horses and our bicycles, we used to swim in a small round reservoir containing the water used for the tobacco seedbeds and play tennis on a clay court made by my father and which I helped maintain. In the late afternoons, my father would try and find time to play a bit of cricket with me in the garden or a game of tennis.

Sadly, neither he nor my mother had much time to relax as they were becoming increasingly concerned about Richard, once they realised the extent of his handicap. He had suffered a loss of oxygen during his birth, which resulted in damage to his brain plus the joints in his elbows, hands, knees and ankles. He was also very shortsighted poor chap. My mother initially refused to accept that anything was wrong with her first born and he was sent to a boarding school near Bulawayo, nearly 300 miles south, for 3 years from the age of 7 until the headmaster there finally admitted he could not educate Richard and that he needed special schooling. However, there were no schools in Rhodesia that could cater for Richard or others like him, so he came home and went daily to the local school in Norton for a year. My parents then found a Rudolf Steiner home in England that would take him, before trying a school near Gwelo some 100 miles from home and then another Rudolf Steiner home at Hermanus near Capetown. Everywhere Richard went he found it difficult to fit in and his severe autism was not identified until much later. He could not help being disruptive, intolerant and impatient, causing my parents enormous heartache and worry. They were determined to provide a better future for him and other mentally handicapped children in Rhodesia. Working together with a group of parents, they set about solving the problem and formed an organisation called Hopelands. My father was elected Chairman and my mother helped with much of the secretarial work. A generous couple donated a place intended as a holiday home for children in Umvukwes to Hopelands, which first started with about ten boys. Soon afterwards another location in Salisbury was offered by the Mashonaland Diocese and, later, two further homes were set up in Bulawayo and another near Salisbury. Both my parents increasingly dedicated much of their lives to mentally handicapped people, on top of coping with the farm. On reaching 21 years of age, Richard joined Homefield, the Hopelands home for adults close to Salisbury and at last became more settled.

My mother loved us all dearly but her constant worry about Richard took its toll and she (understandably) became obsessed with his uncertain future. Hopelands became her main focus. She worked voluntarily as a secretary for the charity two days a week in Salisbury and much of the rest of the week in a small room next to her bedroom, tapping away on her old typewriter with a cigarette hanging from her mouth (she smoked more than 40 cigarettes a day for many years and suffered later from cancer.) She had little interest in the farm and found it difficult to relate to the Africans because she sadly lacked a sense of humour.

She never indulged herself and generously encouraged and supported me throughout my upbringing, but tended to be possessive and often reminded me of just how lucky I was compared to Richard and others like him, brooking little disagreement with what she thought. For her, enjoying life was self-indulgent, while duty, dedication and service were paramount. I sometimes felt guilty when having a good time. It was, perhaps, just as well that I went to boarding schools from the age of 7 where I learned to be myself rather than trying not to upset my mother.

As I became older, I much enjoyed helping on the farm during the school holidays and got to know my father well, despite being away from home for 9 months each year at school. I grew to respect and cherish him the better I knew him. He had been a successful soldier, winning a Distinguished Service Order (DSO) in Italy during the Second World War with his Gurkha Battalion, but my mother did not like the Army and cajoled him to leave during the turbulence in India after the War. Having first tried selling life insurance after settling in Salisbury from India, he adapted far better to life as a farmer. He was instinctively friendly, firmly believing that one 'reaped what one sowed' and treated with people exactly as he expected to be treated himself. He had a wonderful sense of humour and told me captivating stories about his own upbringing in Jersey, his military experiences, the people he had met and the sports he had played. He was always stimulating and encouraging, setting and expecting high standards. Having lived through the Quetta Earthquake, the Second World War and the Indian Partition and seen how easy it was for people to lose their lives and homes, he never set much store in material possessions but placed far more emphasis on human values. He would sometimes take me with him on study days at neighbouring farms during the winter months when the farmers had more time to discuss farming trends and share ideas. I well remember one particular event where a neighbour had organised a meeting to explore pest control and to which the Minister of Agriculture had been invited, together with a retinue of civil servants from his department. About eighty local farmers participated and the meeting started with the neighbor explaining that that there were many kinds of pests in Rhodesia which threatened our crops and our livestock. He mentioned a variety of the pests before focusing on ticks, which he pointed out were "a very real danger to cattle, sheep, goats, horses, dogs and all our animals. There are many different kinds of tick including the brown tick, bont tick, red-legged tick, hard tick, soft tick and many other species and we spend a great deal of effort, money and time on trying to control these ticks. They are cunning, nasty and persistent ..." He paused, looking intently at the Minister and his retinue before continuing "But the most persistent tick of all and which is impossible to eradicate is the Civil Service Tick! Over to you Minister and welcome to my farm!"

My parents both encouraged Richard, Julia and me to read. Tales from 'The Jungle Book' and 'Jock in the Bushveld' were firm favourites. Once I reached 5, I attended kindergarten at Norton School, some 3 miles from our farm, for 2 happy years. Much of the time was spent playing outside the classroom, but I also learned to read, write and cope with basic arithmetic, encouraged by a tolerant teacher. During my second year there Richard (then aged 10) joined me, although in a higher class. He had spent the previous three years as a boarder at a prep school near Bulawayo nearly 300 miles from home but, because of his handicap, he could not cope and my parents hoped that life would be easier for him as a day pupil at Norton. Kids everywhere can be cruel, and Richard's classmates soon picked on him because he was different, and I often witnessed him being teased by the older boys and girls. There was nothing I could do to stop it. I confronted those doing the teasing, even throwing stones at them, but they simply laughed at me, told me to go back to my own classmates and carried on with the teasing. I was only six and no threat to them. Richard was incapable of standing up for himself and I was too small to help him.

Aged seven I started as a boarder at Ruzawi Prep School, 80 miles away near Marandellas (now known as Marondera). The first few days were a little daunting as it was the first time I had been away from home and us new boys, known as 'Kippers' were right at the bottom of the pecking order. After only a few weeks in the bottom class I was suddenly moved up a class, because my reading, writing and arithmetic (thanks to Norton school) was ahead of my classmates, many of whom had not attended any previous schooling and so were starting from scratch. From being at the top of the class in Form 1 to the bottom of the class in Form 2 with 20 other older boys, who had already been together for the previous year, was a rude awakening. I gradually found my feet, made good friends with my new classmates and in time caught up with them.

The overall ambience of Ruzawi was impressive with Cape Dutch style buildings and appealing grounds, surrounded by attractive bush countryside. Maurice Carver, one of the original founders of the school in the 1920s, was the Headmaster. He was a kind man who knew all the boys well and had recruited some very dedicated teachers. Life at the school was robust with early morning swims at 6 o'clock before breakfast, plenty of sport, firm discipline and regular homework, with a strong ethos of encouragement to "always do your best and try your hardest". There were about 120 boys. Many were sons of farmers in Southern Rhodesia and all were pretty self-reliant. The dormitories and classrooms were spartan, but we had everything we needed. We were given an 'English old-style' education, learning Maths, English, French, Latin, History, Geography, Divinity – but no African languages such as Shona or Ndebele, although we were taught about the Zulu Wars, the Boer War, the Mashona and Matabele Rebellions and the early pioneers in Southern Rhodesia.

Games and physical activity were strongly encouraged, I especially enjoyed cricket, achieving unexpected success as an opening bowler. Unexpected because I bowled off the wrong foot, stubbornly refusing to modify my action, but it seemed to surprise batsmen and I took a lot of wickets, bowling in-swingers and leg-cutters.

Every Sunday morning after attending chapel and writing a letter home, we would be escorted on a walk by a teacher or matron for one or 2 miles to a kopje (a collection of large rocks and boulders on a hill) where we were allowed to roam free for a couple of hours, scrambling over the boulders, climbing up the rock faces, throwing berries and wild fruit at each other and generally having a great time. Some of the kopjes had challenging routes to the top that could only be reached by climbing up rock chimneys and jumping from rock to rock high above the ground where a fall would have resulted in death or very serious injury. The teacher or matron would invariably be reading a book in a shady spot, away from us noisy boys and oblivious of our dare-devilry. We saw quite a bit of wildlife during these Sunday excursions. Dassies (rock rabbits), lizards, beetles, butterflies and a variety of birds were always around, and we sometimes encountered the odd duiker and steenbok. Occasionally we came across a snake sunning itself on a rock or slithering away to escape from us, but no one was bitten, perhaps because we were all wary of snakes.

While I soon settled at Ruzawi, my brother Richard was struggling at Norton School and the penny finally dropped with my mother that her eldest son was severely handicapped and needed specialist schooling. This was unavailable in Southern Rhodesia and so my parents decided to send him to a school in England. They were worried about him coping so far away from home so arranged to spend some 6 months in England near him, with a temporary farm manager looking after Swallowfield while they were away. They took Julia with them, leaving me behind for 2 terms and the inter-term school holiday, which I spent on a farm near Mazoe with a school friend, whose mother spoiled me so much that I did not miss my own family. When reunited with my parents, my mother noticed that I had picked up a noticeable 'Rhodesian accent' during their absence and decided that I needed elocution lessons to correct this. She arranged these with a large woman in Salisbury who had awful halitosis and who was also very bossy. I made up my mind to do the exact opposite of whatever this woman told me and was soon speaking with such a broad Rhodesian accent that I might even have been mistaken for an Afrikaner. My mother admitted defeat, thankfully, and the elocution lessons were curtailed.

I left Ruzawi aged 12 to start at Peterhouse, also near Marandellas and founded 5 years earlier by a Fred Snell, a Wykehamist who had been teaching at Michaelhouse in South Africa. He was an unusual man, keen to instill a traditional English Public School code along the lines of Winchester College. Somewhat bizarrely it worked, despite Peterhouse being in a very different setting from Winchester, and he was greatly assisted by a number of excellent teachers. It was an ascetic environment with an emphasis on 'team' before 'self' and 'not letting the side down'.

There were some 300 boys (rising to 350 by the time I left), all boarders in 5 different houses. I was in Ellis House where Anthony Mallett (known as 'Buz') was the Housemaster. An inspiring man, he made an indelible impression right from the start. He had served in the Royal Marines towards the end of the Second World War, but he never mentioned his military service. Tough, compassionate and multi-talented, he had played cricket for England and Kent, won a cricket blue and two half blues for squash and table tennis at Oxford and boxed for the Royal Marines. He took no nonsense from anyone but gave enthusiastic encouragement to all of us and took great pride in any of our successes in the classroom and on the sports fields. He really cared about our development. He lived with his family in an adjoining house to Ellis and we saw quite a bit of his wife Vivienne and their 4 young children. Nick, his eldest son, was a mischievous toddler who enjoyed being cheeky while we were lining up before supper, being inspected by the prefects to make sure our shoes were clean. He once grabbed a cane from his father's study and ran behind the line whacking us on the back of the legs, giggling with laughter. Nick later went on to play rugby for South Africa and coach both the Springboks and the Italian National Team. Anthony and Vivienne were both very hospitable and invited all Ellis boys in turn into their home for supper and games of charades and quizzes. These were always enjoyable, relaxed evenings.

We were expected to work hard at our studies and were given a great deal of homework (known as prep), which had to be completed before the next lessons. The focus on work and doing one's best, together with robust encouragement from my teachers, helped me successfully pass all my GCE O and A levels.

On Sundays, after compulsory chapel, all the boys other than those taking their exams and those in the sixth form were not allowed to remain in the school buildings from noon until 4pm. We collected a packed lunch from the dining room and were encouraged to explore the local countryside. A small group of us became interested in raiding honey from wild bees. We made our own protective gear for our heads and faces, using mosquito netting and old pillowcases, wore an extra pair of long trousers and used socks for gloves. The hives were usually located in trees and often near small African villages. We would ask permission from the local Africans if we could take some honey and the deal involved us sharing the honey in return for access to the hives. We would don our ungainly 'Bee Gear' and take turns to climb the tree, armed with a can in which we lit a small fire topped up with grass to generate the smoke which helped calm the bees. With a bit of luck, the climber would pull out some honeycomb containing wild honey (but also mixed with some of the hive's brood) and clamber down to the ground without getting stung. Most of the hive would be undisturbed but sometimes it would go horribly wrong and the bees would quickly attack the climber and anyone else nearby. Our homemade gear did protect us from the worst, but we had some uncomfortable moments. We found that the most effective way of dealing with an attacking swarm was to keep walking slowly through the bush and gradually the bees would disperse. Keeping calm also helped!

One of the boys was very keen on snakes, which he caught and then kept in his locker by his bed, sometimes taking them around with him in his pocket or inside his shirt. He amused the class once when he hid a harmless grass snake in a new teacher's desk drawer as a prank (before a lesson) that immediately brought the lesson to a sudden close when the teacher opened his drawer. He seemed immune to snake bites until one day an adder unexpectedly bit one of his fingers. His arm quickly swelled but he soon recovered after treatment at the hospital in Marandellas and the incident did not diminish his interest in reptiles of all kinds, but especially snakes.

After the O level exams, taken in the fourth form, there were another 2 weeks before the end of the winter term, allowing an opportunity for an expedition to the Chimanimani Mountains, bordering Mozambique. The highest peaks there are over 8,000 feet and the night-time temperatures were very cold. We were away for a week and spent much of this time in separate small patrols of 3 or 4 boys on specific tasks. The group I was with had to produce a detailed map of 2 of the Southern Lakes; beautiful, clear pools. We were completely on our own having carried all our gear there, including food and a large tractor inner tube and foot pump to pump it up so that we could float on top of the water to measure its depth at different parts of the lakes with a plumb line. The scenery was spectacular, as was the array of stars each night from our sleeping bags out in the open. Those few days amongst the beauty, solitude and stillness of the mountains, streams and small lakes, together with some fairly testing walking, were a great experience and I have enjoyed being amongst mountains ever since.

I played cricket for the school in all the age groups until reaching 16 when I then played in the first eleven for my last 2 years. I opened the bowling, which I really enjoyed, and was selected to captain the side in my last year. We played matches against different schools nearly every Saturday, sometimes mid-week, and also played some 2-day matches involving overnight train journeys each way. 'Buz' Mallett was very competitive and challenged us to develop our mental attitude and confidence, as well as our skills. He moved to Capetown to take over as Headmaster of Bishops (where he became very well regarded) and we were most fortunate that Sandy Singleton then came to teach at Peterhouse: another gifted cricketer and generous mentor who had played for the MCC and had captained Oxford University, Worcestershire and Rhodesia. Cricket under his direction continued to thrive and we won many matches. I also occasionally played tennis for the school during my last two years, ran the half-mile as the second string in the athletics team and was in the cross-country team. In the winter term I played rugby and hockey for Ellis House but could not make the school teams. A swimming pool and 2 squash courts were built once I had been there for a couple of years, which were a welcome addition. The only thing we perhaps lacked was a gym, but we had so much else, plus the wonderful Rhodesian weather.

Although grateful for my grounding and education, I was conscious that I was missing something. Peterhouse was relatively remote, far from any town. I loved my home on the farm but seldom met any girls and felt isolated from many of the experiences available to those living in towns and in other countries. I was shy in mixed company and acutely aware that there was a world beyond school and the farm of which I knew little and which I wanted to explore. I was living in a bubble and needed to widen my horizons; it was now time to make my own way, but I had no idea about what I really wanted to do with my life.

My father, with Richard (at the back) and me outside our home in Salisbury before moving to Norton.

The start of the first two tobacco barns The bricks for all the buildings were made on the farm.

The farmhouse in 1955, four years after moving to Swallowfield.

My father with Julia (right aged 4) and me (left aged 6).

The oxen were dipped regularly to kill any ticks they carried.

Ploughing a field using oxen.

A team of oxen hauling a trailer with recently reaped tobacco.

My father towing a trailer with some of the farm workers and reaped tobacco. Julia and I are sitting behind him on the tractor.

My mother along with Julia in a tobacco field, shortly before it was ready for reaping (harvesting).

Rabson was one of the first workers who came to Swallowfield and stayed throughout. He helped in the garden and with the horses.

Julia with Carla (left) and me with a spaniel we'd rescued – in the garden at Swallowfield.

Gingerpop.

Amber.

Winston (right) and Joe.

My father found time to play cricket with me whenever possible during the school holidays. Julia was roped in as wicketkeeper but was always more interested in the cat! The farm cottage is in the background.

My parents with (from left): Julia, Richard and me – 1963.

My father and me by a maize field on Thornbury (the other farm) – 1968.

My parents at Thornbury with Winston and Joe, by a healthy field of maize.

Ruzawi School, which I attended from 1954–58.

One of the kopjes (known as Parrot) climbed on Sunday morning excursions after chapel.

Aerial view of Peterhouse, my school from 1959–64. We had all we needed for our schooling and sport.

2

COLONIAL BOY TO SOLDIER

Very soon after arriving in England I had my first experience of the London underground tube trains. The scale of the network of interlinked tunnels, escalators and stairs, together with the crush of people all rushing for a train was in marked contrast to the much more relaxed Rhodesia Railways where passenger trains passed by our farm only twice a day; one to Salisbury and another to Bulawayo, plus a few goods trains. Having bought a ticket at Piccadilly station I sat down as the train pulled off and held out a hand to introduce myself to the person sitting next to me who recoiled in astonishment, said nothing and gave me an odd glance! Travelling in London was certainly very different from the slow and easy pace of life I was accustomed to back home where one had time to greet everyone. I was very much a simple country boy!

Having failed the entrance exam for Cambridge, I briefly considered applying for one or two other universities but was seeking independence from home plus adventure and instead applied for Sandhurst. I had to wait a few months before the Army's Commissioning Board at Westbury called me for assessment, but Nigel (my father's youngest brother then serving with the Royal

Marines) and his wife Margaret kindly invited me to stay with them in Portsmouth during this period and they and their children, Sarah, Malcolm and Johnny, warmly welcomed me into their home. I found temporary work unloading vans for Knight and Lee, a local department store, until called forward for the assessment. The various tests, interviews and group tasks at Westbury were a little daunting but everyone was encouraging, and I enjoyed the 4-day selection process. I was much relieved to pass and was allotted a place at Sandhurst starting some 6 months later.

I returned to Rhodesia by sea via Capetown and then by rail to Salisbury. I had been away for 9 months and it was wonderful to be back in the sunshine, catching up with family, friends and the farm. I spent a term at Ruzawi, teaching Arithmetic, English and French to eight-year olds and helping with sport. It was a slightly surreal experience, but I enjoyed the boys' enthusiasm and was helped by patient, older staff members. Most Sundays I escaped to play cricket for Norton Country Club, a team of farmers many of whom I had known since a child, against other farming clubs in Mashonaland. My team-mates called me 'Tanglefoot' because I bowled off the wrong foot and they enjoyed the surprise my action generated against opposing batsman. With their encouragement I was fortunate to be selected to play for the Mashonaland Country Districts Team against Malawi and then a Stragglers Team from South Africa, that included Joe Partridge plus the two Pithey brothers who all played for Rhodesia and South Africa. Given the new ball and invited to open the bowling I was nervous in my first over and was taught a salutary lesson by Tony Pithey, who promptly despatched my first few balls to the boundary, until I settled down and bowled better. Joe Partridge was far friendlier when it was eventually my turn to bat at the bottom of the Country Districts' order. An opening

Test bowler, Joe generously bowled me a slow full toss outside my leg stump for my first ball, but his next delivery was a fast in-swinging yorker that uprooted my leg stump! These few months of winter cricket were enjoyable and instructive. The matches were always competitive but also friendly and very sporting, with the added bonus of listening to farmers' stories over a beer after each game.

The weeks rushed by and after a memorable family holiday to Victoria Falls, Wankie Game Reserve and Kariba Lake, I arrived at Sandhurst in September 1965. There were around a thousand cadets at Sandhurst, split into three colleges each of four companies, and two intakes each year with 250 cadets in each intake. The commissioning course covered two years with three terms each year. The first term was an uncompromising introduction to military discipline. I joined a platoon of 23 fellow cadets in Alamein Company, commanded by Major Fidler, a Parachute Regiment officer. Our platoon officer was a large genial officer in the Cheshire Regiment called Captain Phil Oulton. Our platoon sergeant, Colour Sergeant Frank Corrigan from the Grenadier Guards, and our Company Sergeant Major Wally Hammond from the Coldstream Guards had the most influence over us, constantly driving us to become smarter and sharper with a blend of discipline, humour and encouragement. Another instructor whom I admired was Staff Sergeant Williams from the Royal Engineers who was a major influence on my applying for a commission with the Sappers. Our platoon became a close-knit team working hard for each other and developed a genuine respect for our instructors.

My fellow cadets were from a wide variety of backgrounds and included three, like me, from overseas. Graham Noble was a fellow Rhodesian who had already completed a year's training at the Rhodesian Officer School in Gwelo and had been selected to complete his officer training at Sandhurst, before an expected return to the Rhodesian Army. Benji Dorji, from Bhutan, was destined for a series of influential posts back in his home country after Sandhurst. Johnny Masaba from Uganda was a friendly, gentle man, who was sadly killed shortly after returning to his home country after his two years at Sandhurst in one of Idi Amin's purges. Among the rest of us John Ellicock went on to win the Sword of Honour, represented Great Britain (and Cambridge University) at High Jump, succeeded well with 7 Parachute Regiment Royal Horse Artillery and, later, with Burmah Oil; Graham Lilley played rugby for the Army, Combined Services and the Barbarians; Paddy Hughes joined the SAS and has always been a generous godfather to my son; Tony Moorby opened the bowling with me, both at Sandhurst and at the Staff College and I became a godfather to his elder son Mark. We all made friends for life.

The routine was hectic in the first term with a rigorous cycle of drill, weapon training, minor tactics, map reading, shooting, physical training, and signals, interspersed with field exercises in the local training area. The rest of our time was spent cleaning kit; our boots, shoes, leather belts and anything brass until they all gleamed – and our rifles which we kept in our rooms, with the breech blocks secured in a small safe. There was no escape from the confines of Sandhurst until one had 'passed off the square' which involved being judged smart enough by the Academy Adjutant on one's drill and turnout. For this, our first test, I was in a group of three including Johnny Masaba who sometimes had difficulties in understanding English, especially when the words were spoken quickly. We marched confidently towards the inspecting trio of the Academy Adjutant, Assistant Adjutant and Academy Sergeant Major, resplendent in their uniforms, and saluted to the left, to the right and then at the halt immediately in front of them. They inspected our turnout before asking each of us, in turn, a few questions to test our general knowledge about Sandhurst and the British Army. The Academy Sergeant Major asked Johnny something; "Yes Sir" Johnny replied. An eyebrow was raised. "No Sir" Johnny quickly corrected himself. A quizzical head was inclined (nothing said). Johnny exclaimed, "I don't understand Sir". The Adjutant then slowly asked in a cut glass Guards accent "What do the initials of the medal DSO mean?" Johnny visibly relaxed, smiled broadly and replied, "The DSO sign means happy motoring". The Adjutant smiled, nodded his head and said, "Congratulations Officer Cadet Masaba, correct answer." Johnny and my other companion passed off the square that day, but my saluting was adjudged not up to scratch, so I had to return the following week for another inspection, before I was allowed out of the grounds.

There was a compulsory cross-country race for the junior intake shortly after we arrived, where three of us in our platoon ran well and were then automatically detailed to represent the Sandhurst second eight each Wednesday and Saturday afternoon. There was no option of declining the honour as all teams were nominated on Academy Orders, which had to be obeyed! One afternoon a Captain from another platoon who was involved with the Drag Hunt conned two of us runners (Geoff Mathews and me) plus Johnny Masaba to help him out by acting as the fox for a drag meeting the following week. He drove us to the intended venue and quickly walked us around a route of about nine miles through a number of different farms, around hedges, across fields and small streams and we then drew lots to decide the running order. I would run the first leg, Johnny the second and Geoff the last leg. On the afternoon of the meet the following week we were driven to the start to find the riders expectantly waiting for us while having a drink. They impatiently asked us to hurry up. I quickly picked up a scented bag tied to a rope and started running, dragging the rope behind me. After about 10 minutes I heard the hounds barking and realised that they would soon catch me, so I picked up the bag for the next few hundred yards before dragging it again. The break in the trail allowed me to get away from the hounds but I heard them again in the distance as I handed over to Johnny. He shot off very fast, worried that the hounds might catch him, while I made my way back to the start. Some two hours later Johnny and Geoff arrived with the rather disgruntled riders following them. It transpired that Johnny had forgotten the route, which was not surprising as we had only walked it once and did not have a map. With the hounds rapidly gaining on him, he sensibly climbed a tree until the riders called off the dogs, rescued him and sent him on his way again. We were invited to turn out again for future drags but, unsurprisingly, we declined.

Our first overnight exercise in the local training area in early November was bitterly cold with sleet and snow. Having dug in on a defensive position and before setting out on a night recce patrol I mentioned to my trench mate (Paddy Hughes) how cold it was. He agreed, before wriggling into the part of the trench with overhead cover and reemerging with a jersey, which he passed to me. I put this on but then realised that he had taken off the jersey that he had been wearing in order that I should have it. I was both touched and embarrassed by his unselfish generosity; he reckoned that he was more accustomed to the cold than I was because I had been brought up in Africa. Paddy's gesture typified the spirit of teamwork and mutual support within our platoon throughout our training.

The 11th November 1965 was the day we finished this short exercise. On our arrival back at Sandhurst I was told the unexpected news that Ian Smith, Prime Minister of Rhodesia, had unilaterally declared independence (UDI) from Great Britain. I was very disappointed; concerned about Rhodesia's future and worried about my parents on the farm. I had been aware of the tensions between Ian Smith and Harold Wilson and the mood among quite a number of whites in Rhodesia, who were becoming annoyed and frustrated that Rhodesia had not been granted independence whereas Zambia and Nyasaland (now Malawi) and former partners in the Federation were now governing themselves. I was also well aware that the black Africans expected and demanded a larger stake in their country and their growing impatience at being denied 'One Man One Vote'. But I had always imagined that Rhodesia and Britain would reach an agreement because of the latent goodwill between most whites and blacks and between the two countries. I was wrong.

The Rhodesian cadets from the Rhodesian Army were immediately declared 'persona non grata' and had to return home. As a British cadet, I was summoned by my company commander who expressed regret about UDI and then, obviously embarrassed, asked how I would respond if asked to fight Rhodesia, as part of a British Force. "Of course" he added, "this would be extremely unlikely and I'm sure it won't happen, but I've been asked to find out how you feel about UDI and how you might react." I replied that I thought Ian Smith had made a grave mistake but that I would not fight against friends of mine in Rhodesia and would ask to resign from the British Army if ever ordered to do so. "Thank you" he commented, "I expected that's what you'd say. Don't worry, I can't see Britain becoming involved in any such military operation. Forget about what's happening over there, if you can, and concentrate on Sandhurst."

The first term was soon over, and the pace then eased. Terms 2 to 5 were geared more towards academic studies before Term 6 then concentrated again on military subjects, prior to commissioning. There were regular exercises every term which I enjoyed, especially the longer ones where one had time to become accustomed to living in the field, moving at night and developing a better understanding of tactics and procedures at section and platoon level. On the academic side, the military history was interesting but continuing with Maths and Physics, instead of something new such as another language, was pointless for me as I already had good A levels in those subjects. Nevertheless, these four terms gave me more time to experience what Sandhurst offered and provided some extra maturity before becoming an officer.

At the end of the second term, during the Easter break, I was lucky enough to be selected for a winter warfare course in Norway run by the Norwegian Military Academy. I had never skied before. There were about 20 of us from Sandhurst and we spent the first two weeks just outside Voss learning how to ski with rug sacks and pulling pulks (sledges – carrying supplies) and how to live and operate in the snow. We were issued with Norwegian Army clothing as well as skis, rifles and equipment and each morning we would catch a cable car, along with holiday tourists, up into the mountains above Voss and spend all day learning how to ski on cross-country skis, being taught by Norwegian cadets and a very experienced Major. We gradually progressed to a stage where we could move up, down and across slopes with all our kit and with some semblance of order – just! We sometimes shared the same slopes as holiday tourist and one American woman was overheard exclaiming loudly "These Norwegian soldiers sure speak good English but most of them are useless skiers!"

We learned to dig a snow hole, and in pairs, all dug one that we slept in overnight. It was surprisingly comfortable and although the night temperature fell to minus 15 degrees centigrade, it was only minus one or two degrees inside our snow hole. It had to be large enough not to become warmer than the freezing point in order that we could remain dry. We also learned how to use the Norwegian Army tent sheets, building either 4 or 7-man tents by clipping individual sheets together; how to build an igloo; how to construct field defences in the snow. In the third week we moved to an area near Mjølfjell where we went out on a three-day patrol in the mountains, carrying everything we needed and sleeping in tents. At dawn on the last day we mounted a platoon attack on skis on a position occupied by our instructors and surprised ourselves (and them) by not falling over as we swept downhill in the early light! Returning to Sandhurst was a bit of an anticlimax.

I especially enjoyed playing 1st XI cricket as an opening bowler with some gifted players including two other Rhodesians in the side (Mike Ford and Rupert Litherland) and a Jamaican (Abe Bailey). An article in the June 1966 edition of the Field Magazine about a 2-day drawn match between Sandhurst and the Army on 11th and 12th June reflects the slightly old-fashioned, friendly atmosphere and spirit of the game, which also applied to many of our other matches. An extract follows:

"The Army X1 chosen was a shade too strong for its younger opponents who are still in the formative stages of their education but who this year rejoice in an unusually talented and resourceful team. Of interest was the strong element of colour that was introduced by the players from overseas. For instance, the RMA's opening bowler was a slim, tawny-skinned and chestnut-haired cadet from Rhodesia who bowled at a fast-medium pace off his wrong foot. In these days no cricket match of a commonwealth character would

be complete without its leavening of West Indians, and, sure enough there were representatives of one Caribbean island after another. They performed with varying degrees of success, and each displayed the distinctive shots which set a hallmark for his game."

Sandhurst sport was accorded a high priority and I remember being driven back in a Land Rover from Sennybridge early one morning after a night in a trench just in time to get washed and changed for a match and returning immediately the game finished to rejoin my platoon late at night. Meanwhile the exercise had progressed to another phase and it was a challenge to catch up with what had happened while I had been away! With all-day cricket matches in the summer terms nearly every Wednesday, Saturday and Sunday, plus net and fielding practices on other afternoons of the week, the team was spending some 30 hours a week on cricket, but we somehow kept up with our military and academic studies. Unfortunately, my unorthodox bowling action was by now causing me a problem and a strained muscle in my right shoulder would not heal. The first few balls I bowled at the start of every match were always painful, but I enjoyed playing too much to rest the injury properly and kept bowling throughout the summer. In the 6th (and last) term the following year I became Vice Captain and Secretary of Cricket but my shoulder injury recurred and I had to miss a few games.

After a year at Sandhurst I spent my summer leave at home, enjoying the Rhodesian winter sunshine and helping my father on the farm. I also played a bit of cricket with Norton, being warmly welcomed except for one of the farmers who had become staunchly anti-British since the UDI declaration the previous November. At the end of one of the matches, he warned me that he would shoot me if the British Army invaded Rhodesia, calling me a "f----ng" traitor for not joining the Rhodesian Army. The rest of the team told him not to be so stupid and we shared a few beers, but it was an uncomfortable moment. That same farmer was later killed by his own farm workers a few years later having had a reputation for mistreating them. I faced another similar incident at a party in Salisbury a few days later when a previous school friend, who was studying at Trinity College Dublin but (like me) had come home for his summer vacation, told me that I was a traitor. When I challenged him by asking him how long he thought the current regime led by Ian Smith would last, he replied that Ian Smith's government (the Rhodesian Front) was on the right course and that I owed a debt to Rhodesia, even if I disagreed with how it was governed. Although the terrorist war had not started in Rhodesia it was sad that attitudes were hardening and the prospect of a peaceful compromise for the greater benefit of all the population was diminishing.

In the autumn of 1966, after the start of my second year at Sandhurst, I was part of a small group of cadets selected to visit the Theresan Military Academy at Wiener Neustadt, about 30 miles south of Vienna. The Academy was founded in 1751 and is sited in a 12th Century Hapsburg Castle. We were led by a major from Sandhurst throughout our 5-day visit and joined later by the Commandant and his ADC. It was the first British military visit to Austria since before the Second World War and we were treated royally by our Austrian hosts, who went out of their way to make us feel at home, including placing Union Jacks (in miniature) at a table in the officers mess where we shared all our meals with their General. The food was considerably better than our Sandhurst meals and we were also treated to beer and wine with lunch and supper. The Austrian system of officer training was somewhat similar to the

Norwegians; they served a year as a soldier before selection for the Academy where they spent 3 years. Many had also had civilian jobs, so they were all older than us.

We had a very full, interesting programme that included firing their platoon weapons; an introduction to rescuing wounded soldiers from cliff faces; piloting assault boats on the Danube; being shown around their war museum; a visit to the Hungarian frontier where the grim reality of the Iron Curtain with Hungarian soldiers manning machine guns in search towers, barbed wire, searchlights, guard dogs and mines was very sobering. We were also treated to a wonderful visit to the Spanish Riding School, a quick look at Schönbrunn Palace's beautiful gardens, a cocktail party at the British Military Attaché's house, Figaro at the Vienna State Opera and a dance in the officers' mess where the girls and the Austrian cadets were most hospitable. On the 2 evenings where there was nothing formally arranged, we were taken to a local village pub where the wine and beer flowed freely and there were abundant toasts initiated by "Cheerio" rather than "Cheers"! One of our generous hosts insisted we toasted just about everything (in vodka) and enjoyed telling us that "In Germany everything is forbidden and nothing is allowed: in England everything is allowed and nothing is forbidden: in Austria much is forbidden but everything is allowed!" finishing of course with another toast; "Cheerio"!

It took me a few days to readjust to the more spartan regime on our return to Sandhurst and Austria became a distant dream. We were nearing the end of the fourth term when I was summoned by my company commander (now a Major in the Queens Regiment who had taken over from Major Fidler) and told that I would be moving to Burma Company in the New Year for Terms 5 and 6 as the Senior Under Officer (rather like Head of House). I was surprised and asked if there was any chance of my completing training with my existing platoon, all of whom I knew so well, but he vetoed this. Fortunately, Company Sergeant Major Wally Hammond intercepted me outside the office and persuaded me that I should embrace the challenge. He was keen for me to have the chance of the extra responsibility and further explained the unusual distinction of our platoon providing 2 Senior Under Officers; John Ellicock remaining with Alamein Company and me moving to Burma.

Life in Burma Company turned out to be much the same as before once I found my feet. The new platoon, together with the other 3 more junior platoons in the company, made me feel welcome and I felt privileged to have their support. John Webster and Crichton Wakelin were particularly friendly. Crichton later served as the Defence Attaché in Israel towards the end of his military career, his courtesy would have eased any diplomatic tensions. Company Sergeant Major Hayward from the Coldstream Guards also kept a friendly eye on me and ensured that I did not let the company (or myself) down whenever we were on parade or on exercise.

In the Easter break I volunteered for a parachute course, along with about 50 others in the senior intake. It was called the Edward Bear course in honour of a small brown teddy bear mascot which had been dispatched with its own small parachute and harness on every jump carried out by cadets since 1950. The course was run at RAF Abingdon and the first week consisted of a succession of practice drills learning how to exit an aircraft quickly and safely, how to avoid entangling with other parachutists, how to land safely, how to pack a container carrying one's equipment and how to fit a parachute and reserve. We practiced landing on mats after jumping off ramps, swinging from harnesses, jumping from a high platform with our descents on a rope being slowed by a rotating fan and jumping from an exit trainer with a harness attached to a steel wire rope (known as the 'knacker cracker'!). We learned to distribute the shock of landing by configuring ourselves so that our whole body absorbed the landing, rather than just the feet and legs, concentrating on keeping our feet and knees together, our elbows in and our chins on our chest.

Our first 2 descents were from a cage suspended from a tethered barrage balloon soon after dawn on a misty morning at Weston-on-the-Green, a thirty-minute bus drive from RAF Abingdon. We were called forward in turn to enter the cage, 4 novice parachutists at a time with our RAF Flight Sergeant instructor. He took each of our parachute strops from the back of our parachutes and secured the metal ends on to a strong point on the roof of the metal basket. He then gave the order "Up eight hundred, four men jumping". The winch man on the ground repeated the order before releasing the break on the cable drum allowing the basket to lift upwards. Every 200 feet another crewman on the ground would clip a marker on to the cable. We were nervous and could hear the wind whistling softly around the cage, while our instructor encouraged us by singing quietly "When I feel very small"! At 800 feet the winch was applied and the balloon settled, moving slightly in the wind. Our instructor removed the chain blocking the door exit and called us forward one by one to jump. I made the mistake of looking down rather than up at the rigging lines as I jumped. The ground then seemed to accelerate upwards towards me very fast until my parachute opened with a reassuring tug on my harness.

We were soon back up again for our second descent, this time through a hole in the floor of the cage rather than the door, in order to simulate the exits from a Whitley bomber. This seemed bizarre as the Whitley was no longer operational, it was probably a hangover from parachute training during the Second World War. I was nominated as the third jumper, behind an overseas cadet from the Commonwealth, who became spooked just before he jumped through the hole perhaps because he had to look down before he jumped and was therefore more aware of the ground far below. He refused to jump, became agitated, exclaiming loudly "I cannot do it!" The instructor very calmly stated, "Don't worry sir, just step back away from the hole until I sort something out" while at the same time removing the safety bar from the front exit (which was behind him). He then suddenly pushed him out of the exit very firmly telling him "Jump Sir, jump!" The spooked cadet, totally surprised, tried to grab the bottom edge of the cage as he fell out but gravity quickly pulled him downwards until his parachute opened. He landed safely. I was next to jump and did not enjoy falling through that hole! The subsequent aircraft jumps, all from a Hastings aircraft, were very different from the quiet stillness of the balloon. The noise of the engines and the force of the slipstream were exhilarating and there was much less sensation of falling; more a feeling of being buffeted vigorously, as if within the surf of an ocean wave as it breaks on a beach, until the canopy opened. We progressed to jumping with equipment and in simultaneous sticks from the port and starboard doors, before being presented after our seventh jump with a small badge of a parachute. Some weeks later and half-way through the final term at Sandhurst we all parachuted on to Hankley Common on an early Summer evening for a 'Teddy Bears Picnic' along of course with Edward Bear!

The final term rushed by very quickly. I played a lot of cricket, worked hard for the military exams, and enjoyed the final two-week exercise in Germany. I eventually finished tenth in the order of merit and felt both proud and privileged on the Sovereign's Parade, which finished with the Senior Intake marching up the steps into Old College while the rest of the Sandhurst cadets presented arms. Field Marshal Montgomery was our Inspecting Officer that day on 27th July 1967 and gave a typically forthright address, reproduced below:

"Gentlemen, I imagine that here is one aim uppermost in the minds of everyone on parade today and that is to get off parade and get away as quickly as you can: I will help you. But let me say 2 things. The first quite short: I am an old soldier and I have seen a very great many ceremonial parades. I want to tell you that this parade today, from the turnout and the movements on parade, have been completely first-class. Other people may tell you differently. I tell you it has been completely first-class, and you can tell anybody you like about that. The second point may take a little longer, maybe 3 minutes. You and I are soldiers, and as officers our raw material is men. Men are human beings and their lives are precious, not to be risked in battle without good cause or risked when other means will serve. You will have to learn how to command and control men. You will never be able to do that satisfactorily until you first learn to command and control yourself. I was never told that when I was a cadet here, nor was I told it at any time during my first years as a junior officer in the Army. I had to learn by hard experience. I should have been told. You are lucky. You cannot say that you have not been told because I have told you. And what have I told you? – that if you want to command men satisfactorily you have first got to learn how to command yourself. I would wish everyone of you every happiness in the life ahead."

After Sandhurst I attended a Troop Commanders' course at the Royal School of Military Engineering at Chatham, along with another 30 young officers joining the Royal Engineers. There was a great deal to learn ranging from demolitions, equipment and improvised bridging, mine-warfare, water supply, airfield and road construction, field structures, project management, report writing and much more. Disappointingly, too much of our time was spent in the classroom rather than outside and the tempo of the training was very different from Sandhurst. A sobering event was the very sad death of 4 of our young brother officers in a flying accident one weekend. My most enjoyable memories of the course were the good friends I made and playing rugby most weeks for 1 RSME Regiment, along with many others on the same course. I had little rugby ability but could run and so played on the wing alongside Martin Ashmore, another runner. The team was built around some star players that included John Ashcroft (who later captained the Army side and played for Harlequins) a talented half-back pairing of Simon Fogden and John Wyatt, a determined Knobby Reid and a pugnacious Alasdair Wilson who unwisely punched the opposing hooker in the first scrum of a final Sapper Cup match against 9 Independent Parachute Squadron – thus ensuring a very lively game which we lost!

I had hoped to join a Gurkha Engineer Squadron, but was due to start a Civil Engineering degree course within 6 months and there would not have been time to make any useful contribution to the Gurkhas after language training, but was fortunate instead to be posted to 54 (FARELF) Support Squadron on a road project in Thailand. The road was being built in a north-eastern part of the country, some 60 miles from Ubon town, to link a recently completed airfield at Loeng Nok Tha, also built by the Royal Engineers, with a number of small local villages. When I joined 54 Squadron on 1st March 1968, the battle of Khe Sahn, in South Vietnam near the border with Laos, was being fiercely fought between American

Marines and the North Vietnamese, in sharp contrast to the peaceful countryside surrounding our road. We were aware of the war because of frequent sightings of American B52 bombers flying overhead but felt totally divorced from it. However, once an American defeat at Khe Sahn appeared inevitable, we were ordered to cut short our project and return to Singapore earlier than expected, just in case of an overspill of hostilities through Cambodia and into Thailand. I was sorry to leave Thailand so soon after arriving but, nevertheless, experienced an interesting two months there and liked the friendly Thai people. I was based at the forward road camp, 25 miles from the Squadron Headquarters at the Airfield. Within days, the other officers at the forward camp went to play in a rugby tournament in Hong Kong for a couple of weeks, leaving me as the only officer there with some 80 soldiers. Sergeant Cameron, the plant sergeant, gave me some very sound advice saying "Sir, if you just remember to keep quite and let me do the talking it will all work out fine and the road will be built much faster"! He was a very experienced plant operator who knew more about all the machines on the road than anyone else and I certainly listened to him!

Below is an extract from an article I wrote for the Sapper Magazine, once back in Singapore.

"4.30am; time to get up and grab a quick breakfast before climbing aboard a 3 tonner and driving to the road head ready to start work at 6am. The formation team, after checking their machines, gently coax them to life and within minutes the morning stillness is shattered by the roar of engines. The place is a remote corner of North East Thailand and behind us the road has carved a wide swathe through paddy fields and forest. Ahead lies a village called Ban Nong Phok. It is cold in the early morning and it is not long

before a fire is going and some tea ready. However, the machines do not stop. An operator who is thirsty signals to a spare driver who takes over his machine while he has his tea break. After ten minutes he is back in the seat and on the job. It is a race against time and work will not finish until 6pm. This goes on every day except Sunday, when the machines are serviced ready for the next week.

There are many tasks on the road. The dump trucks and tippers are hauling and dumping laterite on the finished formation base, behind the dozers, towed scrapers, graders and rollers shaping it; the bridging team are working on the last bridge; the culvert team are placing culverts ahead; the fitters are working flat out repairing plant that has broken down. By midday the temperature in the shade is around 100 degrees Fahrenheit and it is much hotter on the footplate of the D8 dozers. Everyone is caked in dust and sweat and the plant operators, their faces blackened by dirt and oil, are hardly recognisable. Today it is a Saturday and the District Officer from Ban Nong Phok has laid on a party. Unfortunately, only a few can attend as work cannot stop. Many of the local villagers have gathered to greet us. Coconuts, oranges, papayas, bananas, rice, chicken, cucumbers, onions, chillies and nuts; all this and more is laid out ready for us. There is also beer, rice wine and (strictly illegal) Mekong whisky – a form of wood alcohol, which no wise man would drink! It is not long before there is a real party going and the British soldiers are busy teaching the Thais new songs. I had a moment of alarm when a friendly Thai woman encouraged me to buy her daughter for a wife, but I managed to refuse without causing offence by telling a white lie and persuading her that I was already married!

Monday is payday for the Thai civilians working on the road. Each work site is visited in turn and the Thais gather round to collect their week's wages. This is not always straightforward as friends and relatives sometimes share jobs; a man called Somchit Hong Saeng might turn up to collect Seebon Hong Saeng's pay, as he is working instead of Seebon today. The next week it might be someone else. But the system does have its advantages as there is seldom a shortage of workers; if a man is sick his brother or a friend might take his place until he is fit again. During a week in mid-April there is a water festival called Songkran, held annually to celebrate the arrival of the rainy season. Everyone throws water at everyone. There is no escape and we are frequently drenched by buckets of water hurled by laughing Thai children while driving though villages. Passing vehicles also seem to contain inexhaustible supplies of water and each time a lorry or bus goes by the water is flung at us."

A joint British/Thai ceremony was held on the 19th April 1968 to hand over the road and mark our departure. It included a parade with a band that our squadron commander had somehow cobbled together during the project and which had absorbed more of his interest than the road. It felt slightly incongruous marching past the invited VIPs perched on a saluting dais in the middle of a dusty field carrying a sword and trying to keep in step with music played by an assorted group of combat engineers, plant operators, fitters and tradesmen, none of them musicians but who were versatile enough to persuade our visitors and parade onlookers that they were regular bandsmen!

During our last days in Loeng Nok Tha I was part of a small recce team of 2 other officers and we spent some time carrying out bridge demolition recces on a number of the larger bridges in the local region, writing up our reports each evening. Presumably, these eventually ended up with the British Defence Attaché in Bangkok. Soon the whole squadron departed via Bangkok, where we boarded the LSL Sir Galahad (later sunk in the Falklands War) for our return to Singapore. I spent a week's leave in Penang with a fellow troop commander before joining a major exercise off the east coast of Malaysia for a couple of weeks, providing the lighting and power for Headquarters 17 Gurkha Division in the field. The remainder of my time, before returning to England in September, was mainly spent playing cricket and waterskiing; very agreeable but certainly not much use to my development as a soldier!

Burma Company slow marching past the saluting dais during the Commandant's Parade in April 1967.

The Sandhurst 1st XI Cricket Team in 1967 included three from Rhodesia, pictured in the front row Mike Ford second from left, myself third from right and Rupert Litherland on the right. Tony Moorby, the other opening bowler, is on my left.

Field Marshall Montgomery at our Commissioning Parade on 27th July 1967 escorted by the Sword of Honour Winner, Senior Under Officer John Ellicock. Immediately behind is the Commandant, Major General Peter Hunt.

The Commandant's Rehearsal for the Commissioning Parade on the Old College Square.

Tree clearance on the pilot track, ahead of the road's construction in Thailand.

A Thai girl from a village near the road.

A D8 dozer with a towed scraper moving earth to shape the road formation and a tractor towing a wheeled compactor – just some of the plant used to build the road.

A completed section of the road, also showing a finished bridge.

A farmer ploughing a nearby rice-paddy field with a water buffalo.

3

BOWLED OVER

Shrivenham College, adjacent to Shrivenham village in Wiltshire, provided external London degrees in Engineering plus technical staff training for the Army. There were about 300 young officers plus a few civil servants studying Civil, Mechanical or Electrical Engineering over a 3-year course and around 100 older officers on the staff courses which lasted between 3, 12 and 15 months. The teaching staff were mainly academic professors and lecturers, but there were some senior military officers supervising the technical staff training. The Commandant for most of my time there was Major General Frank King, a much-revered Paratrooper who had been wounded at Arnhem and taken prisoner. The College had recently decided to award its own degree through the Council of National Academic Awards (CNNA) and we were the first cohort to undertake this new CNNA degree course.

The first year was a common foundation year for all the engineering courses and included maths, electricity, electronics, fluid mechanics, strength of materials, structures, geology, engineering drawing and liberal studies. We then split into our separate engineering disciplines for the next 2 years and I concentrated on civil engineering. We attended lectures in the mornings and carried out practical projects in the laboratories in the afternoons which all had to be written up with the reports submitted regularly. There was a lot to learn and I needed to work nearly every evening and also during some weekends to keep up with the course. I was not a passionate engineer but found that the process of studying civil engineering helped instill mental discipline and I did enjoy parts of the course, such as a theoretical design of a bypass around a local village and the ground survey of a local farm. After 3 years there I graduated with an upper second-class honours degree.

Shrivenham had many attractions; beautiful countryside, friendly local pubs, reasonably close to London, excellent sporting facilities and good friends. I played cricket for the College and the Royal Engineers, but also began running quite seriously. We had a strong cross-country team with races every week in the autumn and winter months and I was occasionally selected to run for the Army in a few 800 and 1500 metre races in the summer. I found myself spending more time on athletics than cricket. I lacked the natural sprinting speed to excel at middle distance running and my best times were pretty ordinary (1.57 for 800 metres and 4.05 for 1500 metres) but running was an excellent way of keeping fit. One afternoon, while competing for the Army in July 1971 at 1500 metres against Wales at Cymbran soon after finishing my final exams, the spectators there included a number of enthusiastic school children. The 1500 metres was scheduled near the end of the day, just before the relay events and quite a few children unexpectedly approached me for my autograph before the race. I tried telling them that I was not a famous runner, but they insisted on a signature. My race started slower than usual and I fleetingly imagined that I might just be in with a chance, but the winner kicked hard on the final bend and accelerated quickly to win very easily, leaving me struggling behind. As I walked off the track some of the kids who had badgered me earlier ran up to me giggling and exclaimed "Hey mister, we don't want your autograph anymore; you better have it back"! Although humiliating, it was very funny! I had received much friendlier encouragement from General Frank King after winning the Army's Eastern District cross-country race earlier that year and was touched that he had found time to write a personal letter that included Mary, whom I had married recently.

During the summer leave in 1969 after my first year at university I walked the Pennine Way with a cousin (Malcolm McGill) who had recently been commissioned into the Queen's Regiment. We averaged 25 miles a day in beautiful, at times bleak, countryside and camped most nights by a stream at the end of each day. Finishing the walk at Kirk Yetholm in the Scottish Borders on the morning of the twelfth day, after a very wet and windy night on the Northumberland moors the manager of the Youth Hostel there greeted us with an urgent message for Malcolm. He needed to report as quickly as possible to his battalion who were being deployed to Northern Ireland to help contain the riots that had recently erupted there – and which heralded the start of the Troubles lasting for over 30 years.

I had volunteered to undergo pre-parachute selection training (known as P Company) for the remainder of my leave as I was keen to join 9 Independent Parachute Engineer Squadron after Shrivenham, hoping that there might be a vacancy there for a troop commander. Shortly after bidding farewell to Malcolm I reported to 9 Squadron, who were then in a hutted camp at Church Crookham, for an initial 10-day pre-selection. There were about 15 on the course, including 4 officers, and we were accommodated with 1 Training Regiment

Royal Engineers in another camp at Cove near Farnborough. On the morning of the first day we paraded for a run, dressed in boots, denim trousers and either PT vests (the soldiers) or rugby shirts (the officers). There were 2 junior NCOs from 9 Squadron (Corporal Morgan and Lance Corporal Philipson) in charge – and a black labrador being looked after by one of them. We formed up into 3 ranks with 2 officers leading and 2 at the back and started running. After some 10 minutes we then leapfrogged each other for a period before continuing the run. Another 10 minutes passed before we are told to 'bunny-hop' until we could no longer manage any more hopping and then run again. Soon we were then told to 'duck-walk' which entailed walking in a crouching position with knees bent. When most of us could no longer manage 'duck-walking' we started running again until we arrived at the Basingstoke Canal, only a couple of miles from our start point. We were told to jump in the canal and clear out any rubbish lying at the bottom, such as the odd shopping trolley, broken bicycle, etc. We then climbed out of the canal and were ordered to run as fast as we could towards it and attempt to jump over it; impossible as it was about 25 feet wide but it ensured that we all became thoroughly soaked. We were then told to 'seal-crawl' (crawling on one's stomach using feet and elbows for leverage) up a sand and gravel ditch from the canal alongside a track for about 50 yards before resuming our run. By now we had sand in our underpants chaffing the inside of our thighs – and the dog was in seventh heaven having become excited by all the jumping in the water and having, in turn, jumped all over us while we were crawling along the ditch! After a further 20 minutes we reached 9 Squadron's barracks and were halted outside the gym. After a short break in a café close to the camp we returned for an hour's circuit training in the gym, with bunny-hops between each set of exercises. Most of us were now struggling to keep moving. At last the order to stop was shouted – what a relief! We formed up outside to find 2 long telegraph poles placed on the ground. We ran with the poles, to the nearby Tweesledown Race course where we were split into 2 teams for a race around the course. The poles had to be passed over the horse jumps but we could run around them. After one circuit of the course our efforts were (of course!) deemed unsatisfactory and we were told to do it again, whereupon a couple of the potential paratroopers gave up and asked to be returned to their units. "What!" exclaimed Corporal Morgan, "We don't need to waste any more time on wankers like you! Get back to your units; I don't want to see you dossers again". He turned to the rest of us and told us to be ready for a run that afternoon at 1400 (in 90 minutes time) at Cove. In the meantime, we were to make our own way back there, clean ourselves up and have lunch. We jogged the 4 miles back to our accommodation, had a shower, dug out some clean kit, grabbed a quick bite to eat and were ready just in time. I was wearing the same boots.

The depleted squad were taken on a run and march for 2 hours, covering 10 miles. There were, thankfully, no more bunny-hops or 'duck-walks' but during the run we all, in turn, had to clamber up the main girders of an overhead truss bridge which crossed the canal and then walk along the narrow diagonal struts of the bridge some 15 feet above the road to the other side of the bridge and then return via the same route. We were back at the camp by 1600. It had been a very challenging day!

During the night a couple more had decided that they did not fancy anymore days like the first one and had asked to return to their units. We were now down to 11 and the numbers continued to dwindle day by day, but mainly due to injury rather than attitude.

Both Corporal Morgan and Lance Corporal Philipson became friendlier, but each day was very intense. In the mornings we ran to the 9 Squadron Gym, had a short tea break and then did circuit training or played 'murder-ball' (a form of rugby with a medicine ball and no rules) or boxed each other in a style called 'milling' where there was little boxing skill and an emphasis on trying to hit each other as quickly and often as possible. Lance Corporal Philipson loved watching us milling and would sometime pit two of us against a third, changing round after a minute so we all endured being one against two. He also especially enjoyed taking the mickey out of the officers and would pair two of us off before blindfolding us and then telling us to hit each other. Of course, we could not see a thing and he would sneak up and jab one or other of us with a boxing glove so that we thought it was our opponent. The soldiers thought it hilarious! In the afternoons we would either go for a run for 2 hours wearing webbing weighing some 25 pounds or a march with webbing and a backpack containing 4 house bricks wrapped in a blanket. One afternoon we were taken to the Aldershot trainasium where we had to negotiate a range of obstacles without hesitation, high above the ground, in order to check if we would subsequently have the confidence to parachute. The last day of the course was a 'rest day' which entailed marching to Guildford and back (a distance of 22 miles) each carrying 44 pounds in our webbing and pack and carrying a light machine gun with 4 magazines. The time limit was 4 and a half-hours. The next morning, only 4 of us were deemed suitable to proceed to P Company run by the Parachute Regiment at Browning Barracks in Aldershot. Throughout this time, we had been in the sole charge of Corporal Morgan and Lance Corporal Philipson with no officer or Senior NCO from 9 Squadron attending any of our pre-selection. Despite the 2 junior NCOs being excellent blokes it seemed that their aim was to ensure a 100% pass rate on P Company from those potential 9 Squadron members, rather than preparing us for P Company and allowing the P Company instructors to select those suitable to join Airborne Forces. I was suffering from a bruised heel but was otherwise feeling fit and strong.

P Company was run much more formally than the ad hoc pre-Para regime I had experienced in 9 Squadron. There were about 80 on the course from all the attached arms (artillery, engineers, signals, logistics, medics) in 16 Independent Parachute Brigade. The Parachute Regiment soldiers did not undergo P Company as it was reckoned that they did similar training and selection during their recruit training, but all Parachute Regiment officers had to pass the course. We spent the first morning in the gym on circuit training and an indoor assault course and the afternoon on a run in the local area around Long Valley. I had aggravated my bruised heel during the morning and found the run very painful despite finding the pace relatively easy. The next morning, I could not put any weight on the heel and certainly could not run or jump. I had to withdraw from the course. It was the first time ever that I had not completed something that I had started, and I felt gutted. I was unable to start another selection course straight away because I had to return for the start of the second academic year at Shrivenham, but was determined to have another attempt and hoped for a posting to 9 Squadron sometime in the future. At least Knobby passed the course and some years later served in 131 Independent Parachute Squadron, a TA sapper unit closely associated with 9 Squadron. On arriving back at Shrivenham to start my second year of the degree course, I heard the devastating news that Martin Ashmore had been killed in a traffic accident in Greece during the summer leave, along with another young sapper officer; a tragic waste. Martin was endearingly modest, despite being highly intelligent and a multi-talented athlete. He had won the Queen's Medal at Sandhurst (awarded to the officer cadet achieving the highest marks in military, academic and practical studies) and he represented the Army at basketball and in the 5,000 metres and steeplechase. I visited his mother a number of times over the next few years; she never got over her loss.

In the late autumn of 1969, during my second year at Shrivenham, I was invited to the 21st birthday party of Anna Fleming, whom I had known since childhood in Rhodesia. The party was near Guildford and Anna soon introduced me to her cousin Mary with very striking looks and a wonderful smile. I was immediately smitten and felt a natural sense of kinship with her. We were soon seeing more of each other and I asked her to marry me a few months later in a pub one evening while en route to London from her lovely home near Chichester. To my great relief she accepted, and we were married on 5th September 1970 in St Richard's Church, Chichester, with the reception generously arranged by her parents at her Grandmother's home in Havant. It was a very special day and Mary looked stunning. My parents had flown over from Rhodesia for the wedding and my great friend John Ashcroft was the best man. We had a short honeymoon in the Lake District before returning to Shrivenham where I completed my studies. Prince Philip presented the degrees and prizes to all those of us graduating in July 1971, accompanied by Mary's father who had recently been appointed his Private Secretary. After a bit of leave and a short refresher course at Chatham I was posted to 12 Field Squadron, part of 25 Engineer Regiment, in Osnabruck, Germany. There was no married accommodation available in Osnabruck so Mary went to stay with her parents in Kensington, London, until I could find somewhere for us both to live.

Ever since meeting Mary, I have counted my blessings that she agreed to share her life with me. She always put herself last, behind all her family and friends, and cheerfully coped with the turbulence of Army life with frequent moves and different homes. Throughout my many absences from home on military training or operations, she provided the bedrock of stability and continuity for our two children, David and Anna, while they were growing up and ensured we remained a close-knit family.

Within a few days of arriving in Germany, I was called to the Commanding Officer's office to be told by him that my father had died in a hospital in Salisbury, Rhodesia after suddenly falling ill on his farm. Lieutenant Colonel Jock Brazier, the CO, broke the news as kindly as he could but I found it difficult to imagine that my father, who had always been so fit and vibrant, was dead. I flew to Rhodesia, via Heathrow where Mary met me for a few minutes while I transferred flights and was later met by my mother at Salisbury airport. We drove back to the farm in a somber mood. She had always been resilient and was already making arrangements to manage on her own, but the loss of her husband had not yet truly registered with her. She had however accepted, that she would not be able to run the farm by herself and would need to sell it and move into Salisbury.

The funeral the next day was in Salisbury Cathedral. When my father's coffin, draped in the Union Jack, was carried in by 6 of his friends including Richard Fleming my heart skipped a few beats as I now realised that he really had gone. Amongst the packed congregation from many parts of Rhodesia were most of his farm workers who had made their own way (some 30 miles) from the farm. After the service, my mother, my brother Richard, and I accompanied the coffin to a private cremation at Warren Hills and subsequently placed my father's ashes in a memorial wall at the cemetery. My sister Julia was on her way home from France and unfortunately missed the funeral. Although my father foresaw the inevitable later changes in Rhodesia, at least he was spared the turmoil that has overtaken Zimbabwe. There were many tributes to him from all sorts of people that were a great comfort for my mother. Poignantly, she only really appreciated just what a wonderful man she had married until after he died.

From the Parish Magazine of St Edmund's Church, Hartley: *It was a tragic day for Rhodesia in general, and for this Parish in particular, when Dick McGill passed on. Tragic, because Dick was an outstanding man. A military man, coming from a military family, he served with great distinction in the 8th Gurkha Rifles. A year or two after World War II he came to Rhodesia and settled on a farm at Norton where he soon became a leading member of the Parish. He will long be remembered for his service to his fellows; especially for his creative work, together with his wife, Frances, in founding Hopelands Trust and guiding it successfully for many years. With characteristic thoroughness, he visited and studied similar institutions in other countries so that their informed experience could be brought to bear on the needs of Rhodesia. Nor was he content to organise facilities for retarded children through school, though this in itself represented a very full task; he was determined to secure a future for them in their years after school. He knew, on a personal basis, all the young people of the Hopelands' communities and – what is more – their individual circumstances. Small wonder that they loved him.*

From Hopelands: *What finer tribute can we pay him except quote from a letter received: 'He was about the only man they know of whom everything was good.'*

The next couple of weeks were hectic while Julia and I helped my mother arrange a multitude of issues connected with the farm. We arranged to sell the cattle, auction the farm machinery and to pay off most of the farm workers but could not complete everything before my compassionate leave expired. I had to return to my unit in Germany. A neighbour, Angus Kirkman, kindly offered to cultivate and manage the crop that Dick had so recently planted, ensuring that my mother received a fair share once it was harvested and sold the following year. Angus also completed the sale of all the livestock and the auction of all the farm machinery. The farm (both Swallowfield and Thornbury sections) was eventually sold a couple of years later after my mother moved to Salisbury.

Just married!

Cutting the wedding cake.

From left: Mary's parents, bride and groom, my parents.

A beautiful bride.

With John Ashcroft (best man).

Setting off for our honeymoon in our treasured MG Midget.

Graduation day at Shrivenham with Mary.

Graduation day at Shrivenham with Mary's father.

4

SHORT STRAND BELFAST

Soon after leaving the farm in Rhodesia and saying goodbye to my mother, sister, brother and the farm workers, I was on a divisional field training exercise in Germany. The autumn countryside was beautiful with crisp cold nights and frosty early mornings. Nearly all our movement was at night and we changed locations frequently. Navigating in my ferret scout car in the dark leading a bridging convoy of up to 20 vehicles through unfamiliar German villages and farmland was challenging. While reading the map and directing my driver from the open turret, I also needed to keep up with the squadron and regimental radio traffic plus, on another net, the combat team or battle group my troop was supporting. The combat engineering once on site was relatively straightforward as we were well practiced at our bridging, demolitions and both mine-laying and mine-breaching drills. I was away from the troop quite often, either on recces for future tasks, attending order groups called by my squadron commander or by one of the units we were supporting

The exercise involved over 30,000 troops and included a large number of tanks, guns and other armoured vehicles, which inevitably caused significant damage to fields, crops, fences, roads and tracks.

My troop was tasked with repairing what we could, when not committed to our higher priority sapper tasks. Although the farmers received compensation, I felt uncomfortable about the damage, having been brought up on a farm and knowing how angry I would have felt if anyone had driven over our land. However, the Second World War had finished only 26 years earlier and NATO had to be ready to repel any threat of invasion of Germany by the Warsaw Pact Forces. Most of the local population who lived close to the Inner German Border were surprisingly tolerant; some even welcomed our military manoeuvres.

On return to Osnabruck after a month in the field we were told that we would be deploying to East Belfast some four months later in the infantry role, together with 16 and 37 Field Squadrons under the command of 23 Engineer Regiment stationed in the adjacent barracks. I was sent on an Improvised Explosive Device (IED) course at the Royal School of Military Engineering to learn how to search for and deal with explosive devices that we might find in Belfast. It was a 2-week course and built on my earlier combat engineering training about booby traps. On the first morning all the students built our own 'bomb' using materials that one could easily find in any home, but without any live explosive. Instead we used a small light bulb or a bell or a short length of fuse instantaneous, similar to a safety fuse, but it burnt far quicker, making a small bang when ignited. We then each tried to defuse someone else's 'bomb' without initiating the trigger device that would set off a bell, switch on a bulb or ignite the fuse. None of us succeeded and we would have all been killed or maimed if the devices had been real. It was a very salutary lesson about the danger posed by any homemade explosive devices and drove home just how careful one needed to be if confronted by them. We did not spend any more time on trying to dismantle any devices but concentrated instead on how to neutralise them by either destroying them with a small charge or attaching a cable to them and pulling them (from a safe distance) to somewhere where they could be blown up. We also learned how to search for such devices, how to approach them and how to set up an incident control point from which to coordinate the clearance of such devices. By the time we arrived in Belfast, the responsibility for neutralising IEDs in Northern Ireland had been passed to RAOC Ammunition Technical Officers (ATOs). Royal Engineers remained responsible for searching for them, especially where the risk was assessed as high.

I returned to Germany, this time with Mary, as I had fortunately found a small top-floor flat to rent in the centre of Osnabruck with help from a German wife of another officer in 12 Squadron. The flat was unfurnished, and it took a couple of weeks for us to sort out a stove, fridge, furniture, beds and lights, but it was wonderful to be living together again. Life was hectic while the Squadron prepared for its annual major Fitness for Role Inspection (our role in the defence against a Soviet attack) while at the same time preparing for our forthcoming deployment to Belfast.

In the New Year we focused exclusively on our Northern Ireland training. The days were long, but the time flashed by and we were soon on the streets of the Short Strand, in Ballymacarret, a small Catholic enclave just east of the River Lagan. 16 Squadron were responsible for the other half of Ballymacarret, while 37 Squadron and the Regimental Echelon, including the Workshops and Headquarters Squadron, were based in Sydenham. It was tough saying goodbye to Mary in the early morning of the 15th March 1972. We had had very little time together in Osnabruck and she was still getting to know her way around. The good news was that she was expecting our first child and her mother Anne had kindly offered to travel out to Germany and join her for the drive back to England. Mary would stay with her parents in London while I was away, so would not be alone during her pregnancy.

Ireland has had an uneasy relationship with Britain for centuries. In addition to the Catholic mistrust of the British Army, I was surprised by the hatred between the Catholics and Protestants in Northern Ireland during this, my first, tour and on 3 subsequent tours of duty there over the next 8 years. This most recent conflict from 1968 was known as the 'Troubles'. Over 3,600 people were killed and thousands more injured. There were several attempts to find a political solution, but they all failed until the Good Friday Agreement was signed in 1998. However, peace remains fragile and a number of issues between the Catholic and Protestant communities have yet to be resolved. Operation Banner, the codename for the British Forces deployment in Northern Ireland ran for almost 40 years from 1969 to 2007.

The Protestant majority wanted to remain part of the UK while the Republican minority, who were almost all Catholics, wanted to become part of the Republic of Ireland. Since the 1922 separation of Ireland into Ulster in the north and the Republic of Ireland in the south, the Unionists in Northern Ireland had dominated politics, business and industry. The Catholic minority felt increasingly disadvantaged. A civil rights march in Londonderry in April 1968 had ended in disorder and the tension between Catholics and Protestants continued to rise and British troops were sent to help restore order in 1969. Malcolm (my cousin) went there in August 1969 with the First Battalion of the Queens Regiment, immediately after finishing the Pennine Way walk with me. The situation continued to deteriorate, especially after internment was introduced in 1971. Bloody Sunday on 30th January 1972 further inflamed the sense of injustice felt by the Catholics and the violence worsened.

Six weeks after Bloody Sunday the atmosphere in Belfast was tense. There were 13 battalions in Belfast with more troops in Londonderry and in the rural areas near the border with the Republic of Ireland. Over 20,000 soldiers were deployed in 3 Brigades; 39 Brigade in Belfast, 8 Brigade in Londonderry and 3 Brigade along the border, all under command Headquarters Northern Ireland in Lisburn. Our role was to support the RUC. 1972 was the most violent year of Operation Banner and the year finished with 146 killed from the British Army, the Ulster Defence Regiment (UDR) and the Royal Ulster Constabulary (RUC). There were numerous shootings, explosions and riots, often on a daily basis. Direct rule was imposed from Whitehall on 30th March, which greatly angered the Protestants. A Northern Ireland Office was set up at Stormont, directed by William Whitelaw who was appointed the Secretary of State for Northern Ireland. With the exception of a brief period in 1974, Northern Ireland was to be ruled from Westminster until 1999.

During our first couple of weeks the accommodation in the Short Strand bus depot was ad hoc with some of the Squadron sleeping in the buses, in the inspection pits and on the bus hangar floor. Those poor fellows then had to move once the buses were started each morning and find somewhere else to stow their personal kit or catch up on sleep before their next patrol. Initially, there were only 2 showers for over 100 of us until a portacabin with extra loos and showers was delivered and plumbed in. Some additional accommodation huts were also installed so that every soldier eventually had his own bed space, but they were very cramped, with the field troops of four 6-man sections sharing a hut and the men sleeping in bunk beds. The huts were protected against blast bombs by sandbag walls around each side and a sloping roof covered in wire netting. The OC had his own room in the bus depot offices while us other officers shared a space next to the Ops room, screened by a blanket. It was very noisy with the constant radio traffic, telephone calls, briefing and debriefing of patrols. Despite the noise, we had little trouble sleeping! We settled into a three-day cycle where each field troop rotated every twenty-four hours; patrolling the streets on foot and in vehicles, on standby with two sections at immediate notice to move and two at ten minutes notice and guarding the bus depot, which also involved searching every bus each time it returned to the depot and checking every visitor's identity at the main gate. Two sections were out in the streets all the time, either both on foot patrol or with one of the sections in an armoured vehicle (a Pig or a Saracen) or in 2 armoured Land Rovers. Either my staff sergeant or I was always with one of the sections on the ground and one of us would always move with the reserve sections whenever they were deployed to an incident. Each of the troop commanders also took our turn on manning the Squadron Ops Room in 4-hour shifts during the night between 9pm and 9am.

The Catholic Short Strand area was small, with dingy terraced houses facing dirty streets and backing on to filthy alleyways. One could smell the poverty and deprivation. Many of the houses had just one tap, located in the kitchen with an outdoor loo in the small back yard by the alleyway. It was a very tight community where everybody knew each other and where any stranger was regarded with suspicion, often hostility. During one of my first patrols a little girl, aged about 4, threw a brick at me which glanced off my leg with no force as the toddler could barely pick up the brick. Her mother screamed abuse shouting at me to "F... off back to England

and leave us alone" while at the same time patting her daughter on her head and praising her action. I was surprised by the hatred and vitriol towards us expressed by so many in that small, bitter enclave but soon became used to it. However, I sometimes wonder what happened to that little girl as she grew up.

We also had responsibility for a much larger Protestant area, south, east and north of the Short Strand. The Protestant mothers were very generous with tea and biscuits for any soldier and most welcomed us into their homes. Some even insisted on doing the laundry for some of our soldiers! The Albert Bridge Road, running east to west and across the River Lagan into the City Centre, bordered the Catholic area at its southern interface with the Protestant area. This interface was the scene for regular aggravation, taunting, rock and bottle throwing, the odd petrol bomb in a bottle and many violent riots throughout our time. The 2 sides might disperse if one could manage to reason with the respective mob leaders, before the numbers built up. If the stone-throwing and other missiles, such as steel ball-bearings and pieces of metal fired by catapults, had not started in earnest, I would try and talk to each side, wearing a beret and not a helmet. As I approached one of the crowds the missile throwing would generally stop (not always!) while the dialogue lasted but would start up again as I left to talk to the other side. They, in turn would cease throwing rocks or bits of paving stone while we talked, but would resume the barrage against the other side as soon as I moved away. If mediation was pointless, I donned my helmet and became a target for both sides! Our worst injuries resulted from the steel fragments fired by catapults, which caused cuts and bruising to any unprotected parts of our bodies; legs, arms and hands, but we fortunately escaped any major injuries. The rioters were always wary of arrest from a snatch team following-up a baton charge or a volley of rubber bullets and kept their distance.

Many of the riots were prolonged, violent and malevolent. Street lampposts would be torn down, pavements ripped up, buildings trashed and destroyed, cars and buses hijacked and set on fire and the crowd on either side would be intent on infiltrating into the other's streets and wrecking their houses. We forced ourselves between the 2 sides and kept them apart with baton charges and by firing rubber bullets. We had to be on the lookout for snipers, especially in the Ballymacarret streets where the IRA would attempt to take advantage of any distraction to take a shot, and we always deployed sentries to cover us. During one particular nasty riot, which started in the evening and died down well after midnight and then suddenly flared up again early the next morning around 5am, my troop fired well over 100 rubber bullets and made numerous baton charges to prevent us being over-run. Along with the rest of the squadron and a strong RUC presence, we were all stretched before restoring calm.

We spent a lot of time on the streets checking vehicles using a couple of Land Rovers or pigs parked across the road as temporary vehicle control points (VCPs) and also checking the identity of pedestrians. While this deterred the movement of weapons and explosives through the area, it also frustrated many innocent people. Some remained surprisingly tolerant about being checked so often, because they realised that the threat from shootings and homemade bombs was ever present. We also searched a lot of unoccupied premises, sheds, waste ground and any derelict houses on a random basis, always taking precautions against possible IEDs. We very seldom found anything but did have a major success 5 weeks into our tour when we discovered a significant haul of explosives which included 568 electric detonators, 58 safety-fuse detonators, 6 blast bombs, some gelignite, a shotgun, 78 shotgun cartridges and 78 x .303 plus 11 x .45 rounds of ammunition. During the night immediately after our find, 3 blast bombs were thrown over a sidewall of the bus depot. Two damaged the side of a bus and one failed to explode. The next night 2 more blast bombs were thrown into the depot; both went off but fortunately caused no injuries. We erected some lights on the top of the wall, overlooking the area from where the bombs were thrown alongside Anderson Street and were never troubled by bombs thrown over the wall again. Additionally, the locals living in that street were delighted because they had had no street lighting for a long time.

The squadron undertook a couple of local community projects, working on them whenever there was a quiet period. 3 Troop built a children's playground in an empty yard overlooking the River Lagan for the Catholics and 1 Troop (my troop) took on the refurbishment of a hall in the Protestant area for old age pensioners which included electrical rewiring, repair of some of the roof, redecorating the inside of the hall and clearing up debris caused by vandals who had tried to wreck the building. The soldiers enjoyed these small projects because they were constructive and contributed in a small way towards improving the local area. The pensioners were extraordinarily appreciative but, sadly, the children's playground was not used as much as expected because the IRA discouraged any amenity provided by the Army and it was soon vandalised.

During the last week of April we were tipped off that some wanted IRA leaders plus some arms and explosives were in two houses in our area. The squadron searched the houses but found nothing. My troop provided the entry party for the second search at 3.30am and I could not help feeling sympathy for the family as we burst in through the front door and rushed upstairs and into the back to prevent anyone escaping. The father was nervous. If there had been an IRA leader in the house, he had long gone. We may perhaps have been given a false tip off, perhaps provided by someone with a grudge against him or his family. The squalor in the house was distressing. In the main bedroom 2 young boys shared a bed with the parents while in the corner were 3 children sharing a 2-tier bunk. Two other young boys were in the second bedroom. During the search, a little girl went to spend a penny, in her bare feet, in the filthy back alley and then climbed back into the bed she shared with one of her brothers. A couple of milk bottles were in the bedroom, both full to the brim with urine, and the whole house stank. The father had fouled his pants, probably because he was frightened. We went back the next day to mend the lock on the front door. I felt frustrated about a pointless search, resulting from false intelligence, which must have alienated the family even more against the British Army.

On Sunday 28th May I spent nearly all afternoon and evening with some of my troop at a VCP on the Albert Bridge Road. We stopped and searched over 300 cars but found nothing suspicious, nor any wanted member of the IRA or the Protestant Ulster Volunteer Force (UVF) or Ulster Defence Association (UDA). Soon after returning to the bus depot well after midnight and some 10 minutes after falling asleep, I was woken by a huge blast and a violent shaking of the wall by my bed. I immediately thought that the IRA had attacked the bus depot but it soon transpired that a large homemade bomb had detonated accidentally while the IRA were unloading it from a stolen car; a case of 'Bombers' Justice'. Four IRA men were killed plus 4 local catholic civilians; a total of 8 including one woman who was still missing the day after the blast and who must have been blown completely away. There were also a few injured people and a number suffered delayed shock. Many of the houses were severely damaged, with roofs blown off, windows shattered and walls badly fractured.

I was at the scene about 5 minutes after the explosion. There were legs, arms, a head and bits and pieces of flesh all scattered around in Anderson Street. A few hours later, soon after dawn, we found a head on the other side of the depot, part of a woman's torso just outside the Ops Room, an arm on the roof of my troop's hut and a leg on the bus hangar. Human remains were scattered everywhere. I saw a dog sniffing around and chased it away but not before it had managed to grab a severed hand with its mouth. The locals were scrabbling about in the wreckage of their houses shouting at us because they blamed us for not stopping the car, which they claimed had been driven there by Protestants. We helped clear the debris, board up the houses still habitable and tied tarpaulins over some of the damaged roofs. Later on in the day (Monday 29th May) some of the locals reluctantly accepted that the bomb was an IRA mistake and a few even offered tea to the soldiers helping them. This 'rapprochement' did not last long.

Unknown to us, secret talks had been initiated between the British Government and the IRA, although Whitelaw refused to speak to them in public. Provisional IRA prisoners were granted special status and a ceasefire was agreed on 26th June. The Protestant community had become edgy and sensed, from their perspective, that the IRA were being treated too softly by the British Government. The UDA had set up a number of roadblocks in East Belfast and other areas of Belfast and began to confront the Army and RUC more aggressively. They paraded in large numbers close to the interface and these gatherings often developed into sporadic aggravation, bottling, stone throwing and rioting throughout much of June.

A month after the Anderson Street bomb, on Sunday 25th June, someone fired 7 shots in a street close to the bus station. I was on patrol with a couple of sections and rushed towards the 3 houses near the source of the shooting. 2 Troop went into another house on the same street. We found nothing but a Catholic crowd quickly formed and subjected us to a hail of stones, bottles and abuse. It was obvious that the gunman was still around and being protected by the locals. Because of the impending truce we could not follow-up more aggressively but had to pull back while they set fire to a couple of vehicles in Thompson and Beechfield streets. We were restricted simply to ensuring that the violence did not spread.

The next day (Monday the 26th June and just before the start of a so-called truce[1] (due to take effect at midnight) there was a lot of shooting in the rest of Belfast. In the evening some kids set fire to some old bits of wood in the Short Strand, prompting a surge of local youths to gather around the fire. The Protestant Tartan youths on the other side of the Albert Bridge Road became excited and lit their own fire. The situation soon escalated with the rival crowds shouting abuse at each other and we were called out. My troop drove straight through the small Catholic fire and we positioned two 4-ton trucks on the road between the two crowds so that they could not see each other. The Catholic children danced around excitedly shouting "We are the IRA" and "The IRA has got the Army on the run" plus screaming much ruder abuse. The Protestants retaliated with their comments and gestures, but surprisingly there was no

---

1. The IRA had earlier split into the Official IRA and the Provisional IRA. The Official IRA had agreed a ceasefire on 30th May 1972 but was occasionally still involved in attacking British troops afterwards. The Provisional IRA (PIRA) became the largest and most violent Nationalist terrorist organisation and was commonly called the IRA as well as PIRA.

stoning. A bus driver returning to the depot stupidly entered the Short Strand and I just managed to stop him by sprinting alongside and banging on the side of his bus and telling him to get the hell out of it which he fortunately just managed. This angered the children as they missed their chance to set fire to the bus.

We were very aware that the IRA in our area were planning to shoot a British soldier before the truce began as we had had a couple of warnings that they were boasting that they would. Just before midnight a small blast bomb was thrown in Beechfield Street, some 500 yards from the bus depot and just outside of 12 Squadron's area but within 16 Squadron's area. A mobile patrol investigated, and shots were fired at a Land Rover and hit Staff Sergeant Banks; one killed him instantly. The incident happened 3 minutes before midnight. It was a tragic event. With hindsight, the blast bomb was obviously a 'come-on' to lure a follow-up patrol into an ambush. I knew Staff Sergeant Banks quite well as we had both attended the same IED course in Chatham before Christmas. He was a good man who would always do his best to protect the local population and had been closely involved with a project to help handicapped children from both the Catholic and Protestant communities. His death left a wife and 2 young boys without a husband and father.

The days after the start of the truce were tense but passed reasonably quietly. The UDA continued erecting barricades and developing some 'no-go' areas in response to the IRA 'no-go' areas in Londonderry and West Belfast. The Protestant marches and processions during this period passed off peacefully but they all required close monitoring and we spent many hours either on street corners or on standby for riot control. One of the marches contained 42 bands and over 5,000 people. Two cars, each with 100 pounds of explosive were found parked in the Short Strand area but neither bomb exploded properly. One burnt, rather than exploded and in the other one only the detonator went off. We were not sure who planted these homemade and rather amateur devices; It could have been either Protestant extremists or the IRA in a cunning ruse to persuade the locals that the Army could not defend them.

The truce soon broke down on the 9th July and a spate of shootings and bombings all over Belfast immediately followed. It was obvious that the IRA had used the period to replenish their arms and supplies. At about 3am on the morning of the 10th July a gunman fired about 10 rounds from an M1 carbine from an alley at one of my sections, patrolling in a pig, injuring Sapper Cook (the driver) and Corporal Pike (section commander). Sapper Cook was lucky as a bullet went through the driver's seat backrest and lodged in his flak jacket only giving him a nasty bruise. Another 7 rounds went through one of the portholes in the side of the pig and Corporal Pike was hit by 4 of them; one bullet cut the underside of his chin, near his throat; two bullets hit an arm and another one went under his arm and lodged somewhere near his collarbone. He was immediately driven to the Royal Victoria Hospital in West Belfast where he received excellent care. He remained cheerful throughout his treatment with nurses fussing over him. He was later moved to the military wing of the Musgrave Park Hospital to complete his recovery.

During our last few days in the Short Strand, local Catholic vigilantes kidnapped 3 Protestants who took the wrong turn from the Albert Bridge and strayed accidentally into a corner of the Catholic area. Such was the mutual hatred that they were instantly suspected of trying to infiltrate into the area and do some damage. The more likely reason was that they had simply drunk too much and mistakenly did not turn right immediately after leaving the bridge. Very early the next morning, the Squadron Sergeant Major found the 3 men on some waste ground in the north of our area. They had all been shot; 2 were dead and the third was still alive but he had all the skin from his neck flayed, as well as skin from parts of his face and his eyelids, before being shot. It was very sobering that such medieval torture could take place in the United Kingdom.

During the afternoon of Friday 21st July, subsequently known as Bloody Friday, the IRA set off 19 bombs over a period lasting just under 80 minutes across Belfast. The bombing caused chaos in the city, killing 9 people and injuring 130. Television images of fire fighters shovelling body parts into plastic bags at the Oxford Street bus station were shocking.

A few days after Bloody Friday[2] our Op Banner tour came to an end. We were relieved by The Life Guards and returned to Osnabruck. A week later I went on leave and had a precious time with Mary before she was admitted to the Middlesex Hospital in London for David's birth on 5th August. It was lovely to be reunited and to be with her in the hospital while David was born.

2. Following Bloody Friday, the British Army was ordered to clear the "No-Go" republican areas in Londonderry and Belfast. Operation Motorman was launched in the early hours of 31st July and all the barricades were very soon destroyed.

Short Strand Bus Depot.

Wire netting and sandbags protecting 1 Troop's hut. A Saracen parked alongside.

A car and driver being checked at a VCP.

Corporal Pike – before he was seriously wounded by the IRA.

A member of the UDA keeping watch Photo from The Belfast News Letter – 12 June 1972.

A peaceful Orange Parade.

A Catholic pub in the Beersbridge Triangle torn down by Protestant rioters.

Standing by for expected trouble. The armoured vehicle behind me is a pig.

The completed playground near the bus station, built by 3 Troop.

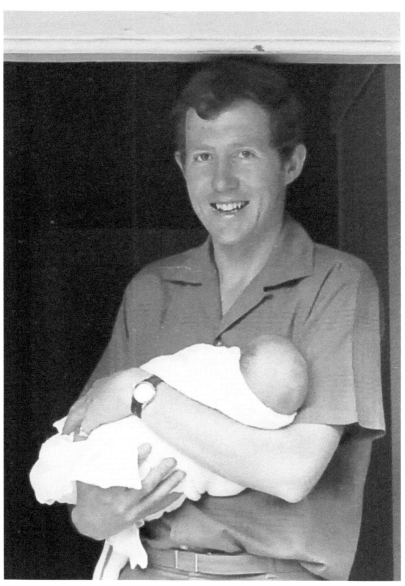

Proud father with David soon after his birth.

5

COMMANDO ENGINEER

My leave with Mary passed all too quickly and I soon returned to Germany. After the tour in Belfast 12 Squadron had to readjust to our main role as a mechanised field squadron and we needed to sort out our vehicles, kit and procedures, ready for the autumn manoeuvres. We were soon out in the field on a succession of squadron, regimental, brigade and divisional exercises. Mary and I had been allocated a flat in Osnabruck, hired by the Army, which I had made ready for her and David's arrival. The week before she was due to join me, I was sent on a 2-week attachment with a French Amphibious Engineer Regiment near Breisach in southern Germany, close to the Rhine. No sooner had she settled into the flat, I rashly drove some 400 miles to see her at the weekend and then drove back with her and David to rejoin the French Regiment, only to find that I would (unexpectedly) be deployed on exercise with a French engineer company for 5 days. Mary was left on her own with David, who was just a few weeks old, in an unfamiliar French officers' mess. Fortunately, she is a fluent French speaker, but I was not popular! A week later we drove back to Osnabruck and I spent the next 6 weeks in the field with my troop on exercise.

Soon after the autumn exercises were over Mary and I were on the move again; this time to Plymouth. I had volunteered to join 59 Independent Commando Squadron and was delighted at last to receive a posting order with a reporting date the week before Christmas in 1972. We were warmly welcomed by Major Graham Owens and all ranks of 59 Squadron and soon settled in an Army quarter only half a mile from Crownhill Fort, the Squadron's home. I spent much of my Christmas leave preparing for the Commando course with long walks over Dartmoor carrying a bergan and circuit training in the Gym in Seaton Barracks, which the Squadron shared with 40 Commando. The other military families near us were all very friendly, as were the local shopkeepers in Crownhill village, a couple of miles north of the centre of Plymouth. I was taken aback the first time the local baker and butcher welcomed Mary by greeting her in a friendly Devonian drawl with "Hello my lover, what can I do for you today?" but soon realised that they greeted all their female customers the same way! We immediately felt at home.

In early January I formed up with a few other Sapper hopefuls at Crownhill Fort. We spent a week on a pre 'beat-up' to ensure we would be ready for the following three-week 'beat-up' run by 29 Commando Regiment, Royal Artillery. This would select those going forward to the five-week All Arms Commando Course at Lympstone, the home of the Royal Marine Training Centre. We spent the next 3 weeks on runs and marches over Dartmoor, circuit training in the gym, tackling the assault course, abseiling down the walls of the Citadel and on a couple of 2-day exercises on the moor. We also spent many hours practicing regains on a rope stretched across a water tank. Done successfully, one kept dry but if one could not regain position on the top of the rope a ducking was inevitable. The regain practices invariably lasted until every one of us eventually ended up in the water! Some early mornings started with a log-run around the outside of the Citadel with a break half-way by the sea when we would put down the logs, remove our webbing, jump into the water and swim across a stretch between two sets of rocks. We would then continue with the log-run. Being, mid-January it was bitterly cold. Amongst us was a Gunner sergeant who was a non-swimmer and who bravely (and very foolishly!) did as he was ordered. The first morning he jumped unhesitatingly into the sea only to reappear in alarm, spluttering and frantically waving his arms. Fortunately, I had jumped in just before him and managed to reach him and drag him to the shore. It was then belatedly agreed that I and another officer should in future always jump in before the non-swimmer and rescue him before he drowned. Every subsequent log-run with an inevitable dip into the sea must have been a frightening ordeal for him, but he never faltered and showed tremendous determination to remain with the group.

Around 20 survivors from the 'beat-up' reported at the Commando Training Centre, Lympstone at the end of January, joined by a group of Iranian PT NCO instructors and an Iranian Army officer. The then Shah of Iran was an admirer of the Royal Marines and was keen to have a Commando Division in his Forces, organised along the same lines as the British Commando Brigade. These Iranians had been chosen to undergo the Royal Marine All Arms Selection Course and would then form the initial nucleus to initiate similar commando training within the Iranian Forces. There were also 2 Royal Navy padres on the course who had been posted to Commando units. We were treated rather like raw recruits at the start; very irritating but perhaps inevitable, and there were a few jibes such as "you'll never make a Royal Marine". A Sapper volunteer for 59 Squadron always cheekily replied "I don't want to be a Royal Marine; I'm a Sapper!"

Overall, I enjoyed the course and it helped that our instructors clearly wanted us to pass so long as we met the set standards and worked well as a team, especially while out in the field. Most days in the barracks included some classroom instruction on Fieldcraft but we spent most of the day in the gym or on the Assault course and the Tarzan course (a combination of an aerial confidence test and assault course) or on runs and marches. Each week we also spent some days and nights on field exercises on the nearby Woodbury Common or on Dartmoor. We also had an interesting day on the coast at Poole learning how to embark and disembark from different types of Royal Marine landing craft, rigid raiders and RIBs.

The Iranians were strong physically and impressed us all by the ease with which they climbed ropes and tackled obstacles, but nearly all of them struggled on the exercises in the field and on the longer marches, apart from their officer and just one or two others. They were not unaccustomed to living in the field in wintry conditions with wet and freezing weather; nor could they cope with lack of sleep. On one occasion they all jumped out of their trenches and ran away during a defense exercise on Woodbury Common when we were subjected to a mock enemy night attack that also included CS gas. The 2 padres, to their credit, gamely attempted everything despite one of them suffering from rope burns on his hands after slipping down a rope too quickly near the start of the course. They did not carry a rifle but instead each had to carry two additional full water bottles and a bible in order to make up some of the weight difference.

During our 5 weeks at Lympstone, we had to pass a number of tests. These included covering 6 miles in 60 minutes and 9 miles in

90 minutes (with fighting order weighing 25 pounds and a rifle), completing the Assault, Tarzan and Endurance courses within specified times and climbing a 30-foot rope with fighting order and rifle. The Endurance Course started on Woodbury Common with a series of obstacles for the first 2 miles before a 4-mile run finishing at a range at Lympstone where we fired 10 rounds at a target. The pass time for officers was 70 minutes (for soldiers a bit longer) and we all had to score enough hits on the range. The obstacles were 3 narrow underground tunnels, negotiated on hands and knees and by crawling on one's stomach, a large pool of cold, muddy water up to one's chest which we waded through and a culvert completely submerged under water. As we did for all the other tests, we carried a rifle and fighting order and it was vital to keep our rifles clear of any mud or dirt so that they remained fit for firing on the range at the finish. The test was undertaken in three-man teams because it needed one man to push and a second man to pull the third man through the underwater culvert (in turn). The rifles were not taken under water but were placed to one side until all three were through the culvert. The ensuing 4-mile run to the range with soaking wet equipment and clothing was a good way to get warm!

The anticipated test of a 30-mile march followed by an interrogation ordeal had very recently been scrapped because the interrogation techniques used were similar to those banned earlier in Northern Ireland, such as hooding, noise, lack of sleep. Instead, our final 3-day exercise on Dartmoor involved some long marches with little sleep. The temperature was well below freezing at night and visibility was very poor with fog and mist, but at least the rain held off. We had been briefed not to bring any chocolate or snacks because our ration packs would offer ample nutrition. One of the padres was determined that he would not go hungry and hid a stack of chocolate bars and other snacks in his clothing. This was inevitably found during an early search and confiscated by the instructors. While tramping across the moor, one or more of the instructors would sneak up in the mist alongside the disconsolate padre, munching on a portion of the confiscated 'nutty' (the term used by Royal Marines for chocolate, snacks and sweets) and thank him for his generosity!

All that remained now was a rerun of the endurance course test, which I had already completed well within the required time the week before, and the 30-foot rope. Called forward for my final attempt on the rope I climbed until reaching the metal bar from which the top of the rope was suspended but then lost my grip and fell from the top. I landed flat on my back, was knocked unconscious and came to in the medical centre some 30 minutes later. Fortunately, my webbing had absorbed some of the impact (my mess tins in a rear pouch had been crushed flat). The good news was that the instructors reckoned that I had climbed to the top of the rope and so had successfully passed that test. The not so good news was that my back was very badly bruised. I was incapable of bending and unable to attempt the Endurance Course the next day. I formed up with the others and ran with them (very stiffly) around the course but could not tackle the tunnels because I could not crawl or bend low enough to get through them. I was a reluctant bystander at the parade the next day where those who had passed were awarded their green berets. I returned to Lympstone the following week, once I had regained some flexibility in my back, and completed the Endurance Course with 2 generous course members who kindly returned to accompany me. I was awarded my green beret at the finish and joined 59 Squadron the next day as 3 Troop Commander.

3 Troop was affiliated to 42 Commando nearby at Bickleigh, on the edge of Dartmoor. We were based in Crownhill Fort along with 1 Troop (affiliated to 40 Commando in the adjacent Seaton Barracks) and Squadron Headquarters. Support Troop (with all the plant, heavy equipment and vehicles) was based in Seaton Barracks; 2 Troop was in Malta with 41 Commando and Condor Troop was with 45 Commando in Arbroath, Scotland. The total number in the Squadron was just over 250. Everyone felt proud to belong to an elite unit and I was very fortunate to have excellent NCOs and Sappers in 3 Troop. Staff Sergeant Joinson, Sergeant Sims and the four Corporals, Alum, Evans, Howell and Lewis quickly helped me settle in, as did John Moore-Bick who handed over the troop in very good order before he moved to Condor Troop.

The Squadron deployed to Kansas soon after Easter. My troop provided the freight party and we spent 2 days in a Hercules C-130 flying from RAF Brize Norton to Kansas with an overnight stop in Gander, Newfoundland. While drinking a beer in the Flyers Club in Gander close to the hotel we were billeted in, I unexpectedly heard an announcement "Is there a Lieutenant McGill in the audience?" whereupon some of my troop immediately cheered, grabbed me by the arms and led me to the stage where an attractive stripper (dressed as a cow-girl) handed me her Stetson hat and invited me to try and trap her naked breasts with the hat while she rotated them in opposite directions and gyrated to the music. I was dressed in boots, combat trousers, a heavy shirt and pullover and was soon feeling very hot and also slightly embarrassed at my repeated failures with the hat! The girl, known as 'Diana Does – Sheriff of Horney Hollow' thought it all a hoot and kindly presented me with a signed photograph of herself straddling a toy donkey! I was much relieved when the music stopped and was allowed to leave the stage and return to my troop, who had thoroughly enjoyed my inept performance!

In 1973 the United States Army's war in Vietnam was about to finish, as was American conscription. Those stationed at Fort Riley were interested to see how an all-volunteer British unit operated when living alongside the 1st Infantry Division (Big Red One). We were hosted by an American engineer battalion who provided our vehicles and engineer plant and arranged our accommodation. The Divisional Commander, Major General Duquemin, spent a lot of time with us and seemed intrigued, amused and impressed by the Squadron. While there we completed a number of engineering tasks at a nearby nature reserve which included a breakwater, a dirt road and a sewage pond together with its associated pumping station plus the connecting pipework and we also joined in many of the activities on the huge Divisional base. We played rugby against a variety of teams and everyone had an opportunity to spend a few days on adventurous training in the beautiful Rockies. Towards the end the Squadron put on an immaculate parade with a Royal Marine Band, followed later that day with a display of commando skills that included soldiers abseiling from helicopters to take out a group of terrorists 'hiding' in the display area, others abseiling from a scaffold tower and a third group demonstrating unarmed combat skills. In the evening, the Squadron officers then hosted General Duquemin plus officers from our host Engineer Battalion and some others at a traditional-style Dinner Night. This finished well after the meal and the toasts, with the General drinking port while perched precariously on a chair hoisted up high by some of us standing on a table so that his head was almost level with the ceiling! Fortunately, no one fell over! All in all, it was a most interesting three months for us, and in turn, the Americans enjoyed the Squadron's versatility, expertise and humour.

On return to Plymouth, Graham Owens handed over command of the Squadron to Garth Hewish, a big friendly bear of a man whom the men immediately took to their hearts. Formerly an officer in 9 Independent Parachute Squadron, he had passed the Commando Course at the age of 38 and had a natural affinity for people, especially soldiers. He became an enthusiastic member of the Squadron rugby team, relishing the contests in the scrum, looking 10 years older when he removed his false teeth before running onto the pitch! He was also a gifted violinist and seeing him playing the violin tucked under his jaw presented an image very different from a paratroop commando who loved soldiering, rugby, boxing, canoeing (and all sport) and parties. Within a few days of becoming the OC he came to visit my troop while we were building a bailey bridge for spectator access to the Royal Naval Air Show at Culdrose in Cornwall. He stayed until well after the main span had been lifted into position and he had spoken at length to every single NCO and Sapper present. By then it was long past midnight.

Soon after the bridge task at Culdrose I joined 42 Commando on a major NATO exercise in Turkey which included 3 Commando Brigade, 16 Independent Parachute Brigade, a substantial number of Royal Naval ships and forces from other NATO countries. 42 Commando deployed earlier to Cyprus for some work-up training, with the Commanding Officer's command group, in which I was included, departing by air and the main party following on in HMS Bulwark.

Lieutenant Colonel Jeremy Moore, the CO, had been awarded an MC on operations against the Communist insurgents in Malaya in 1952 and a bar to his MC ten years later in a hostage rescue operation in Borneo. In 1982 as a Major General he commanded the UK Land Forces during the Falklands Campaign. He closely mentored all those in his Command Group in planning and then conducting detailed ground recces for rehearsing 42 Commando (once it arrived) in 4 different phases of war (Advance, Attack, Defence and Withdrawal) in the 2 British Sovereign Base Areas in the west and east of the Island. I learned a great deal about tactics in those few days, was made welcome and felt part of a close-knit team.

Once HMS Bulwark arrived close to the Cyprus coastline, we were picked up by 2 Wessex helicopters after dark one evening and flown aboard. It was the first time I had flown on to any ship and found the experience exhilarating. After landing on the flight deck we were led away quickly before climbing out of our survival suits and life jackets. I was then shown my cabin, shared with 3 others, stowed my kit and went to find Corporal Howell and the others from 3 Troop, who were relieved to see a familiar face after 10 days living below deck. The next day the Commando Group deployed ashore in a continuous cycle of helicopter lifts, which required detailed synchronisation between 42 Commando HQ, the ship's Air Operations officer and the Fleet Air Arm's embarked Helicopter Squadron. We were organised into tactical groups which were marshaled by chalk number below deck, before being lifted up to the flight deck and called forward to an assigned helicopter and dropped off at nominated landing sites near Episkopi in the west of Cyprus. The whole operation appeared to go without a hitch, but it soon transpired that some of the chalks had been dropped in the wrong place, due to an error in the sequencing of the later chalk numbers. It took the rest of the day for some sub-units to locate their vehicles and equipment and reorganise. Once the mix-up was resolved, 42 Commando moved forward during the night for a dawn attack on the 'enemy' on a plateau, with the assault engineers from

42 Command and 3 Troop sappers providing the battle simulations. These were explosive charges detonated in sequence to simulate artillery, naval gunfire and air support and marked with white tape to ensure no one approached the charges too closely. Having secured the plateau, we all dug in to defend it against the inevitable counter-attack and stayed there for 3 days living in trenches, when not on patrols. On the fourth night of the exercise we made a tactical withdrawal and were lifted back to HMS Bulwark from landing sites a few miles from the plateau at first light. That evening in the ship's wardroom after supper the friendly banter between the Royal Marine officers, the ship's officers and the helicopter pilots suddenly became tense when a few marines blamed the pilots for dropping them in the wrong place 5 days earlier. Within minutes a serious brawl broke out, but it was soon over, and any hard feelings were quickly patched up over a couple of beers.

After a day on the ship sorting out kit and being briefed on the next exercise, the Commando Group was lifted ashore once more, this time at last light to an area near Dhekelia in the east of Cyprus. My small team of sappers had an initial backbreaking task of digging a hole large enough for a MEXE shelter, backfilling over the top of the shelter to provide the overhead protection and making it suitable for the Commando Tactical Headquarters. It took all night and much of the next day, but we were encouraged by the CO, who unexpectedly helped for a couple of hours at the start and proved surprisingly handy with a pick! He explained that, having given his orders before leaving the ship, there was nothing he could do to influence events until all his men were deployed and so he might as well make himself useful. I imagine it was more likely that he was using it as an opportunity to get to know us, but it was a generous and impressive gesture. Once the MEXE task was completed we rejoined the assault engineers and spent the remainder of the exercise providing battle simulations – much more fun than digging! The final day involved a withdrawal in contact with the 'enemy' which proved quite testing as the sub-units leap-frogged each other from one tactical bound to another. After returning on board, cleaned up and debriefed, we had a welcome day off on a 'banyan' (a picnic) on one of the more remote beaches where we all relaxed over a few beers and a barbeque.

Within a few days we were ashore again, this time in Turkey. The 3 Troop section had been tasked with providing the battle simulations for a demonstration brigade attack, which was to be witnessed by a group of senior NATO observers. I arranged for more than a ton of plastic explosive, together with detonating cord, detonators, switches and safety fuse to be drawn from one of HMS Bulwark's magazines. On arrival at the designated area for the attack (due the next day), we found it contained a large herd of goats and a number of children milling around from nearby villages; clearly unsuitable as a place to stage any attack. The helicopter had already left, and we were stuck amongst a small crowd of friendly onlookers while we tried to relay a message from a man-pack radio. Eventually a liaison officer turned up to inform us the demonstration had been cancelled and we were picked up later by a helicopter and returned to HMS Bulwark. The unused explosives were certainly not welcomed back, and I suspect may have been tipped over the side rather than running the risk of restocking the magazine. We were soon retasked to help 2 Troop who had deployed on the exercise with 41 Commando but who had been urgently reassigned to set up a decontamination point to clean all the vehicles from 3 Commando Brigade before they left Turkey. There was, apparently, a possibility of some sort of parasite being picked up from the soil in the area and all vehicles had to be thoroughly washed before being re-embarked. Tim Hodinott and his troop welcomed some extra hands to cope with such a monotonous task.

At the end of the exercise I flew back with Garth Hewish and his radio-operator (Lance Corporal Wobbly Roberts) from Istanbul on a Hercules aircraft, arriving at RAF Lyneham in Wiltshire around midnight, before catching an RAF bus to Salisbury and boarding an early morning train to Plymouth. Garth (as a Major) was entitled to a first-class seat and invited Wobbly Roberts and me to join him as the train had very few passengers at that early hour and he was the only passenger in his compartment. We were all looking forward to a hot drink but there was no buffet service so Wobbly produced a mess tin and water bottle, lit a hexamine block on a little cooker issued with every 24-hour ration pack and started brewing up a welcome mug of tea for all of us on the floor of the compartment. As the water was just about to boil, the flabbergasted conductor entered to check our tickets and it says much for Garth's charm that we were not thrown off the train!

The Squadron had two remaining commitments before Christmas leave. The first was our participation in a visit to 3 Commando Brigade by HRH the Duke of Edinburgh, Captain General of the Royal Marines. The event was on Dartmoor and there were a number of stands, manned by different units. The weather on the day was wet, windy and cold; by the time HRH arrived to meet my troop near the end of his visit he appeared somewhat disgruntled. We had almost finished building a medium girder bridge and had it poised so that he could witness the final launch over a stream on to rollers on the far bank. He rather acidly remarked that he could not see the point of a bridge from nowhere to nowhere! Understandably, he probably wanted to get off the moor as soon as he could.

The second commitment was a Brigade logistic exercise. We embarked on HMS Fearless at Portsmouth, spending a few uncomfortable days afloat in stormy weather in the English Channel, much of the time dressed in NBC protective suits and wearing respirators, while the Royal Navy practised amphibious procedures and we kept out of the way. After disembarking at Lulworth Cove we completed a few relatively simple tasks to assist the Commando Logistic Regiment move its trucks disembarked from other shipping to and from different locations in and around Salisbury Plain. The trucks were loaded with simulated ammunition, fuel, rations, equipment and other stores and our tasks included a long section of trackway from the beach at Lulworth Cove, a bridge over the River Avon and a brigade water point. Although this exercise did not challenge the Squadron, it demonstrated the scale of logistic support required by amphibious operations and the complexity of linking the sea tail to units deployed forward ashore. After Christmas our focus switched to our forthcoming deployment to Northern Ireland in March.

After 2 months of pre-deployment training and a short spell of leave the Squadron arrived on 21st March 1974 at Antrim Bridge Camp, located on the edge of Loch Neagh about 15 miles north-west of Belfast. We were providing the Sapper support to 39 Infantry Brigade (Headquarters in Lisburn) and its battalions based in Belfast. 3 Troop was tasked with supporting the First Battalion Royal Highland Fusiliers (1 RHF) in Anderson Town and Turf Lodge, in the west part of Belfast, and were soon busy constructing sangers (built with high density concrete blocks and sited on scaffold towers), anti-rocket screens and cover from view screens (large sightscreens) in order to provide defensive protection for the soldiers in their company bases. Most of the construction work was at section level once I had confirmed with the company commanders and the CO what they needed, recced each task and ordered the stores. Staff Sergeant Joinson and Sergeant Sims had moved on and my two Senior NCOs were now Staff Sergeant Roberts and Sergeant Jones, who helped with the planning and supervision of the different tasks. Our most difficult job was to build an anti-rocket chain-link screen around a 4-story high block of flats in Lenadoon, Anderson Town to protect an RHF Observation Post (OP) against possible RPG 7 rocket attacks. The screen had to be cantilevered from the roof and tied to scaffolding, on the roof and around the block to provide a ten-foot standoff from the walls. Any rocket fired at the OP would detonate against the screen and most of the explosive energy would thus be dissipated before it reached a wall. Throughout the task my soldiers were very vulnerable to IRA snipers as there was no cover and they were working on the roof and high up around the sides. I coordinated the work with the company commander and his infantry patrol plan to ensure they only worked outside the building while patrols were on the ground to cover possible sniper positions. We also had infantry protection on the roof. The day the task was finished, and the covering patrols withdrawn, the Provisional Irish Republican Army (PIRA) fired an RPG 7 at the OP. Thankfully it detonated harmlessly on the screen without harming the RHF soldiers inside the building.

I saw a lot more of Belfast and the surrounding area while working in the Sapper role than during my infantry tour two years earlier in East Belfast and generally had a more interesting time. While visiting the various task sites my Land Rover was often stoned, especially in and around West Belfast but I saw little rioting, in comparison with the Short Strand area in 1972. Along with the other troop commanders and troop staff sergeants in the Squadron

I took turns to be on duty for 24 hours at Girdwood Park, in the New Lodge area of the city, where the Squadron had a plant section on permanent stand-by to assist with riot control and road clearance. This section was equipped with armoured wheeled front-loading tractors and tipper trucks. Whenever there was a riot, crowds of youths would try and hijack buses, lorries and cars, set fire to them and block the roads. The tractors would pick up cars and load them into the tipper trucks and they would also nudge the buses and lorries to the side of the road. A local Catholic priest in the New Lodge made it his business to warn the local people in the area that the British troops were evil men and that they should have nothing to do with them. Long live the Easter Spirit! One old woman who sometimes gave soldiers a cup of tea challenged him by asking if that was how a Christian really should behave. The priest had no answer and that same old dear was frequently threatened by the PIRA and her husband beaten up simply because they were friendly towards soldiers. 42 Commando were based in Girdwood Park, so I always enjoyed being there as it was a chance to catch up with some of the officers I had been with the previous year in Cyprus and Turkey.

The RHF soldiers, known as 'Jocks', were always friendly towards us and we felt comfortable working on our sapper tasks in their area, knowing that their patrols were an effective deterrent against PIRA snipers. They took no nonsense from the local community and reacted very quickly to any terrorist incident. In early April there was a surge of violence with the PIRA hijacking buses, lorries and cars in the Falls Road area, placing bombs around the city and making a number of hoax calls. They also started shooting in the Anderson Town area, which included 2 separate daylight unsuccessful shootings targeted against the OP in the block of flats while my section from 3 Troop were on site and a third unsuccessful daylight shooting on a sanger overlooking a cover-from-view fence which another of my sections was replacing.

During this period the Jocks were involved in a number of more serious shootings at night, when we were back in Antrim. In one incident someone in a car opened fire on a patrol with a machine gun; the soldiers returned fire but could not follow up until the next morning when they found the abandoned car with two bullet holes in the back and another hole in the passenger back seat. There was a pool of blood in the car and they then arrested a man in a nearby house who was burning blankets from a hijacked ambulance. From his house to the car was a trail of blood, in the car there were pieces of a weapon and parts of a nail bomb. The following night the OP in the flats was nail-bombed and shot at again. The soldiers fired back at the gunman who was using a crowd around a chip van as cover. They hit someone because they followed up a trail of blood the next day. The next night, the PIRA fired a rocket at a sanger in another RHF base, which just missed the sentry inside although he was peppered with concrete debris and bruised from the blast. This rocket attack was followed by a burst of firing from an armalite rifle and, shortly after, the Jocks arrested a young woman who was carrying an armalite rifle under her coat. A week later, on the 19th April after a shoot up near the Woodburn Hotel, a Jock OP saw a car pull up, 3 men drag a fourth man out and shoot him in the knee. The Jocks reported the shooting on the radio and a patrol rushed to the scene as the car was leaving. The car did not stop but was driven at the patrol who opened fire on it. The rifle fire damaged and stopped the car. Three PIRA men ran off and were chased by another patrol. They went into a house, leaving one wounded man behind who escaped. The other two ran straight into the arms of a third patrol but one of these also escaped. The third patrol could not shoot him as they were not certain that he was connected with the shooting; all they had seen was the men running. So, the incident ended with one man captured, one wounded and two pistols recovered. Overall, it was an eventful fortnight in Anderson Town with more than 200 rounds fired by the PIRA in over 15 different incidents, one rocket attack and a few blast bombs. Not one soldier was hurt but they wounded a number of PIRA, found a number of weapons and made some arrests.

We were also tasked for searches where there was a high risk of IEDs. The PIRA were increasingly using hides to conceal their weapons, retrieve them prior to a sniping attack or an ambush and then hide them again. Some of these hides were cleverly concealed in houses but they also used derelict buildings and waste ground in Republican areas of the city, in order to reduce the chances of arrest. Many of the derelict buildings were filthy, crawling with lice and fleas, so the search teams wore coveralls for these searches instead of their Commando smocks. Afterwards, the coveralls would be burnt, and the soldiers would be deloused. We did not find many weapons, but the searches undoubtedly forced the PIRA to store their weapons in less convenient places (for them) and made it more difficult to move them before and after a shooting. The risk of booby traps was always present in any derelict building and vividly demonstrated in an incident involving a search carried out by an infantry battalion soon after dawn on 5th May close to Grosvenor Road. The battalion had received a tip-off that that there was something suspicious about this particular building and one of the search teams found a .22 air rifle with a telescopic sight, concealed by a rug to make it appear like a sniper's rifle. The Corporal in charge of the team was very careful as he suspected a trap so he attached a cable and hook to the air rifle and began to unwind the cable towards a safe place some distance away from the rifle, from where he intended to pull the rifle clear. Unfortunately, all sorts of other military people had barged into the building, taking photographs, and generally milling around. A Royal Military Police (RMP) Finds Team member stupidly picked up the air rifle before it had been pulled clear. As suspected, it was booby-trapped and the RMP soldier lost an arm and suffered blindness and loss of hearing in the explosion. The infantry search team corporal lost an eye (and later the sight of his second eye). It was a senseless tragedy that should never have happened. One of my sections had to search the house in the aftermath in case there were any further booby traps, but found nothing.

For some time, the Protestant Community had become increasingly disillusioned with events in Northern Ireland. Their sense of alienation came to a head during the Ulster Workers Council (UWC) strike from 15th to 28th May 1974, called in protest at the British proposals to give the Republic of Ireland influence in how Northern Ireland would be governed. The strike brought down the short-lived Northern Ireland Executive, established on 1st January 1974, and direct rule was reimposed from Westminster. A key factor was the support for the strike in key industries such as power generation, gas and petrol distribution. Robert Fisk (a prominent journalist) commented in the preface to his book 'The Point of No Return: The Strike Which Broke the British in Ulster'.

"During those fifteen days, for the first time in over fifty years ..., a section of the realm became totally ungovernable. A self-elected provisional government of Protestant power workers, well-armed private armies and extreme politicians organized a strike which almost broke up the fabric of civilized life in Ulster. They deprived most of the population for much of the time of food, water, electricity, gas, transport, money and any form of livelihood."

During these 2 weeks my troop was employed in the infantry role, under command of B Squadron, the Blues and Royals, a cavalry squadron responsible for Antrim and much of the surrounding area of Belfast. Their operations officer, Peter Rogers, was an old friend from my Sandhurst days, delightfully casual and laid back. We carried out a few vehicle checks, patrolled during the night and day, stood by one day with a company from the 1st Battalion Royal Regiment of Wales for a riot that did not kick off and cleared a number of roadblocks. Two of these roadblocks consisted of trees felled across the road with a couple of 5-gallon cans by the side of the trees, with wires connected to a battery. In each case I radioed to ask for an ATO to clear the devices. On blowing open the cans, the ATO found that they contained explosive but no means of setting it off; the devices were elaborate hoaxes. Some of the troop also helped to run petrol pumps taken over by the Army and wire up the pumps to emergency generators.

It was a slightly surreal time because we did not feel threatened or hated by the community in and around Antrim, as we did in some parts of Belfast, but we felt annoyed that a bunch of hardline Protestants were holding the British Government to ransom and getting away with it. It seemed to me that both sides were so intransigent that there was no realistic prospect of an agreement acceptable to both the Protestant and Catholic communities ever being negotiated.

A few days after the UWC strike finished, I was posted to 9 Independent Parachute Squadron as the Second in Command. Although delighted to be joining 9 Squadron, I was sad to be leaving 3 Troop with whom it had been great fun to serve. They were an extraordinarily decent group of men, always ready to tackle whatever task was thrown at them with humour and determination and I learned a lot from them. On the morning that Albert Whitley, a good friend, took over the troop they surprised me by presenting me with a Commando Dagger beautifully mounted below a Squadron plaque on a larger wooden shield inscribed with the words "From the Lads of 3 Troop. Good Luck Chief!" As I waved farewell afterwards at the Antrim Camp gate to them deploying on different section tasks in Belfast, I felt humbled by their generosity.

Emerging from the water culvert on the Endurance Course.

Helping the next man through.

The flight deck on HMS Bulwark.

Waiting to be called forward to fly ashore.

A walk with Mary and David (in the papoose) on the edge of Dartmoor. We were fortunate to live close to the Moor.

A Medium Girder Bridge being launched across a Dartmoor stream on a wet Autumn day for HRH The Duke of Edinburgh, Captain General Royal Marines.

Staff Sergeant Joinson (my Troop S/Sgt) briefing HRH about the bridge. I'm standing on HRH's left and Major General Pounds (Commander Commando Forces) is on his right.

Building an anti-rocket
screen to protect an OP
in Anderson Town. The
chain-link netting was
delivered by helicopter and
hung from the top, secured
to a scaffold frame on the
top and sides of the building.

Staff Sergeant Roberts
marshalling an approaching
helicopter.

Lance Corporal Wobbly Roberts
linking the netting together.

Corporal Ben Allum belaying Wobbly from the roof with a sentry from 1 RHF keeping watch.

View of the completed screen from the road.

6

AIRBORNE ENGINEER

Mary and I enjoyed a blissful short break in Cornwall on my return from Northern Ireland in June 1974 before packing up our belongings in Plymouth and moving in with Mary's parents in London. I reported to 9 Independent Parachute Squadron at Rhine Barracks, Aldershot at the beginning of July to attend Pre-Para and P Company. The Squadron was in Hong Kong but had left behind a small rear party. I asked Corporal Peter Bates (then assistant Chief Clerk and back in Aldershot having recently completed a Round the World Sailing trip with Chay Blythe) how I could get hold of some kit needed in Wales for the last few days on P Company. He cheekily remarked "Why bother? I reckon you won't last long enough on P Company to even get to Wales!" After passing the course and taking over as 2IC he handed me my P Company Report (with an A grade) remarking with a grin, "Got that one wrong didn't I Sir! Welcome to the Squadron!" He typified the confidence of all 9 Squadron soldiers, who believed that they could take on anything and come out on top. They were fiercely loyal to anyone in the Squadron, but one first had to earn that loyalty by passing the selection course. Peter Bates left the Army the following year to seek his fortune in Civvy Street where he became a very successful security consultant and earned a fortune.

Mary was expecting our second child, due in early August, and she had made arrangements for the birth at the Middlesex Hospital, where David had been born 2 years earlier. Soon after starting P Company, I arrived at her parents' home one Friday evening to find an ambulance outside the house. Mary had been bathing David before his bedtime when she suddenly felt the baby's umbilical cord emerge unexpectedly. She dialled 999, packed some overnight belongings in a small suitcase, lifted David out of the bath and dressed him ready to accompany her. When I arrived, she was stoically walking towards the ambulance, calmly holding David's hand, but I could see that she was very concerned. The ambulance crew were wonderful, quickly taking charge and setting off immediately for the Middlesex. All sorts of scenarios were flashing through my mind and I was desperately hoping that all would be fine. I could not help thinking about the circumstances of my brother Richard's birth that resulted in him being multi-handicapped all his life. Fortunately, the consultant who had carried out an emergency caesarean to save both the baby and Mary confidently reassured us both that all was well. What a relief! Anna (our new baby) had arrived 4 weeks prematurely, weighing a little over 4 pounds and she spent her first fortnight in intensive care. Fortunately, she had been in a breech position when the birth started and one of her tiny feet had been trapped in the birth canal with the chord, rather than her head. This resulted in a bruised foot but at least no cut-off of oxygen and no brain damage. We felt enormously lucky to have 2 healthy children. During her recovery from the traumatic birth Mary remained in hospital with Anna until returning to her parents, while I completed P Company.

As on my first attempt 5 years earlier, the course was tough, but I escaped injury this time. We had been joined by members of the British potential Olympic Ski Team who joined in most of the training except for the long marches in the local area and the last few days in Wales. I remember Konrad Bartelski (who became a famous skier) just beating me on the assault course and me just beating him on the steeplechase. The course had many parallels with the Commando Course and essentially sought to identify the same characteristics. There was less emphasis on upper body strength but more on speed with the tabs (marches) and the runs considerably faster. There was no attempt to teach tactics. The instructors all carried the same weight as the students. Our course numbering about 50 was split into different sections, with just one other officer in my squad, John Scott, who was joining the Parachute Regiment and who had just returned from a climbing expedition in the Himalayas. He made the interesting comment that he experienced more team spirit and camaraderie on P Company than he had on his climbing expedition where individual climbers were so intent on getting to the top first that many put their own needs above those of their fellow climbers. Our section instructor, Sergeant 'Smokey' Lloyd, was firm but fair as were all the instructors and the course soon developed a strong sense of fellowship.

The first 3 weeks was spent at Browning Barracks, the Parachute Regiment Depot and named after General Browning who commanded the 1st British Airborne Corps at Arnhem. I was 'ambushed' just before lunch in the first week by the Commanding Officer (CO) of the Depot who insisted that I join him at the bar and would not allow me to leave until I had downed 3 pints with him. When I mentioned that I was on a tab in the afternoon and would prefer a soft drink he would not hear of it, saying

"Nonsense boy – beer is just what you need!" Despite enjoying his stories, I thereafter had to sneak into the Mess at lunchtime through the kitchen, not the front door, in order to avoid him. He was a hard, uncompromising officer decorated with two MCs who had served with the SAS.

The tests in the third week comprised the assault course, steeplechase, trainasium (an aerial obstacle course), milling, the log race (6 men carrying a telegraph pole over a 2-mile cross-country course running as fast as possible in a race to beat the other teams), a 10-mile tab with rifle, webbing and bergan in an hour and fifty minutes and a fast 20-mile tab along part of the South Downs. Perhaps the most challenging was the log race although it only lasted for a lung busting few minutes. In the milling, I was drawn against a Senior NCO who was a good boxer and he knocked me down 3 times. Fortunately, I just managed to stand my ground as he tired, landing a few blows of my own, but my head was buzzing after the bout.

The last part of the course was spent in and around the Brecon Beacons. We were transported to Cwm Gwdi camp, near Brecon at the bottom of Pen Y Fan in the back of a couple of four-ton trucks arriving in the early evening. The next morning, we set off by sections at intervals with rifles, fighting order and a bergan. Our route was a strenuous climb straight up Pen Y Fan and then across the hills to a hilltop RV 22 miles away, which we reached 4 and a half-hours later. There the officers were each given a jerry can and told to collect water for everyone from a water bowser at the bottom of the hill about a mile away. By early afternoon we had established a patrol base, posted sentries, had some food, replenished our water bottles, and were briefed to be ready for a night tab across Llangattock Moor and then further west, leaving at 2am. Until then we rested.

We again set off in sections, this time in the dark and feeling a little stiff. I was map-reading (in our section) and followed compass bearings very carefully until it started to become light around 4.30am shortly before sunrise. By then we were off the moor and on forest tracks that provided easy walking and we reached our next RV just before 7am having covered another 20 miles. Here we were treated to a welcome surprise of a cooked breakfast of porridge, bacon and eggs, bread and tea, provided by our instructors, before mustering for a 12-mile speed march back over Pen Y Fan to Cwm Gwdi. Within minutes some were struggling with the pace and the course soon became strung out. I, along with a few others, went back repeatedly to fetch the stragglers and needed all my endurance, thankful for the fitness I had gained over previous years as a runner. Well before the summit of the Fan the instructors split us into groups, and I found myself in the leading section now led by the Major who commanded P Company. He had been on many of the tabs throughout the course and always set a blistering pace, despite being well into his forties. I developed cramp in my legs just below the summit but added a couple of salt tablets to my water bottle, gulped the mixture down and was soon back on my feet, running to catch up and finishing with the leaders 2 hours after we had started. We had covered over 55 miles in a little over 24 hours with some long climbs.

The next morning those of us still on the course formed two 12 man teams for the final test; a 10-mile race from Cwm Gwdi carrying a stretcher along minor lanes and up a long uphill track skirting around the western edge of Pen Y Fan finishing close to the Storey Arms Inn. Each stretcher weighed 16 stone, the weight of a wounded soldier with his equipment, and was carried by 4 men at a time in relays. We also had our rifles and webbing but passed our rifles to another team member when it was our turn on the stretcher. We set off at a brisk pace alternately jogging and speed marching, with an instructor telling us when to change over every few minutes. Inevitably, there were some who dropped out and with over 4 miles still left until the finish our team was down to 6 so we were all taking much longer stints on the stretcher. Fortunately, we remained resolute and reached the finish in just under 2 hours. Anyone who dropped out failed. We staggered on to the trucks parked near the finish and crashed out in the back, fast asleep, until arriving back in Aldershot. After cleaning our rifles and returning them to the armoury we cleaned ourselves up and the whole course met up in a local pub with the instructors for a farewell celebration. It had been a very intense but invigorating few days and the terrain in the hills had truly tested us.

The next morning all those who had completed the course assembled in the gym at Browning Barracks to be told who had passed. The CO of the Depot was present, along with all the P Company staff. Sitting on the floor in our depleted squads, our names were called out in alphabetical order by the Company Sergeant Major, a charismatic Irishman. We stood up in turn to be told by the CO brusquely, "Pass" or "Fail" and sat down. For those of us who passed it was a tremendous relief, coupled with a great sense of achievement, but it was devastating for those who failed despite them sticking with the course until the end. Failing P Company must have been a very personal blow because the course exposed more than physical fitness or frailty; it laid bare one's character under stress.

The next week I collected Mary plus David and baby Anna from her parents' home, and we settled into our quarter in Knollys Road, very close to the Headquarters of the 16 Independent Parachute

Brigade's Officers Mess blown up by the Official IRA 2 years earlier. The Mess building was still boarded up and unoccupied, providing a stark reminder of the terrorist threat. Our new home was only a 5-minute walk from 9 Squadron; very convenient. It was lovely to be reunited again but there was no time to relax as the Squadron was due to deploy to Northern Ireland within a few weeks, 4 months since I had left 59 Squadron in Antrim and 2 years since leaving the Short Strand in Belfast. Mary was becoming used to coping on her own.

Meanwhile I needed to attend a parachute refresher course at RAF Abingdon as my last jump was in 1967 while at Sandhurst and I was out of date. Once that was over, I could finally concentrate on my new job and find my feet in a hectic preparation for our tour. In addition to 2 weeks search training at Chattenden for the search teams and advisors and some basic construction training in the local area, we undertook infantry training under the guidance of the Northern Ireland Training and Advisory Team (NITAT) at Lydd and Hythe, together with a Gunner Regiment who were deploying to Belfast City Centre. The CO of the Gunners could not cope with the Squadron's exuberance when we were acting as enemy in the Rype Training Village and requested that we should only be allowed to use the ranges and not train in the village with his men. Mike Payne (our OC) therefore decided that it was not worth remaining and we formally marched out of Lydd Camp the next day – to the astonishment of the Gunners and the quiet amusement of the NITAT trainers. We felt we were ready for whatever we would encounter in Northern Ireland.

Not long afterwards the Advance Party arrived at Castle Dillon near Armagh on 5th October 1974 to take over from 3 Field Squadron, followed soon after by the Main Body. The normal areas of responsibility for each field troop, were: 1 Troop with Jim Snape in South Down and South Armagh, 2 Troop with John Mulvaney in North Armagh and East Tyrone, 3 Troop with Martin Richardson in West Tyrone and South Fermanagh, while Support Troop deployed wherever plant and specialist driver support were needed. Each field troop provided 2 construction sections and 3 dedicated search teams. Paul Scoble had been left behind to run the small rear party and help the families and Sergeant Dave Weaver also remained in Aldershot with the P Company staff, keeping an eye on potential new recruits to the Squadron.

All the Sappers in Northern Ireland were under the command of the Commander Royal Engineers (CRE) at HQNI at Lisburn with the three field squadrons each supporting a brigade. We were supporting 3 Infantry Brigade, commanded by Brigadier Wallis-King, in the south and southwest of the Province. 33 Independent Field Squadron at Antrim supported 39 Infantry Brigade in Belfast; the Field Squadron from Germany based at Ballykelly supported 8 Infantry Brigade in Londonderry. 325 Engineer Park (which provided our resources back up and additional construction plant) was co-located with 33 Squadron at Antrim. Although 9 Squadron was by no means new to Northern Ireland it was our first tour there in a rural environment. The tasks were very varied and widely spread throughout 3 Brigade's area. We were usually tasked direct by 3 Brigade, keeping the CRE, Lieutenant Colonel Morris, and his small staff closely informed, and the CRE visited us regularly. I represented Mike Payne at the daily morning briefings at HQ 3 Brigade and formed a very close working relationship with the brigade staff.

In the construction role we supported some 50 Security Force bases ranging from section to battalion strength and which included the Royal Ulster Constabulary (RUC). The biggest challenges were movement and logistics. Vehicle movement was often very limited, especially to any site close to the border, and needed to be closely coordinated with the infantry. The country lanes between Bessbrook, Crossmaglen and Forkhill posed the greatest risk and movement by military vehicles of any sort in South Armagh was unsafe. Civilianised, covert vehicles were often recognised by terrorists and we used helicopters whenever possible.

We closed 30 unapproved border crossings, usually by blowing craters at the crossings but we were often restricted to using plant to position Braithwaite tanks (steel tanks filled with concrete) as obstacles, in order to prevent blast damage to nearby buildings. Border closures were often controversial because of their impact on the community; although they did disrupt movement across the border for short periods, they alienated the locals in the longer term. We felt that they were counter-productive as obstacles because the infantry seldom had enough manpower to provide any sort of over watch on them and the local farmers nearly always reopened the crossings using their tractors and other farm machinery. We far preferred to use explosives because cratering was much quicker than deploying a long convoy of plant down narrow lanes close to the border. On one memorable day we closed 2 crossings with a total of 42 separate cratering charges (28 on one and 14 on the other) that created significant obstacles, but even these crossings were eventually reopened. On another border closure, gunmen from across the border in Monaghan opened fire but were surprised by the immediate weight of fire returned by the infantry cordon and the sappers and soon fled. We twice had to close a crossing some 6 miles south of Newry and adjacent to the main railway line from Belfast to Dublin. The limited time that the infantry were prepared to remain on site meant that we had to use cratering charges, as it would have taken too long using plant, but it was therefore inevitable that the blasts would deposit a fair amount of earth on the line. The tasking order from 3 Brigade for the second closure directed that no debris was to fall on the line – difficult! This did not daunt 1 Troop who completed the task without disrupting any train movements. On another operation soon after our arrival some local yobbos made the mistake of stoning a plant convoy on its way through Armagh City en route for a border closure further south. They were astounded when the column stopped and men from 1 and Support Troops jumped out of the vehicles and ran after them, giving them a lesson that the Squadron would not be intimidated. Thereafter we encountered very little stone throwing when moving through or around Armagh City.

During the third week of October 1974, the Republican prisoners and internees in Long Kesh (also known as the Maze) rioted and also set fire to their compounds. More than 40 platoons from infantry units from all three brigades in Northern Ireland were rushed to contain the riot and the Squadron was tasked to help clear the debris, carry out searches and help sort out damaged accommodation for the prisoners. The IRA had cleverly arranged to leave one hut undamaged in each of their compounds as they realised that they would need some shelter to return to after the riot. All the soldiers and most of the population would have been happy to allow them to endure this arrangement throughout the winter as they had after all orchestrated the riot, but 36 Engineer Regiment was soon deployed from Maidstone to rebuild all the Republican accommodation. It seemed to us that the prisoners had escaped any retribution for their actions.

Soon afterwards, on 5th November 1974, the Republicans attempted a mass breakout of Long Kesh from a tunnel but fortunately one of the early escapees was shot by a member of the Prison Guard Force, which encouraged those prisoners behind him to surrender. A few had already escaped, much to the chagrin of those responsible for running the Prison. 9 Squadron was asked to return and search for more tunnels. None were found but Mike Payne forcibly pointed out to the Prison Authorities that they would certainly have found the tunnel used in the escape if only they had regularly searched each compound. However, the Prison Guards were no doubt intimidated by the IRA who knew where they and their families lived and it is perhaps unsurprising that some of them left the prisoners and internees alone and failed to report the concealed spoil from the tunnel. Thereafter, 9 Squadron search teams were tasked fairly frequently to search both Republican and Loyalist huts, sometimes finding very realistic looking weapons made in the prisoners' wood-working workshop, but we did not find any more tunnels.

Our main emphasis soon became focused on search operations, which later also included Heavy Goods Vehicle (HGV), searches in an attempt to thwart the movement of arms and explosives across the border. By the end of the tour the Squadron Search Teams had completed over 250 search tasks, most of which were high risk Improvised Explosive Device (IED) search and clearance operations in support of an infantry company group. This figure does not include the several hundred HGV searches for the RUC. Search concepts, procedures, skills and equipment were continuously modified and improved. The role of High Risk Search, undertaken only by RE search teams, was crucial not only in clearing safe lanes for Ammunition Technical Officers (ATOs) to enable them to deal with IEDs, but also in the clearance of routes, derelicts and hides. Our search teams and advisers established a very professional rapport with the infantry units, the ATOs, the Reconnaissance Intelligence Centre (RIC) who provided up to date air photo analysis of the locations of planned searches, pilots from both the Army Air Corps and those based in Aldergrove with the Support Helicopters and the RUC. RE search tasking was coordinated from the Squadron Ops Room and the planning sometimes took days in order to collate all the latest information available and avoid needless risks. The tasking unit retained overall command and control on the ground but, during each operation, the local unit commander would delegate command of the search phase to the Search Adviser and the clearance phase to the ATO.

The relationship on the ground between the ATOs, search advisers and search teams was always good but we experienced unwelcome obstruction from the Chief ATO in HQ NI (known as CATO) who attempted to ban the Squadron from using explosives unless there was an ATO present. He also banned our search teams from using an earlier model of an IED wheelbarrow (no longer needed by his ATOs who by then had newer models) to prove safe routes in appropriate search scenarios. His attempt to ban us using explosives was soon rescinded as everyone recognised it as absurd, but he jealously guarded his wheelbarrow and would not budge. His insistence that 'cap-badge politics' took precedence over operational safety and effectiveness was senseless.

Sadly, 2 ATOs were killed by IED devices in November; one near Stewartstown, south of Cookstown, and another near Kinawley in Fermanagh. In hindsight the ATOs perhaps took avoidable risks but the PIRA were extremely cunning, and these incidents highlighted their skill in setting lethal traps for the unwary or the impatient.

The incident near Stewartstown was initiated by an explosion near an electricity sub-station. On arrival at the scene the ATO proceeded to make his way around the site without first tasking a search team to clear a safe route for him. While moving through an opening in a hedge line, with a policeman and an infantry senior NCO, a massive second explosion killed all three. 3 Troop's Search teams were immediately deployed to carry out a full IED search and clean-up operation, working alongside another ATO because 2 Troop's search teams were already deployed on a follow-up to a sniper's killing of two soldiers in Crossmaglen. The Kinawley incident involved 2 separate IEDs. The first was a collapsing circuit and explosive in a milk churn, which killed the ATO who decided to disarm the device by hand rather than neutralising it remotely. The second, linked IED was 100 pounds of ANFO (a homemade mixture of Ammonium Nitrate and Fuel Oil) connected to a firing mechanism tied to the command wire by fishing line and designed to catch the search team following up the command wire from the milk churn. This second device was fortunately thwarted by the vigilance of the Search Adviser, Sergeant Kevin McGrath.

A third very nasty device was uncovered successfully in early December by Sergeant Peter Kershaw and 2 Troop's search teams in a follow-up to a shooting near Coagh, between Cookstown and Lough Neagh that had taken place earlier. It was likely that the firing point used in the shooting had been booby-trapped by the PIRA. After allowing a soak period of a few days, the search teams completed a circular search of the area to locate command wires, but none were found. Two sappers were then tasked to clear a path to the firing point, but Sergeant Kershaw became suspicious and halted them because he felt that there was a greater risk of a pressure operated device rather than tripwires. He made up an improvised small explosive hose by linking a number of PE4 charges along a length of detonating cord and flung this towards the suspect firing point. The subsequent detonation of these charges and a second similar charge exposed a 'pressure plate' type device which was linked to 3 separate explosive charges designed to kill anyone approaching the firing point.

A ceasefire from 22nd December 1974 to 16th January 1975 was negotiated between the IRA and the British Government and subsequently renewed on 9th February until 23rd January 1976. The IRA used the truce to buy time for regrouping and rearming. No trust developed between them and the Security Forces. The truce was fragile, and the IRA violated it when it suited them. Once it broke down completely the conflict continued until the Good Friday Stormont Agreement was signed in 1998. The Squadron's tasking continued much as normal throughout the truce, but we ceased any offensive search operations and adopted more of a reactive profile. 3 Brigade took the opportunity to task the search teams to clear as many derelicts and suspected IED sites as possible. Although not directly threatened by the IRA in the three weeks before mid-January, the search operations along the border remained dangerous and no short cuts were taken.

Throughout the tour, including the truce, the high-risk searches in particular provided a most demanding challenge for the teams and search advisers. They were as much at risk as the ATOs and the results achieved enhanced the Army's hard-won searching expertise and sharpened the IED counter-measures in Northern Ireland. Corporal Pete Ellis was awarded a well-earned QGM for his efforts as a Search Team Commander in support of the 1st Battalion the Royal Green Jackets in South Armagh. The CO (then Lieutenant Colonel Jones who later became General Sir Edward Jones and, after retirement from the Army, Black Rod in the House of Lords) was a firm supporter of the Squadron and regarded the two teams permanently attached to his battalion at Bessbrook as an integral part of his unit.

One of our search teams was caught out in a particularly devious 'come on' in Lurgan in November 1974. The battalion responsible for the area had received tip-offs about a rifle hidden in one of the houses on a particular street and were keen for it to be found. Somewhat reluctantly, as we were suspicious of a trap, a search operation was eventually planned. Towards the end of the day and after searching a number of occupied houses, a search team from 1 Troop were just about to enter an unoccupied house when a local resident approached to tell them that he had a key and would let them in, claiming to know the owner. The search team commander asked him if he was happy to go inside and demonstrate that it was indeed safe, while they observed from some distance away. He readily agreed and soon returned to confirm that there was nothing there. The first pair of searchers (Sappers Froth Beer and Dave Garrard) donned their protective equipment before they entered the house, but inevitably their guard was down as they now believed the house to be safe. A sideboard door on the ground floor was slightly ajar and was opened by Sapper Beer, resulting in a massive explosion which destroyed the house and severely injured him. Sapper Garrard received superficial blast injuries which included temporary damage to his hearing. The local key holder appeared extremely shocked as he claimed not to have known about the booby trap and was relieved that he had not opened the cupboard himself. He was also angry because his young daughter had been playing close by in the street outside and was lucky not be harmed. This incident clearly demonstrated just how callous and ruthless the IRA were and their readiness to risk the lives of innocent bystanders in order to kill a soldier. Froth Beer lost a leg at the hip, some loss of sight, damage to his right hand and one or two other injuries. Throughout his painful and protracted rehabilitation he never lost his sense of humour; while at the Queen Elizabeth Military Hospital in Woolwich he was allowed out one day with another soldier who had also lost a leg and they went to buy one pair of shoes between them, totally baffling the poor sales girl! He was medically discharged from the Army in 1976 but has since achieved a great deal in his life, becoming an expert yachtsman sailing around much of the world. Soon after leaving the Army he completed the strenuous Devizes to Westminster Canoe Race, with another soldier who had also a leg so that they were able to 'balance' the canoe and he also carried out a number of parachute descents into water in aid of the British Limbless Ex Servicemen's Association (BLESMA).

The tour was not 'all work and no play' and the Squadron participated in sports whenever possible. The Rugby Team won the Northern Ireland Minor Units competition, and also managed a few games at the Portadown Rugby Club. Our Boxing Team somehow found time to train as and when they could, coached occasionally by an Oxford Boxing Blue, Captain Robert Nairac (subsequently murdered by the IRA). They regrettably lost the Army Minor Units Final to a very good team from the Royal Pioneer Corps who had travelled to Lisburn for the event. The Cross-Country Team comfortably won the Northern Ireland Minor Units Championships and our Basketball Team reached the Army Minor Units Final.

We came home in style, parachuting on to Hankley Common on 14th February 1975, with our 'Valentines Day Return' being widely reported in the National Press and on TV and depicted in a Giles Cartoon two days later. General Sir Frank King, GOC Northern

Ireland at the time, was keen to jump with the Squadron but his commitments prevented this at the last minute; nevertheless, he saw us off from Aldergrove and sent Captain Max Gandell (his ADC) in his place. It felt surreal to parachute on to Hankley Common within an hour of leaving Aldergrove on a sunny afternoon with a crowd of onlookers, mostly family members, welcoming us home. We all landed safely but Mary wrenched her knee very badly while running across the heather, while responding to Press demands for photographs of her greeting me. She was taken to the Cambridge Military Hospital by her father, who had come with her and our children to watch the jump. Her left leg was bandaged in a cast from her thigh to her ankle for the next 2 months and we needed to employ an au pair girl to help her until the bandage was removed long after I returned to work after post-tour leave. Later, the doctors decided to remove her left kneecap and she has since suffered permanent discomfort and weakness in that knee. For her, that homecoming was 'bitter-sweet'.

It was now almost 5 years since my father had died so suddenly in Rhodesia. My mother had sold the farm and moved to Salisbury (now Harare) while my brother Richard had settled at Homefield, one of the Hopelands' homes not far from Salisbury. However, a long-term secure future for Richard in Rhodesia was increasingly uncertain so they both moved to England and my mother managed (just) to buy a small house in Fleet with the rather meagre proceeds of the sale of her Swallowfield and Thornbury farms. She and Richard were now close by; my sister Julia also soon left Rhodesia to live near Exeter, having met her future husband in Capetown when he was visiting South Africa. My mother, at the age of 65, found it difficult to adapt to her new circumstances, but she fought hard to find somewhere that would look after Richard and eventually found a residential home in Aldershot for about 20 men and women all struggling with some form of learning disability. Richard was moved from there shortly afterwards into a house (also in Aldershot) with 3 other disabled men that was run by a charity. Sadly, the house was soon taken over by a sheltered housing association (not a charity) and the standard of care and supervision for Richard declined markedly over the years. He regularly came to stay with Mary and me (and Julia) and we kept in close touch with him, helping to sort out a variety of issues for him, especially his debts. He was often difficult, selfish and rude, but he did at least try and get about and not simply accept his misfortune. Eventually (thankfully long after my mother died), the housing association callously evicted Richard when he was almost 70 years old. Julia and I arranged, through Hampshire Social Services, for him to be taken in by a nursing home for the mentally infirm in Aldershot where he received very compassionate care from Nepalese, Filipino and Eastern European care workers until he died. He was there for over 4 years, eventually becoming demented, deaf, almost blind and incontinent towards the end of his life.

After our post Northern Ireland leave, the Squadron deployed on a variety of very different exercises for the next 6 months. These included a night parachute insertion and a testing week's infantry training on Stanford Training Area in Norfolk; an inter-troop competition with a night parachute descent on Salisbury Plain before then moving to Wales for a series of challenging combat engineer tasks; 3 weeks in Bavaria where we qualified for our German Parachute wings at their Parachute Training School at Altenstadt, learned about the German Army's Armoured and Amphibious Engineers in Munich and Ingolstadt and experienced some mountain walking in the Bavarian Alps; 6 weeks in Cyprus with an attached troop from 1 Parachute Logistic Battalion, where 2 Troop built a ski hut, Support Troop cut a series of terraces in a remote, very steep area of the Troodos Mountains to assist a local village and the Squadron Diving Team carried out a survey of an underwater mole in preparation for a future build of a jetty. While in Cyprus we were challenged to a rugby match by the Welsh Guards, losing a very fast, exciting game by a narrow margin. Our runners won all the cross-country races they entered and set a record by winning the Dhekelia Dash Relay with our last runner home well before any of the other teams, had completed the penultimate leg. While the bulk of the Squadron was in Cyprus the other two field troops were in Italy and the Sudan.

Wherever we were, the Squadron's indomitable spirit and infectious humour were ever present. I remember an incident involving Lance Corporal Chalky White and Sapper Ginge Shipway who had attempted one evening to break into the local NAAFI in Aldershot on return from their bricklaying course while the rest of us were in Northern Ireland. They were bored and looking for some excitement. They were subsequently identified by the Military Police, charged, and remanded for a Court Martial. I was handed the task of Prosecuting Office some months later once back in Aldershot. Throughout the trial I was given a seriously hard time by the Permanent President of the Court Martial who was a grumpy, overweight, elderly Major who clearly did not like paratroopers. Throughout, the two accused behaved impeccably and readily admitted their guilt. Eventually the Court was adjourned in order that the members could discuss the case and decide sentence. During the adjournment, Lance Corporal White approached me, annoyed by the President's attitude and keen to cheer me up, despite the fact that I was prosecuting him and that he was facing an inevitable sentence of some months in Colchester Military Prison. He remarked, with a friendly grin: "I'm sorry Sir. It's us who've done the business but it's you who's getting all the hassle and grief here today. Why don't I go and sort out that old geezer for being such a rude and ignorant bastard. He's got no right to speak to a 9 Squadron officer like that!"

I persuaded him that such a course of action would not be wise! He and Sapper Shipway accepted their sentence without any bitterness, with a very honest acknowledgement that they had been foolish and with genuine regret that they had let 9 Squadron down. They both left the Army after their release but kept in touch with the Squadron for many years afterwards. During all my years with the Squadron as 2IC and later OC, this was the only court-martial involving anyone in the Squadron. Our soldiers were certainly high-spirited and sometimes mischievous, but they were never malignant or vicious.

In late 1975 Mike Payne handed over command to Gerry Taggart, fresh from his recent posting with the Royal Canadian Engineers School at Chilliwack, British Columbia. Everyone in the Squadron was aware that 16 Independent Parachute Brigade was soon to be disbanded and we would lose our independence and become part of 36 Engineer Regiment in Maidstone. The future was uncertain, but Gerry who had been a troop commander in 9 Squadron in Aden, understood the airborne ethos and we were all pleased to welcome him. He was a big, genial Irishman who had played rugby for the Army, the Combined Services and London Irish, but was invariably courteous and tolerant. We felt confident that he was the right man to lead the Squadron through a difficult transition from being independent to becoming part of a regiment with a different 'modus operandi'. Within a few months of Gerry's arrival, 2 Troop (now commanded by Roger North) deployed for an emergency construction task to fortify the Security Force Base in Crossmaglen against IRA mortar attacks. Not long after their return, the whole Squadron was preparing for another deployment to Northern Ireland and I moved to Chatham to attend a civil engineering course.

My P Company Section with Sgt Lloyd our instructor I am front right with John Scott between me and Sgt Lloyd.

One of the obstacles on the Trainasium.

Proud parents with David and Anna outside 9 Knollys Road (our quarter in Aldershot).

David trying on my red beret!

Anna by the garden door.

Closing a border crossing point in South Armagh with explosives to blow craters in a minor road.

Returning from Northern Ireland by parachute on to Hankley Common Valentines Day, 14 February 1975 (Photo from the Keystone Press).

Mary's greeting on the DZ! (Photos (above right) from the Guardian and (above left) from the Associated Newspapers Group, 15 February 1975).

A copy of the Giles cartoon in the Sunday Express two days after our return, kindly presented to 9 Independent Parachute Squadron by Giles.

7

CHANGE OF SCENE

The last 5 years had been fulfilling for me, but I was seeing very little of Mary and our children, due to spending so much time away in Northern Ireland and on exercises both overseas and in the UK. I had especially enjoyed my time in both 59 and 9 Squadrons with their close bonds of brotherhood between all ranks, but was less sure about the wider Army where procedures were more formal and where the focus, understandably, was on deterring the Soviet threat in West Germany rather than reacting to events further afield that were more likely to be tackled by Commando and Airborne Forces. I had been warned to expect a posting to Germany after 9 Squadron, possibly as a junior staff officer with an armoured brigade, but I wanted to experience something different and also spend more time with my family. I therefore took the chance to extend my civil engineering knowledge by attending the Long Civil Engineering Course at the Royal School of Military Engineering at Chatham, which included 2 civilian attachments; the first with an engineering contractor and the second with a consultant. The experience would provide me with a better understanding of civil engineering and the construction industry;

it would also highlight some key differences between military and civilian attitudes and management.

Mary and I moved to Chatham in October 1976 where I joined 8 other Sapper Captains and Majors on the course, including Joff Johnson, an Australian who was a fanatical cricketer and excellent company. For me it was hard work because I was also preparing for the Staff Exam in order to have a chance of attending Staff College; there had been no time for that while in 9 Squadron. I would get up early each morning at 5am and do 2 hours revision, plus write 3 or 4 essays most Saturday mornings, on top of the civil engineering studies I did during the rest of the day and in the evenings. Life became much easier once the Staff Exam was over in early December! The civil engineering subjects we covered included foundations, soil mechanics, reinforced concrete, pre-stressed concrete, structural steel, temporary works, survey and setting out, bills of quantities, codes of practice, plus a number of other areas and we had to submit a design assignment (for example; a bridge deck, a coffer dam, etc.) with detailed drawings every 2 or 3 weeks, which we completed over a weekend. It was very different from the much more varied lifestyle I had become used to, but at least the engineering was interesting and practical – and I saw my family every day.

After this 6-month crash course we were all attached to different companies and I went to work for Gleeson on the M25 Westerham to Sundridge contract, which comprised 8 bridges and almost 7 kilometres of rural motorway across undulating countryside overlying gault clay. It entailed another house move, our seventh in 7 years of marriage, and we were quartered in Maresfield, East Sussex some 30 miles south of the project. Mary needed our car for the children, so I bought a small second-hand motorbike to commute to work and enjoyed the early morning rides across Ashdown Forest to the site.

I was responsible for 2 of the bridges. The first was a skewed single span deck to carry the motorway over Croydon Road, constructed of pre-cast pre-tensioned concrete beams with a top cast in situ top slab. The abutments were reinforced concrete walls, each side of the road and each supported by a reinforced concrete pile-cap supported by bored piles down to a depth of more than 20 metres. There were 248 piles in total and each had to be positioned using a theodolite and a level before being bored by a rig mounted on a crane. The second bridge at the other end of the contract (also skewed) carried Sundridge Road over the motorway. The deck had a total length of 80 metres, was supported by 2 abutments and 3 intermediate supports of 2 tapered columns and was cast in situ. The abutments and intermediate supports were, in turn, supported by pile-caps each carried by 14 bored piles varying in depth to 26 metres. The whole structure was reinforced concrete with the 2 centre spans being voided to reduce the deck weight. I also designed a temporary structure to support a bridge deck for a three-span bridge on the same contract and helped with other bridges for short periods while engineers were away.

Some of the management team had previously worked together on an M4 motorway contract in Wales, so knew each other well. They lived in mobile homes or caravans on the site and were a close team. Many of the workforce were itinerant, hired on a weekly basis, but key tradesmen and plant operators remained throughout my period. The hours were long; 7am to 7pm Monday to Friday and 8am to 1pm on Saturday during the summer months; 8am to 6pm Monday to Friday in the winter. When necessary (for example during a concrete pour for a foundation) I would check everything was ready as soon as it was light at around 5am and work would finish once the pour was completed which would sometimes take until midnight. Later, we had to close the Croydon Road overnight and used a large hire crane to position the pre-cast deck beams on to the bearings on top of each abutment either side of the road. We worked right through the night to complete that task. Everyone on the site was always friendly, but I was surprised by the lack of trust at senior level between the contractor (Gleeson) and the consultant (South East Road Construction Unit (RCU), Ministry of Transport, who had designed this section of the M25). There was bickering about payments, especially when there were changes to any designs, between the RCU Resident Engineer and the Gleeson Project Manager. A cooperative partnership would have been more effective, and I was never comfortable with the 'point-scoring' that seemed to drive the contractual negotiations. I was fortunate to work with RCU site engineers on my bridges who were keen to get the bridges built quickly and we worked together in a spirit of cooperation when setting out the exact locations and levels of the different parts of each bridge and when checking the shutters and steel reinforcement before starting any concreting. This saved time and we trusted each other, but it was disappointing that our mutual respect was not replicated by the respective bosses on the project.

The size of the workforce varied but it averaged around 200, roughly the number in 9 Squadron where we had all known and respected each other. In contrast the Gleeson Project Manager showed little interest in the workforce. One morning on his way to work an elderly carpenter, known as Bill and who worked in the main site workshop constructing the larger shutters for the concrete abutments and piers for the various bridges, had an accident in his car. He was taken to the nearest hospital with a broken leg and some other injuries. I only found out about his plight a few days later and went to visit him that evening, surprised to find that I was his first visitor. He was anxious about losing his job as his leg would take at least 6 weeks to heal enough for him to get back to work, and asked me to let the Project Manager (John) know he was looking forward to returning as soon as he was fit. The next morning, I approached John to relay the message, and also to let him know how Bill was doing. To my disappointment, I was told that Bill would be laid off as he was no use while in hospital and that the financial pressure on the contract meant that no unproductive worker (even if temporary) could be afforded on the payroll until he recovered. And, in any event John reckoned that it would be easy to find another carpenter! I protested, telling John that the rest of the workforce would surely take note of his attitude because they all respected Bill as a skilled, hard-working tradesman and would now be less willing to give that little bit extra for the project if required. It was to no avail; Bill never returned and from then on, I sensed the men on site had less regard for John. He moved on a few months later but before he did, we had another encounter when he turned up at the Croydon Road Bridge one mid-afternoon expecting to find Mick, the ganger on the site. Mick was on a short tea break in the small hut I used as a site office, right by the bridge, his only break on that very warm afternoon. John demanded, rather petulantly, to know why I had allowed him to take a few minutes off. I in turn asked him how many cups of tea he drank in the afternoon, knowing full well that he usually had a cup of tea on his desk whenever I passed his office. He replied, "What's that got to do with Mick and his team here?" I pointed out that should he stop having tea in the afternoon he could then rightfully ask the men to follow his lead, but that it made no sense for them to work without anything to drink from 2pm until 7pm every day and expect them to work accurately. To my surprise he commented, "I'd never thought of that!"

The fields by our quarter were safe for the children and they spent much of their time outside, close to the house. Mary took David to the local village school each day but there were few other children for Anna to play with and we were relatively isolated. I played village cricket on many Saturday afternoons in the summer for Maresfield Second XI, often rushing to the different venues straight from the project. The games were always very friendly, great fun and keenly competitive. I opened the bowling and it was just about the only vigorous exercise I managed during that time, except when I sometimes stopped on my way home on a weekday evening for a run in Ashdown Forest. The rural countryside around Maresfield was beautiful and we enjoyed family walks most Sundays.

Just before Christmas Mary and I had moved again with David and Anna, this time to our own house (our first home purchase) close to Camberley. David settled in well at a very good local school while Anna attended a small play school in the grounds of Sandhurst. I commuted daily to the M25 project for a month in January before starting my next attachment with L G Mouchell and Partners in West Byfleet working in their Bridge Department. There I designed one of 13 bridges on a section of the M63 Stockport By-Pass; my bridge was a simply supported, skewed single span post-tensioned reinforced concrete bridge over the motorway, supported by reinforced concrete walls founded on spread footings in sandstone. I found a more professional attitude in Mouchell with the associate partner running the Bridge Department, John Harrington, taking a keen interest in everyone working for him. He was most helpful to me throughout my 8 months there, investing considerable trust in me and allowing me to get on with the design. I found the daily office routine boring, stuck at a desk and immersed in detailed calculations for the bridge, but managed to exchange my small motorbike for something larger (a Honda 400/4) that provided an exhilarating commute between Camberley and West Byfleet at the start and end of every day.

In late August I was back at Chatham, along with the others I had started with 2 years previously, and it was interesting to compare notes about our different attachments. I was very thankful to have gained an insight into the construction industry and valuable experience to subsequently qualify as a Member of the Civil Engineers and a Chartered Engineer. However, my time away from the Army convinced me that I was better suited to soldiering than engineering so I decided to attend the Army Staff Course, having been selected for staff training after passing the exam over which I had sweated so much effort earlier.

My first 3 months of staff training were spent at Shrivenham on a basic introduction to military technology before moving to Camberley in January 1979 to join 180 others, comprising a few officers from the Royal Navy, Royal Marines and Royal Air Force, around 40 officers from NATO, the Commonwealth and other countries, plus 2 civil servants from the MOD. At Camberley, the course comprised 5 terms, each of about 2 months, and we were split into syndicates that changed every term. The 5 terms covered staff duties, brigade level tactics, counter-revolutionary warfare, divisional level tactics and joint services cooperation. We also had a short introduction to the MOD and went on some interesting external visits. I still remember visiting a very deep coalmine in Nottinghamshire and being impressed by the skill, fortitude and teamwork of the miners; a striking parallel with soldiers. But by far the most interesting part of the course was a battlefield tour to Normandy where veterans from the Second World War recounted their experiences to us over 3 days. Hearing their stories and having the chance to mix with them in the evenings was both inspirational and sobering and provided a precious insight into the realities and human costs of war. I was enthralled, not only by their remarkable achievements but also by their courtesy, humour and modesty – and by the obvious mutual respect they all had for each other, including a German veteran who had fought against some of them after the landings.

Aside from the battlefield tour and the external visits, I found much of the instruction at the Staff College rather too prescriptive. The approach taken by some of the Directing Staff appeared to be "This is the Gospel according to Camberley: read it, study it, learn it, regurgitate it;" instead of encouraging us to think more innovatively and challenge the accepted norms. Nevertheless, I learned a great deal about other parts of the Army, something about the Royal Navy and Air Force and especially enjoyed meeting such a wide cross-section of people. Mary and I made some life-long friends and the officers and families from other countries much enhanced the whole year. The sporting and social activities were great fun and I played a lot of cricket in the summer months, opening the bowling again with Tony Moorby whom I had last bowled with at Sandhurst! It was an extensive fixture list; so much so that it was difficult finding time to play in the matches especially when I joined the Free Foresters, thanks to Tony's sponsorship. I finished with a good report and encouraging comments from the Commandant, Major General Frank Kitson, who wrote: "... undoubtedly an officer of above average ability who is capable of holding down a demanding staff appointment. I expect that he will be even better as a commander as I feel that he has the ability to make men want to give of their best."

M25 construction with Gleeson, near Westerham, Kent: Above – Earthworks at the start of the contract, near the Croydon Road Bridge. Below – Boring a pile shaft, prior to lowering steel reinforcement and filling the shaft with concrete.

Above: Base of the eastern abutment of the Croydon Road Bridge showing tops of 124 piles. Below: Western abutment under water from flooding, with starter reinforcing bars visible.

Croydon Road Bridge taking shape (above) and nearing completion (below).

Sundridge Road Bridge.

Preparing to lay the concrete slab on top of the sub-base on the north carriageway.

David and Anna having fun outside
the Army quarter we lived in at
Maresfield.

Checking out my motorbike outside our home near Camberley.

8

RETURN TO SOUTH ARMAGH

It was with a sense of elation that I returned to 9 Squadron as the OC a week before Christmas in 1979. I knew it would be a very busy two years but was delighted to be serving again with such committed soldiers.

During the Christmas leave a detachment led by Lieutenant Peter Wall, who later became General Sir Peter, Chief of the General Staff in 2010, deployed to Rhodesia for 3 months as part of the Commonwealth Monitoring Force on Operation Agila. Individuals from the 9 Squadron detachment were widely dispersed on the operation providing support at a variety of RVs and assembly areas at a very tense time. Fortunately, the high standards demonstrated by all the Commonwealth soldiers ensured an unexpected, relatively peaceful integration of ZAPU, ZANU and Rhodesian Security Force units into the new Zimbabwe Army. The Monitoring Force withdrew in March 1980 and we all welcomed the safe return of Peter and his men. Peter then acted as the Squadron 2IC because the actual 2IC (Chris Guthkelch) had broken his leg very badly on a night parachute descent the month before and was still in hospital. I had been on the same jump with Chris and there must have been an inexperienced pilot in our Hercules as we were despatched much higher than normal, at around 1500 feet rather than 800 feet, so that a number of us drifted away from the DZ. I ended up in trees but was fortunately hung up by the parachute only a few feet off the ground and it was easy to drop out of the harness. Other soldiers in the Squadron, apart from Chris, also suffered broken limbs.

Soon afterwards a visit from Lieutenant General Sir George Cooper, GOC South East District and a Sapper with a fierce reputation, started badly and finished disastrously with him climbing into his staff car, exclaiming "Bloody 9 Squadron – if that's how you treat a 3-Star General I'll sort you out!" The visit had been arranged by my predecessor and was a 'fast ball' to field just 3 days after returning from the squadron commanders course. I was due to see the Brigade Commander, Brigadier Jeremy Riley, the next day for my initial meeting with him and was naturally a little apprehensive about what he would say. He had his feet on his desk and was smoking a cheroot as I entered his office but immediately put me at ease, saying that he had a lot of time for 9 Squadron and that the Squadron had always delivered what he had asked of them. He then calmly asked what my priorities were, listened carefully and wished me success as the OC. His encouraging attitude was in marked contrast to General Cooper's approach. The Squadron typically all got behind me after this incident but many years later, I was surprised when General Cooper (then the Chief Royal Engineer) wrote to congratulate me for sorting out 9 Squadron!

That same month a section led by Lance Corporal Hunnibel was deployed at short notice for 10 weeks to assist the 1st Battalion the Parachute Regiment (1 PARA) in Hong Kong, engaged on preventing illegal immigrants crossing into Hong Kong over the border with China. The section was split up among the 3 platoons of A Company, 1 PARA, and Colour Sergeant Pringle, commanding one of the platoons, wrote to commend the 5 men from 9 Squadron in his platoon:

"My sole reason for writing is to say how pleased I am with their work rate, enthusiasm and professional attitude. All have slotted into the platoon very well and mix with my Toms[1] as though they have known each other for years. One big advantage they show some of my younger soldiers is their maturity and acceptance of some hard graft. All five Sir are a credit not only to your Squadron but to Airborne Forces. Perhaps on future tours we may well be blessed again with the attachment of some of your soldiers."

The Squadron deployed to Wyke Regis in late March 1980 on a 36 Engineer Regiment combat engineer concentration that culminated in a bridging gallop, building a series of bridges over a number of obstacles, back to Aldershot immediately after Easter. Tragically, Sapper Hopwood from 2 Troop had his lower body crushed by a D4 Dozer during a night build of a Medium Girder Bridge (MGB) over the River Avon on Salisbury Plain, when he tripped and fell behind the dozer while the operator was moving his machine to help free a bridging pallet that had become wedged on the tailgate of one of the vehicles. It seemed that neither Sapper Hopwood nor the dozer operator (Lance Corporal Phillips) were aware of each other in the dark and the noise from the dozer's engine meant that Hopwood's belated cry of alarm was not heard by Phillips. A group of us rushed to pick up Hopwood, put him on a stretcher and ran with the stretcher to the nearest vehicle, parked some 400 yards from the site. We drove to the hospital in Salisbury; all the time Hopwood

---

1. Soldiers in the Parachute Regiments were often called 'Toms'

was alert and we left him there with a sense of relief, feeling that he had a good chance of survival. Very sadly, his condition deteriorated, and he was transferred to Southampton Hospital where he died of his injuries a few days later. I remember meeting his parents at the hospital with Charlie Crawford, his Troop Commander. We both attempted to comfort them on their devastating loss and were very moved by their dignity and how proud they were of their son. The father had been in 9 Squadron many years earlier and they both understood the close sense of brotherhood within the Squadron. As a result of Sapper Hopwood's death, we commissioned a trophy called the Hopwood Trophy which was subsequently awarded to the winning section of future inter-section competitions. The first section to win it a couple of months later was commanded by Corporal Strettle, whose elder brother was also in the Squadron.

Almost immediately after the Bridging Gallop was over, 36 Engineer Regiment organised an inter-squadron athletics competition in Maidstone. There was no time to train but 9 Squadron did well and both Paul Scoble, our quartermaster and by far the eldest competitor, and I surprised ourselves (and everybody else!) with him winning the shot put and me winning the 1500 metres.

Within a few days we were back on Salisbury Plain on a major field training exercise for our parent formation, 6 Field Force commanded by Brigadier Jeremy Reilly. Lieutenant General Sir George Cooper was the Exercise Director. Towards the end of the exercise, General Cooper attempted to catch us out by suddenly changing the location of an MGB night build over the River Avon, while also ensuring the Squadron was fully engaged on demolitions and some other sapper tasks elsewhere. The timings for the build remained the same despite the new crossing being a much wider gap. The order for the change was deliberately delayed as late as possible and only transmitted to Squadron HQ after 2 Troop (building the bridge) had left its harbour area and was en route for the original site. The men were slightly baffled on arrival in the dark at a new site they were not expecting. Flexible as always, they responded well, and the bridge was completed in time for the Brigade units to cross the river as scheduled. After this little 'test' General Cooper's hitherto critical attitude towards us softened slightly. I received an encouraging note from Brigadier Reilly congratulating the Squadron's performance.

It would soon be time to start training for our forthcoming Northern Ireland tour in October. We were to return to Castle Dillon, but first we enjoyed some parachute training. Once caught up in the Northern Ireland cycle there would be few opportunities for this and it was crucial to nurture our airborne ethos and expertise, as we were now the only Royal Engineer unit with a parachuting role. The Squadron's parachute strength had fluctuated around 200 while it was independent just over 3 years earlier. However, we were now part of 36 Engineer Regiment and supporting 6 Field Force with much more emphasis on combat engineering and little priority accorded to parachuting. We had more vehicles and plant but less men and more effort had to be spent on equipment maintenance.

The Squadron had undergone a high turnover in all ranks after losing its independence, especially among the Junior NCOs, and we were now only established for a 50-man troop in the parachute role plus 20 reserves. The numbers of trained parachutists in the Squadron had fallen to 110 and only 70 men received parachute pay at any one time. In order to spread this as fairly as possible I asked the Sergeant Major to allocate it so that the para-trained Junior NCOs and soldiers received it every alternate month, Senior NCOs every third month and the officers every fourth month. Fortunately, and it says much for the calibre of the men, parachute pay never became a major issue. I also had a close look at our Pre-Para training with Paul Scoble the Quartermaster (QM) and one of the fittest men in the unit although double the age of many of them. We devised a more progressive preparation for P Company and Paul ran the first couple of Pre-Para courses on the principle of 'Train In' rather than 'Select Out' before I handed back control to the Pre-Para NCO. There was an immediate improvement in our P Company pass rate and the para-trained strength of the Squadron steadily increased, eventually reaching more than 160 over the next 18 months.

In June 1980, a joint Anglo–French operation was launched very suddenly in response to a rebellion led by Jimmy Stevens on Espiritu Santo, one of the many islands that formed Vanuatu previously known as the New Hebrides. Jimmy Stevens wanted independence from the remainder of Vanuatu. The British component of the Joint Task Force comprised 42 Commando Royal Marines, then the Spearhead Battalion, with elements from other arms and services. Just as 42 Commando were about to deploy, the planning staff in HQ United Kingdom Land Forces (UKLF) realised that it would be relatively easy for Jimmy Stevens to deny access to the airfield runway on Espiritu Santo and I was suddenly ordered to send a 12-man detachment with the Marines. The section's role was undefined but a possible, although unlikely, task for it would be to launch a parachute assault on the runway, together with the Recce Troop from 42 Commando, and then clear the runway of any obstacles so that reinforcements could be flown in.

On 14th June 1980, with Independence Day due on the 30th July, the Joint Task Force flew to the capital, Port Vila, on the main island of Efaté. The sapper detachment found work repairing a former wartime airstrip, building an assault course for the local college and jungle training with the Royal Marines. As events unfolded, a parachute insertion was not needed and the Independence Day celebrations on Efaté passed off successfully. Most of the detachment sent to Vanuatu was from 3 Troop but every man in the Squadron had been keen to go, especially with a possible opportunity (however flimsy) of an operational Parachute jump. During the short period before the detachment left, Lance Corporal Pashley from 2 Troop expressed his intense disappointment at not being chosen and asked for an OC's interview. I explained to him that he was shortly due to start his Northern Ireland training the next week as a search team 2IC and that there was a much greater chance of being involved in a real operation in Northern Ireland than there was in Vanuatu. Nevertheless, he was especially keen and requested to be removed from his search team in order that he might then be reconsidered for Vanuatu. I refused but, in order to soften his disappointment, reminded him that he had just married and suggested that a sudden deployment to Vanuatu followed immediately by his joining the squadron in Northern Ireland was not an ideal start to any marriage. I also pointed out that he would undoubtedly have other chances of seeing action as a professional soldier. The conversation proceeded as follows: "Permission to speak Sir please." "Of course LCpl Pashley." "How do I get a divorce?" (said in jest with a huge grin!) Sadly, less than 2 years later and after I had left the Squadron, Lance Corporal Pashley was killed in the Falkland Islands during a diversionary attack in support of the 2nd Battalion Scots Guards assault on Mount Tumbledown.

While Staff Sergeant Turner, Corporal Lovely and the detachment were away in Vanuatu, the rest of the Squadron prepared for Northern Ireland. By now, both Peter Wall and Chris Guthkelch had moved on to other units and Freddie Kemp had taken over as the 2IC. The Squadron's pre-tour preparation included the search advisers course in mid-June, followed by the search teams and advisers training, individual construction and plant courses plus a wide variety of specialist courses, all fitted in around infantry and military skills training, first aid training and shooting. We had a break with 3 weeks leave before the Northern Ireland training package on the Lydd and Hythe ranges and in Rype Village in late September. Ready for the tour, the Advance Party departed in mid-October, soon followed by the Main Body.

We took over from 59 Squadron in Castle Dillon on 22nd October 1980, after an excellent and very friendly handover. 9 Squadron's strength was 188 men and we were reinforced by an additional 40 pioneers from 518 Company, Royal Pioneer Corps, plus a few additional individuals from 36 Engineer Regiment and 6 Field Force. We had left a small rear party in Aldershot under Dick Barton. We were now under command of the CRE Northern Ireland, Lieutenant Colonel Mike Stancombe, and in support of 3 Infantry Brigade, commanded by Brigadier Muddy Walters. Search was a high priority with 8 search teams earmarked in that role. 1 and 3 Troops (commanded respectively by Richard Willett and Alan Jones) were committed to building the new bases at Crossmaglen and Forkhill while 2 Troop (commanded by Staff Sergeant Joe Houlston) carried out all the other construction tasks in the eastern part of 3 Brigade's area. A troop detached from the Field Squadron in support of 8 Brigade in Londonderry undertook the construction tasks in the western area.

Searching procedures and equipment were constantly developing, especially the techniques to counter the remotely controlled Improvised Explosive Devices (IEDs). Search could be 'offensive' as well as reactive and could also be very useful in gaining intelligence about the terrorists' methods and capabilities.

The level of sophistication of the PIRA devices was high and every high-risk search operation needed careful planning and control with consistent standards across the Brigade. Charlie Crawford, now Support Troop Commander, took on the crucial coordination of our search tasks. We had 5 trained search advisors, one each permanently deployed at Bessbrook, Omagh, Armagh and Portadown and one at Castle Dillon, who was also the Intelligence Sergeant in the Ops Room. Hence there was unbroken continuity in the planning and execution of any search operation, which reduced risk and enhanced effectiveness. Two teams were permanently based at Bessbrook, on immediate standby and frequently working out of Crossmaglen and Forkhill. The search advisers, search teams, ATOs and the infantry had to rely on and trust each other. Search operations on this tour were not as numerous as those on the 1974/75 tour, perhaps because the PIRA recognised that the Army's capability in this field was now so well-honed that it was more effective to inflict casualties on the Security Forces by their homemade improvised mortars and by their sniping attacks. There was a constant danger from mortars to the soldiers in Crossmaglen and Forkhill but the IED threat also remained high, especially culvert and roadside bombs. The Squadron's search teams carried out a total of 141 high-risk searches, of which 22 proved positive, including 20 IEDs. Sgt Strettle was awarded a BEM for his outstanding contribution as a Search Adviser.

By 1979 the PIRA had developed the Mk 10 mortar, which could be fired from the back of a flatbed lorry, tipper truck or from the inside of a specially modified delivery van with a range of about 100 metres. There could be as many as 10 tubes, each approximately a metre in length and made from modified oxyacetylene cylinders, bolted to the floor of the vehicle with initiation charges connected by detonating cord. The size of the charge in each mortar bomb varied but, ranged from 20 kilograms upwards of homemade explosive and the mortars posed a very dangerous threat to any Security Force base, especially those close to the border in South Armagh. At Crossmaglen, the infantry lived in a very basic reinforced concrete shelter, dubbed the 'concrete submarine', rapidly constructed by 2 Troop, 9 Squadron on its emergency deployment in 1976 and the RUC were protected by a brand new three-story station, with a sacrificial top story, heavily reinforced concrete walls and blast proof windows which had just been finished by 59 Squadron. At Forkhill the military accommodation comprised timber huts reinforced with sandbags and with very limited overhead protection sited behind the brick-built RUC station. The accommodation for the sappers at both bases was even more vulnerable than for the infantry. A new design for blast and mortar-proof accommodation for the soldiers at both Crossmaglen and Forkhill involved substantial three-story steel-framed buildings with sacrificial top stories. This would prevent a mortar penetrating through the roof and also limit damage solely to the top floor, thus protecting soldiers living on lower floors. The buildings would also have thick reinforced concrete walls and blast proof windows to limit damage from a mortar bomb landing on the ground beside them.

1 Troop had the task of building the new Army three-story block in Crossmaglen. It was roughly 30 by 12 meters in plan and included a kitchen, dining room, a junior ranks club, sleeping accommodation, toilets, showers, and ablutions for a company group. The site was very restricted and an early priority was to erect a tower crane, on hire from a civilian company in England who sent out a specialist to help the troop erect it and show them how to operate it. This crane was controlled from the ground because of the ever-present

threat from snipers. The civilian specialist fitted in well with the troop for the few days he was with them but questioned why those erecting the crane with him seemed very wary when up high on the tower or the boom, because he always thought that parachutists were comfortable with heights. When they pointed out to him that they were anxious about snipers, not the height, he thought that they were exaggerating the danger. He did not appreciate the threat because it had been minimised by the extra infantry patrols and OPs deployed from the base during the building of the crane.

Shortly before the crane was ready, the crane specialist was up high near the junction of the tower with the boom checking some electrical connections with the troop electrician, Lance Corporal Hall. An IRA sniper, armed with a Garand rifle, seized the opportunity and shot him. Fortunately, the round hit the safety rail first before then wounding the man in his backside and almost knocking him off the tower. Lance Corporal Hall showed great courage and strength in carrying him safely down the tower by himself, while still very exposed to further shooting. The specialist was evacuated to the Musgrave Park Hospital and eventually recovered. Lance Corporal Hall earned a GOC's commendation for his quick thinking and prompt rescue.

1 Troop worked extremely hard throughout the winter months. They started with the foundations and drainage works for the building, a dirty task in cold and wet conditions. By early March 1981 they had almost finished the outside shell. The interior fittings, decoration and finishing works would be started by the troop that followed them. It was a demanding project with a challenging logistic chain and some unforeseen technical issues that were all solved by a determined and resourceful team on site. When possible, members from the troop went out on the odd patrol with the

infantry in order to escape the close confines of the base and see something of the outside world. These occasional breaks from their restricted working site helped maintain a sense of perspective.

3 Troop's task at Forkhill was to complete the first building, designed to house the RUC and some of the infantry, and to erect the frame and shell of the second building which would eventually house the rest of the infantry. As with Crossmaglen, it was a complex task with a complicated supply chain delivering a great variety of construction materials ranging from steel girders and pre-cast concrete panels to detailed plumbing, electrical and finishing items. Over 200 engineering drawings had to be interpreted and the project absorbed up to 70 working on site. Living conditions for the sappers and the RPC were basic but not nearly as cramped as they were for 1 Troop in Crossmaglen. Towards the end of the tour Alan Jones was posted to his next job in Germany and Robbie Burns took over as 3 Troop Commander. As with 1 Troop the men worked a punishing routine, finishing everything that they were tasked to do and handing over the project on schedule for the next troop to take forward. It is worth noting that soon after the buildings in Forkhill were finally completed a year later, the PIRA fired 5 x Mk 10 mortars into the base on the 17th April 1982. These destroyed the vacated RUC station but caused only superficial damage to the new accommodation. The hard work and determination shown by the different sapper squadrons during the build had undoubtedly saved soldiers' lives.

Only men, small items of equipment and some materiel could be moved by helicopter. All major stores such as bulk materials, pre-cast concrete panels, structural steelwork and construction plant had to be transported by road and stored until needed in the already grossly overcrowded bases. Redundant materiel and plant had to be removed when it was no longer needed. We carried out 2 major resupplies, known as Op Tonnage during the tour, the first in early December 1980 and the second at the beginning of February 1981. The 1st Battalion Queen's Lancashire Regiment (1 QLR), the battalion at Bessbrook, and the 2nd Battalion the Parachute Regiment (2 PARA), based at Ballykilner, first had to secure the ground overlooking the routes from Bessbrook to Crossmaglen and Forkhill throughout each operation. Once the infantry patrols were deployed, the route was carefully searched by our search teams. These searches were speeded up as much as possible by deploying 2 search groups simultaneously from Bessbrook and Crossmaglen and 2 more search groups from the half-way point, one working back towards Bessbrook and the other working forward to Crossmaglen. Each search group contained a search adviser, two search teams and a trailer with the electronic monitoring and suppression equipment. An ATO was on standby to move as soon as a potential IED was identified. Once the route to Crossmaglen was clear the search effort was switched to Forkhill and the road convoys, organised into packets each of up to 8 vehicles, delivered construction stores, first to Crossmaglen and then to Forkhill. The infantry remained picquetting the routes and the convoys continued non-stop until all the loads had been delivered and any equipment no longer required at either base had been removed.

Op Tonnages were complicated operations that needed detailed planning and liaison. Troop commanders at Crossmaglen and Forkhill first ensured that their stores bids were accurate. The QM and his resources staff pre-stocked the stores at Castle Dillon during the preceding weeks. Extra vehicles, low-loaders, tippers and plant, together with additional drivers and escorts, were concentrated there before the operation started. The size of the Squadron just prior and during each Op Tonnage grew to around 300 all ranks, with the extra drivers and escorts. The operations needed coordinating from both Bessbrook and Castle Dillon; the 2IC deployed the Squadron Tactical HQ forward with 1 QLR, while the QM at Squadron Rear HQ despatched the convoys when ordered, ensuring that an inbound convoy loaded with stores did not meet an outbound convoy on the narrow roads south of Bessbrook and block the route. I had the privilege of leading the first packet into Crossmaglen to prove the route. There was a constant danger of roadside and culvert bombs, but we trusted our search teams implicitly. There were occasions when there was an urgent need to move a vital piece of equipment to either Crossmaglen or Forkhill which was too heavy for a helicopter and which could not wait until the next Op Tonnage. Once authorised by the brigade commander, a 'flit' would deliver the crucial equipment to site by means of a small convoy moving rapidly down the narrow lanes in the dead of night. We only used a 'flit' twice during the tour; once to deliver the mobile crane needed to construct the tower crane at Crossmaglen and once more towards the end of our tour.

Appropriate routes in South Armagh for the heavy road convoys were very limited. Very shortly before our second Op Tonnage, we received a report that there was a partial collapse of the road between Bessbrook and Camlough, which if true, would necessitate a diversion with all the additional planning for high-risk search and picquetting of the new route. Freddie Kemp and Charlie Crawford undertook a covert reconnaissance using a car brought in from Enniskillen, and therefore unknown in the local area, first checking in at Bessbrook before continuing further south. 1 QLR required all drivers to book in and out of Bessbrook under their Standard Operating Procedures. This was to confirm back-up arrangements with a Quick Reaction Force on standby in a Wessex helicopter at

Bessbrook. Shortly after checking out of Bessbrook, Freddie, who was at the wheel, noticed in his rear-view mirror that a black Ford Granada was following close behind them. By this stage, they were committed to driving down the typical South Armagh road with high stone walls on each side and the occasional entrance into small fields. As Freddie felt uncomfortable being followed by an unknown vehicle, he forced the Granada to overtake by suddenly braking hard and turning into a field. Almost immediately there was a massive explosion which threw up a large amount of debris. Freddie, fearing an ambush linked to the explosion, immediately reversed out of the field and headed back towards Bessbrook, with a dented bonnet and a shattered rear windscreen from the falling debris. During the follow-up operation over the next few days, while the Op Tonnage operation was still underway, it became apparent that a local man who ran a small business near Crossmaglen had been driving the black Granada. His car had been sent flying nearly 200 metres by a culvert bomb consisting of an estimated 400kg of explosive. The command wire from the culvert was traced to a firing post on a hillside and our search teams discovered there was a well-planned escape route for the terrorists. Fortunately, the section of the route approaching the culvert was invisible to the firing point, due to the high walls. The bombers, who had been warned by the PIRA OP overlooking the Bessbrook base that the 'next car' was the target, therefore mistakenly detonated the bomb under the Granada that, at the critical time, had just overtaken the 'target car'.

As an aside, during that Op Tonnage, the CRE, Lieutenant Colonel Mike Stancombe, was the driver of one of the heavy goods vehicles in a convoy from Castle Dillon to Crossmaglen in the early hours of the morning, because he wanted to see for himself what the drivers experienced and how the operation was run.

The tension in Northern Ireland was always high but was further exacerbated by a hunger strike in the Maze Prison, initiated in October 1980 by IRA Prisoners who wanted to be granted special status as political prisoners. This hunger strike finished with no deaths in December but another more serious one started on 1st March 1981, led by Bobby Sands the IRA leader in the Maze, and ending on 3rd October 1981 after we had returned to Aldershot. Ten Republican prisoners starved themselves to death in support of their demands, including Bobby Sands, who was the first to die after 66 days without food. By then he had become a British MP, having bizarrely been selected for the Fermanagh and South Tyrone seat on 9th April 1981. During this second hunger strike there was an upsurge of violence in Northern Ireland to a similar level as experienced in the early Seventies. Although the British Government made no public concessions to the hunger strikers, the consequence of the deaths was that the Sinn Féin Party emerged as a much stronger political force.

Our rugby team, led by Staff Sergeant Andrews, won the Northern Ireland Minor Units Final and the Army Final, played later during the post-tour leave in Germany. Our cross-country team easily won the Northern Ireland Minor Units Championships. We all returned home safely on 9th March 1981 after a successful Squadron's sixth tour in Northern Ireland. Brigadier Waters summed up our tour by writing:

"The major task of the Squadron has been the building programme at Crossmaglen and Forkhill. This is a back-breaking major engineering project made none the easier by the winter weather conditions. The Squadron has also provided general engineer support for units in the brigade and in particular search teams for clearance

of explosive devices. In all these demanding and at times dangerous tasks, the high morale and determination of the Squadron has been most apparent."

Once back at work after our post-tour leave, we were soon on a round of exercises and commitments. These included a Regimental military and adventure training fortnight in Scotland where we joined the rest of the Regiment by parachuting on to the DZ at Barry Budden; a Regimental combat engineer exercise in the Maidstone area; the Freedom of Rushmoor Parade and March through Aldershot; our own squadron-level combat engineer exercise in and around Wyke Regis. Our new brigade commander, Brigadier Edwin Beckett who had taken over from Brigadier Reilly, visited us just outside Weymouth and was surprised that the men did not take to him after he questioned the value of airborne troops. Fortunately, the next day his comments were soon forgotten after a visit by Major General John Cowtan (long retired) who could not hide his delight at being back with the Squadron he had commanded just after the Second World War. Two new officers joined: Lieutenants Peter McManners and Jon Mullin who took over 2 Troop and Support Troop respectively. Whenever in Aldershot, the men soon became bored and amused themselves (and sometimes others!) by playing the odd joke. One night before a special parade the next day by the 1st Battalion the Royal Regiment of Wales (1RRW) a couple of sappers sneaked into the pen where the Battalion's mascot was stabled (Taffy the Goat) and shaved off one side of the goat's beard. 2 PARA were the suspected culprits!

In the autumn we were part of a United Kingdom Mobile Force (UKMF) major deployment in Denmark, to rehearse NATO's deterrence options against the Soviet threat in the

Baltic area. While units were concentrating near Copenhagen, we reconnoitred a large number of sites, especially bridges and major road junctions, for possible demolitions as part of a UKMF General Deployment Plan, in case of a Soviet assault. Once the exercise started we completed an extensive minefield before preparing a bridge for a reserved demolition and then guarding it for a couple of days, as part of a 2 PARA battalion group under command of Lieutenant Colonel H Jones (later killed in the Falklands and awarded a VC). During the final phase of the exercise we were employed as infantry under 36 Engineer Regiment.

The Army was now rebuilding its parachute insertion capability 5 years after the disbandment of 16 Independent Parachute Brigade. HQ 6 Field Force moved to Tidworth while HQ 8 Field Force moved to Aldershot and was renamed 5 Airborne Brigade, under a new commander, Brigadier Wilson. The brigade was to include two in-role parachuting battalions with a slice of combat support and combat support arms. This resulted in our parachute establishment in the squadron being increased to two field troops plus a reserve and we soon felt an integral part of the new formation.

The Christmas lunch for the Junior Ranks in the Squadron turned out to be very different from normal because quite a few soldiers failed to show for the traditional lunch in the cookhouse, served by the officers and Senior NCOs. Those who had not bothered to turn up were ordered to parade the next morning, dressed for a speed march and carrying bergans, ready for a long tab around Long Valley. The morning would finish with a Christmas lunch in the field and they would then be allowed to go on leave. Soon after setting on a very wintry, cold December morning with the ground covered in snow, many of the men pulled out Christmas hats, the banter grew, and the miles soon passed. On arriving at the RV where lunch had been laid out, bergans were opened and Christmas decorations, balloons and the odd can or more of beer pulled out to supplement the excellent meal produced by Sergeant Paddy Boyce and his chefs. We all had a thoroughly good party – so much so that the men cheerfully asked if they could have the same arrangements every year!

Soon after Christmas leave, 5 Airborne Brigade started planning a brigade concentration in the Stanford Training area in mid February 1982. My tour as OC was sadly at an end and I handed over on 11 February 1982 to a good friend, Chris Davies, before moving to Canada with my family for my next posting. I felt a tinge of sadness as I knew that I could never return as a serving member of 9 Squadron, but felt enormously privileged to have had the honour of leading such talented and lively soldiers who thrived on challenge and fun. Commanding them might perhaps be likened to driving a very fast car without any brakes and a steering wheel but I was lucky to have excellent, high-grade officers and NCOs who helped me steer the Squadron! I, like everyone else, had no inkling that they would all be preparing for war in the South Atlantic within two months and regrettably missed being with those I knew so well, when they courageously fought in the campaign as part of the Task Force to recover the Falklands from Argentina.

9 Squadron parachuting on to a DZ on Salisbury Plain – without equipment.

The 9 Parachute Squadron Contingent in 1981 leading the Freedom of Rushmoor Parade passing the saluting dais by the Princes Hall, Aldershot.

A safe landing from the balloon.

Starboard Stick
(Cpl Lacey leading)
getting ready to jump as
the C-130 approaches
a DZ on Salisbury Plain.

Posing prior to jumping! The Squadron ever ready for a smile!

Captain Peter Wall, 1 Troop Commander waiting to parachute. Peter became Chief of the General Staff.

A Gazelle helicopter about to land inside the Army Base at Crossmagle.

An aerial view of Crossmaglen village. The Army base is in the centre of the photograph, surrounded by the cover from view screening.

The new "mortar-proof" accommodation under construction inside the base. The steel frame has yet to be completed and the pre-stressed concrete cladding will follow. The photograph on the right shows the top section of the tower crane being assembled.

One of the accommodation blocks at Forkhill under construction.

A Plant Team on standby at Castle Dillon, ready to be called forward for riot control.

A road convoy with construction material about to leave Castle Dillon, our base in Armagh.

A search team on a route clearance task near the border in South Armagh.

An ATO is manoeuvring a wheelbarrow device to deal with a suspect IED.

The Squadron officers in N Ireland: Rear (L to R): Charlie Crawford, Richard Willett, Robbie Burns, Alan Jones Front (L to R): Dick Barton, Freddie Kemp, me, Paul Scoble.

The Cross-Country Team with the NI Trophy: Rear (L to R): Me, Cpl Gaz Doyle, LCpl Jinks, LCpl Runner Costen Front (L to R): Spr Lee Hackett, LCpl Scouse Hogan, Spr Bridge, Spr Staples.

9

CANADIAN INTERLUDE

We arrived in Ottawa in March 1982 towards the end of a Canadian winter, with snow still lying deep on the ground and the temperature hovering around freezing. It was not long before we had settled into our new home in Minnetonka Road in one of the Ottawa suburbs, having taken on the lease from Simon Hill from the Parachute Regiment, whom I was replacing at the Canadian National Defence Headquarters (NDHQ) as an exchange officer. We had bought all Simon's furniture and household electrical equipment (fridge, cooker, washing machine), which saved time and administrative hassle for both of us and I hoped that my successor in 2 years time would do the same for us.

Anna started at a nearby school where all the lessons were in French but very soon moved to another school which suited her much better and where she quickly made good friends. She was remarkably adaptable and had coped very cheerfully with the long flight and interminable waits at RAF Brize Norton, Dulles, Baltimore and Ottawa Airports on the outward journey plus the move to another completely strange house. It was all 'a great adventure' for her! We had reluctantly left David behind to continue his schooling at Fernden Prep School near Haslemere close to Mary's mother's home in Frensham. She generously provided him with a second home, spoiling him every weekend and driving and collecting him from Heathrow for his regular flights to join us during his school holidays. He soon joined us for the Easter holidays in April within weeks of our arrival.

Mary's mother, Anne, was Canadian and had met Mary's father while serving as a Wren in the Canadian Navy soon after the war ended. Her sister Mimi and her husband, Ian Richardson, kindly invited us to spend a family Easter with them in Montreal, where it was lovely to catch up with so many cousins. We immediately felt at home and closely connected to all their family. On our return to Ottawa during the evening of Easter Monday the weather was still very cold with swirling snow and a biting wind. As I neared the crest of a major highway bridge over the St Lawrence River our car, a large American station wagon, began sliding sideways towards the edge. The steering would not respond and there was nothing I could do except fervently hope that we would not crash through the railings and plunge into the freezing water far below. Very fortunately, there was another car between us and the railings that halted our uncontrolled slide as we nudged the side of the car, both cars travelling at 50 mph. As soon as possible I stopped at the side of the bridge to apologise to the other driver and thank him! He was surprisingly relaxed and very understanding about the incident, telling me that the Highway Authorities should have salted the road but clearly had not because of the Easter Break and that the steel deck on the bridge would have been even colder than the road surface either side of the river; it was effectively an ice rink. Outside the car, I could barely stand upright, as the road surface was so slippery. I insisted that I should pay for any damage to his car and asked him to send me the bill once he had a chance to check it properly. Some weeks later I received a friendly note and an invoice for 200 dollars, which I though was very fair and was happy to refund him. But that near-disaster was a very sobering introduction to cold–weather driving in Canada.

At work, I was the NDHQ desk officer responsible for British training in Canada, Canadian airborne training, and military adventure training. It was an interesting job that involved quite a bit of travel and extensive liaison. I spent a lot of time with the Canadian Airborne Regiment in Petawawa, the Canadian Airborne Centre at Edmonton, Alberta, plus the Canadian training bases at Suffield and Wainwright which were used regularly by British battle groups from Germany and battalion groups from the UK. I helped coordinate the support for Royal Engineer projects on Canadian bases, funded by the Canadians but which, in turn, provided valuable construction experience for British Sappers. These projects were readily sponsored by the Canadian Military Engineers who were proud of their links with the Royal Engineers and who always went the extra mile to overcome any last-minute glitches. I also negotiated with Parks Canada for the necessary clearances and permits for the military to use the National Parks for adventurous training. I was the only British officer in the Directorate of Land Operations and Training but there were a few other British officers in other NDHQ departments. We all kept in close touch with each other, and also with the Military Attaché in the nearby British Embassy. Everyone I worked with was invariably friendly and my senior boss, Major General Mitchell, who had attended the Camberley Staff Course, was widely respected by all of us on his staff. During the latter half of my tour he handed over to a French Canadian general who was less friendly but fortunately had little personal influence over me.

I recall him remarking "Ha, McGill you must be the British Gunner who has just arrived" and being unamused when I replied, "No Sir, I'm a Sapper who is just about to leave!" Fortunately, Brigadier General de Chastelain[1] soon joined the Directorate and his courtesy restored the balance.

While finding my feet in the job, I was desperate to find out what was happening in the Falklands Campaign. The British Task Force had set sail on the 5th April 1982, in response to Argentina invading the Falklands on the 2nd April and the conflict ended with the Argentine surrender at Port Stanley on the 14th June 1982 after an incredible series of events. The British achieved a remarkable victory, but at a cost of 255 killed, and won unstinting admiration from the Canadians. Mary and I were glued to the news channels every evening and anxiously watched scenes of Argentine Skyhawks attacking the British ships in wave after wave. Although we never doubted an eventual British victory, the campaign might well have ended in disaster and we both felt an enormous sense of relief and pride once it was over. I was regularly called into General Mitchell's office as he was keen to chat about the unfolding events, even though my only sources of news were the TV and the newspapers plus the odd letter and phone call from England. His active interest, along with everyone on his staff, was heartening and I felt the close sense of kinship amongst them.

My key responsibility in NDHQ was the oversight of the British Army's annual training in Canada: up to seven battle groups from

---

1. Later General de Chastelain, Chief of Canadian Defence Staff and Ambassador to the USA. He became closely involved in the Northern Ireland peace process and was Chairman of the Independent International Commission on Decommissioning, responsible for the decommissioning of arms by paramilitary groups in Northern Ireland.

Germany at the British Army Training Unit Suffield (BATUS), near Medicine Hat south east of Calgary; three infantry battalion groups from the UK at the Canadian Forces Base (CFB) Camp Wainwright, a hundred odd miles south east of Edmonton; a Royal Engineer squadron on an annual construction project; the occasional low-level exercise and a number of adventure training expeditions.

CFB Suffield is in the middle of the prairie on the Alberta plain and the base area is vast; just over a thousand square miles, with a slightly smaller manoeuvre training area. BATUS offered unrivalled live fire training for armoured and mechanised battle groups on a scale not remotely available in Germany or the UK. The training cycle ran from April to October, with a battle group rotating every month and working through a series of challenging test exercises. The tanks, armoured personnel carriers, self-propelled guns and logistic vehicles remained with BATUS and were handed over from battle group to battle group, with an extensive maintenance programme during the winter months. Most units also managed to organise a few days adventurous training in the Rocky Mountains or excursions elsewhere for their soldiers after their month's training. I soon sensed that feelings between the BATUS Training Team and the Canadians on the base were a little strained after my first visit there, perhaps because the British gave an impression of 'owning' the training area and failing to acknowledge that they were guests on Canadian sovereign territory. Another irritant, particularly for the Canadian Base Commander, Colonel Gene Lake, was the frequent lack of liaison and communication at a local level. This was perhaps due to the very intense training schedule for the rotating battle groups but Gene Lake once remarked that "We (the Canadians) have sold the farm to the Brits" after a series of senior British officers from Germany and the MOD had regularly visited the training without anyone letting him know that they were on his base. He was also sensitive to the BATUS Commander's apparent disdain for the Canadian Army. I felt rather the same on my first visit to BATUS being interrogated by a particularly arrogant cavalry officer "What on earth are you doing here and why have you come?" I had to explain that the training lease was due for renewal and that it was my job in NDHQ to organise the Training Conference later that year where all British training issues in Canada, including BATUS, would be agreed jointly by the Canadians and the British. Fortunately, once a new Commander BATUS took over, matters soon improved.

In comparison, the 'Pondjump West' exercises at Wainwright were invariably welcomed at the Canadian base where there was always a spirit of mutual cooperation between the small resident British training team and the Canadian hosts. Each battalion group would train for about 6 weeks working up to a live firing exercise involving all the battalion's weapons with artillery and sapper support.

I counted myself lucky to belong to both the Airborne and Sapper Brotherhoods in Canada; both were extraordinarily hospitable. There was a very strong sense of identity in the Canadian Airborne Regiment and they generously invited paratroopers from other nations as well as Canadians to their annual summer 'Jump Bivouac' in Petawawa. My job at NDHQ was to ensure that aspiring participants were 'bona fide' before they were authorised to attend. Those invited were accommodated by the Regiment, parachuted often, were awarded Canadian Parachute Wings, got to know everyone else at the Bivouac and enjoyed a barbeque and a few beers every evening. It was a most relaxed time that reinforced a friendly mutual respect amongst us all. In the winter I was invited for a few days to join one of the Regimental Companies (called Commandos) on some low-level winter training where the temperature hovered around minus 20 degrees centigrade; a sharp contrast from the centrally heated NDHQ building! The Canadian winter kit was very warm, almost too much so when on patrol in the snow but the heavily insulated boots, gloves and clothing were essential to avoid frostbite. It was a salutary experience to parachute at such a low temperature with the severe wind chill. I later heard about an earlier exercise where some American rangers had flown up from Georgia to join the Canadian Airborne Regiment for some winter training and had not been properly briefed by their officers. One of the US soldiers had packed his gloves into his bergan before leaving Georgia and not put them on after landing at Trenton near Toronto and fitting his parachute. He jumped without them on a very cold night on to the exercise area in Northern Ontario. After landing, having been in the air during his descent for well over a minute and rolling up his parachute, he lost all feeling in his hands and could not open his bergan to get his gloves. He was also disorientated; never having experienced such conditions before, and took some time to find the RV in the dark on the edge of the DZ. His hands became frostbitten and, despite an immediate medevac, he subsequently had to have one of them amputated. The Canadian winter could be pitiless; soldiers had to be trained, motivated and disciplined to avoid cold injuries. I was impressed by the Canadian's cold weather discipline while living in the field and their patience. They never rushed the basic drills, just as earlier instructors had emphasised during my winter warfare course in Norway almost 20 years earlier.

While in 9 Parachute Squadron we had dropped Land Rovers and trailers, light wheel tractors (equipped with a front shovel and back-hoe) and a small D4 Dozer from C-130 Hercules on training exercises. Riggers would prepare the vehicles by securing them on to a platform attached to a number of parachutes (4 for the Land Rovers and 7 for the heavier plant equipment) and the platform would be loaded on to rollers on the floor of the aircraft. On approaching the DZ the ramp would be lowered, the rear cargo door opened and a drogue chute deployed to extract the larger parachutes which, in turn, would pull the platform out of the back of the plane as they filled with air. The cargo would drift down to earth where it would be derigged, and the vehicle or piece of plant driven away. For safety, the heavy drop DZ would be offset from the troops' DZ and the heavy drop loads would be dropped before troops, just in case any drifted and landed on or amongst soldiers on the ground. This tried and tested system worked reasonably well but it sometimes took a long time for us to locate our vehicles and plant after landing, especially in the dark or on a larger exercise with other brigade units taking part and where the platforms might be widely spread. The Canadian's used both heavy drop parachuting and the Low Altitude Parachute Extraction System (LAPES) to deliver certain equipment accurately and quickly. The aircraft approached the extraction zone at a very low height above the ground (about 10 feet). In a similar fashion to the higher altitude drops, a drogue chute was used to pull a cluster of larger extraction chutes out which then pulled the load, lashed to a pallet, out of the plane. The very low altitude allowed for no margin of error; the pilot had to adjust the flight controls to remain level during the rapid shift of the aircraft's centre of gravity while the pallet was extracted from the plane. Once on the ground the pallet would quickly slide to a stop, braked by the extraction chutes.

In 1983 the Canadian Sappers built an ice runway high up in the Arctic, north of the Canadian Forces Station Alert, to support a Canadian Scientific Expedition to study the Alpha Ridge (CESAR), an underwater mountain range running from Ellesmere Island to the Siberian Continental Shelf. In mid-March a number of sappers parachuted on to a very large ice floe, followed by the construction plant (a grader and bulldozer) plus other equipment, supplies and rations delivered by LAPES. Over the course of several days, the sappers levelled the ice with plant and explosives and flooded the site with seawater in a process similar to constructing an outdoor skating rink, before roughing up the surface to provide a braking surface for the aircraft. Once the airfield was ready, the Air Force delivered materiel for the scientists' camp, including kitchen structures, dormitory tents, prefabricated plywood buildings, equipment and food and, later, the scientists. The expedition lasted until May 1983 and the ice runway was still in good shape when the scientists left.

During the winters of 1982 and 1983 Mary worked as a volunteer for the Canadian Ski Marathon helping with the administration, along with Mary Bullock who became a 'friendly aunt' to us, especially Anna, during our time in Ottawa. The event consisted of 10 sections of varying lengths and difficulties in the Laurentians between Ottawa and Montreal, which could either be skied together over the 2 days (5 stages per day), or individually on subsequent days. The 2-day event was open to anyone of any age or ability and there were 2 categories of skier: the *'Coureur des Bois'* starting out each day before dawn to ski the entire distance and the others starting later (around 8am) to ski any number of the 10 sections. The *'Coureur des Bois'* category was broken down into Bronze (ski the whole trail), Silver (ski the whole trail with a pack), and Gold (ski the whole trail with a pack and camp out overnight). The famous Norwegian skier, Herman

'Jackrabbit' Smith-Johannsen,[2] who lived a very long life from 1875 to 1987, was a patron of the Ski Marathon and joined the skiers for the last section (aged well over 100!) in both years that I entered the event – quite amazing! At my first attempt in 1983 I only managed 30 miles each day, running rather ungainly on my skis – and falling frequently! However, in February 1984 I proudly managed to complete the *'Coureur des Bois'* bronze challenge, despite my rudimentary skiing technique.

Before our time in Canada I had never ran a marathon but decided to enter the Ottawa Marathon in 1982 and 1983 as an incentive to keep fit. On my first attempt I went off far too quickly, passing 20 miles in 2 hours before suddenly 'hitting the wall' and feeling as though I was wading through treacle. I staggered through the last 6 miles, eventually finishing exhausted in a time of 3 hours and 10 minutes. The next year I approached the event more carefully, running at a steadier pace throughout, and broke my 3-hour target in a time of 2 hours and 54 minutes. Since then I have never wanted to run another marathon!

During one of many visits to the Canadian Airborne Centre (CABC) in Edmonton, the CO there, Lieutenant Colonel Don Dalziel, invited me to join him and some other runners from the Edmonton Journal (his local newspaper) in the 'Jasper to Banff' relay race. This followed the famous Icefields Parkway among majestic mountain scenery for most of the 170-mile route, which was split into 17 stages. Amongst a carnival atmosphere I started the first leg at noon handing over to a teammate about an hour later

---

2. In 1982, at the age of 107, Jackrabbit Johannsen was inducted into the Canadian Sports Hall of Fame. He was a legend in his own time and an example to generations of Canadians. He died aged 111.

and climbing into our support van for some rest before running one of the later stages in the middle of the night. All those running in the dark were given a small cyalume glow stick that we were assured would deter any bears! Our team finished in Banff the next morning, long after the winners but well in front of a number of slower teams and in good time for a relaxing dip in the Banff hot springs. We drove back to Jasper savouring the views either side of the road from the relative comfort of our van, having enjoyed a very special event.

On another CABC visit that coincided with the Edmonton Air Show, I was unexpectedly invited to parachute with some members of the Canadian Forces Parachute Maintenance Depot from a Chinook helicopter in one of the display events. I asked whether there had be a rehearsal, or at least a briefing before we climbed into the helicopter but was casually told "Just follow the jumper before you; it'll be a cinch". Twenty-four of us climbed into 2 Chinooks with the ramps down. A few minutes later we were over the airfield, watched by many thousand spectators. We stood up, hooked up, checked our equipment and jumped off the ramp one by one. As soon as my parachute opened, I looked around and down to get my bearings, assess my drift and pick out the landing area. I soon realised that we had been dropped almost directly over the spectators instead of the other side of the airfield and were also higher than expected with the wind blowing too strongly for me to steer towards our designated drop zone. If I had tried to reach it I would have ended up landing in the middle of the crowd, so had no choice but to steer with the wind, clear of the crowd and hope I would not land on one of the large hangar roofs. Having cleared the crowd, I pulled down as hard as I could on the rigging lines to reduce my drift and eventually landed close to an enormous hangar and between a vintage sabre jet fighter and a single-engine propeller powered plane, fortunately with its engine switched off! I quickly gathered up my chute and beat a hasty exit to meet up with the others; it turned out that none of them had landed where expected! The helicopter pilot either had not been briefed properly or had simply made a mistake. Fortunately, there were no injuries to any of the parachutists or to any spectators.

The Canadian Brigade based in Alberta with its headquarters in Calgary periodically organised a familiarisation tour of the Canadian Arctic for its unit commanding officers, regimental sergeant majors and the Brigade Staff. In November 1983 they kindly included me and another British Officer. There were about 30 of us in the group and we had a dedicated C-130 Hercules which flew us each day to a different location with the seating rigged much more comfortably than usual and with hot coffee permanently available from a large heated flask at the front of the seating area. Clearly, this flying crew was not from the RAF! We flew first from Calgary to Yellowknife, the capital of the Northwest Territories and then to Whitehorse in Yukon where I saw Sam McGee's cabin and gained some insight into the previous lives of the Klondike gold prospectors and adventurers, portrayed so well by Robert Service's poems. I just had to buy a copy of his poems from the cabin (also a museum), which I brought back for Mary. We moved on to spend 2 nights in Alaska, close to Anchorage, hosted by an American brigade with a very steely commander. We then flew to Tuktoyoktuk, close to the Mackenzie River Delta on Canada's northern coastline and a large base for oil and gas exploration in the Beaufort Sea. The land around Tuktoyoktuk was all tundra; very bare and desolate. Some of the local people were making a living by hunting and fishing but not many of them seem to be employed by the oil and gas industry, staffed mainly by outside workers. We only spent an afternoon in

Tuktoyoktuk before moving on to Resolute on Cornwallis Island, our most northerly destination and the second most northerly community in Canada. It is named after the ship HMS Resolute that searched for Sir John Franklin who disappeared without trace with his crew while attempting to find a route through the North West Passage. It is also known as the 'place with no dawn' because of the long winter night this far north and the 'place with no sunset' in the summertime! It is sometimes called Resolute Bay, after its bay, the waterway into Parry Channel on the southern coast of Cornwallis Island in the middle of the Northwest Passage. It was sad to see rubbish piled outside the huts built by the Canadian Government for the local people, broken window panes that had not been replaced and a number of abandoned, broken snowmobiles. There appeared to be little sense of ownership or pride in the small community. The Inuits were finding it increasingly difficult to hunt for seals, due to restrictions, but could not adapt to a modern western culture, based on a cash economy rather than on their traditional reliance on seal meat and fur, especially when their territory was covered in snow and ice for most of the year and they had few other means of earning a living. They had become reliant on government benefits and would not bother to repair a window because they could simply turn up the heating in their huts, all paid for by the state. Nor was it possible for most of them to look for work away from their traditional homeland, unless, they were prepared to forget their heritage. Their exposure to the modern world seemed to have done them no favours and I wondered about their future prospects. After leaving Resolute we flew back to Calgary via Rankin Inlet, a small town on the west coast of Hudson's Bay built in the 1950s to house Inuit miners for the Rankin Inlet Mine producing nickel and copper. When the mine closed in 1962 the town had a population of around 500 Inuits, nearly all miners, but appeared rather desolate in 1983.

I found this Arctic tour fascinating. It gave me a much better understanding of Canada's vast geographical size (it is further from its southern border with America to its northernmost tip in the Arctic than it is from its east to west coastline), an appreciation of the Arctic's remoteness and harsh climate and the difficulties of integrating the Inuit into a modern society without destroying their culture. The Arctic contains valuable natural resources yet roughly 75% of Canada's entire population live within a narrow 100-mile wide strip of land along its American border.

Mary and I enjoyed our time in Canada so much that we very nearly emigrated there. The country offered a wonderful outdoor lifestyle and the pace of life allowed plenty of leisure time. I never had to work over a weekend and was usually home by 5pm; very different from our life in the UK. We and the children loved the skiing in the winter, the swimming and cycling in the summer, the scenery, and the clear blue skies. We also took the chance to travel and visit some beautiful places that included Niagara Falls, Toronto, Vancouver, Quebec City and New England and we particularly enjoyed a break with Mimi and Ian in their cottage on one of the Muskoka lakes. The climate was bitterly cold in the winter but there were very few grey winter skies; normally sunny, bright, cold days. The transition from winter to summer seemed virtually instantaneous, almost no spring, but the autumn lasted longer with gorgeous, vibrant colours in the trees. In addition to Mary's Canadian family and Mary Bullock, my cousin Brenda Beament and her husband Ted, together with their daughter Meriel Bradford and her family were also very welcoming, and Anna regarded Ted and Brenda almost as surrogate grandparents. Ted had a very distinguished war record, having served with the Canadian Gunners and on the staff of the 1st Canadian Army as a brigadier general. Although by now well into his eighties he still drove to his barrister's office a few days each week and somehow also found time to support numerous charities. Brenda had been my father's favourite cousin. We also made many friends among our neighbours and those with whom I worked.

After what was almost a 2-year holiday, our time in Canada sadly drew to a close. I was posted to Germany and handed over to Hector Gullan, a decorated Parachute Regiment officer who had served with the SAS and with the Royal Marines. We had both attended Sandhurst at the same time and experienced the same Norwegian Winter Warfare Course as officer cadets; it was a small world! Mary and I knew that we would surely miss the relaxed Canadian lifestyle but were looking forward to seeing more of David and catching up once more with other family members and our friends.

Winter training with the Canadian Airborne Regiment.

Waiting to board a C-130 before parachuting with the Canadian Airborne Regiment.

Mary and Anna cross-country skiing in the Gatineau Hills near Ottawa.

A short hike on a section of the Appalachian Trail in New England.

Anna (above) and David (below) enjoying themselves on a lake in Quebec.

10

OUT OF AREA

Just before leaving Canada, Mary had a very nasty fall on the icy road surface outside our house and broke a wrist. A nearby hospital in Ottawa set it as best as they could before we flew to England, en route for Germany, but she was in constant pain. Once we arrived in Hameln, she needed another operation that involved resetting the bones and screwing a metal plate into her wrist. It was an uncomfortable transition for her but we both grew to like Hameln, rich in heritage. Soon after our arrival Anna and other children from her school took part in the Pied Piper Play celebrating the 700th Anniversary of the legend in the main square by the Town Hall. The beautiful town buildings, streets, shops and surrounding countryside were always immaculately tidy and well kept.

The town, with the River Weser running through it, was an ideal location for 28 Amphibious Engineer Regiment which trained on and near the river for much of the time. I was the Second in Command of the Regiment and we provided rapid bridging across rivers and canals within the Corps' area, using M2 vehicles (also known as rigs) and later replaced by M3s. These were extraordinary pieces of equipment, capable of driving at up to 40 mph on the road as a wheeled vehicle and moving on water at speeds of up to 8 knots. When driven into the water a rig would fold out to form a flat deck and be propelled by rotating water jets, making it surprisingly manoeuvrable. The rigs could be joined together by ramps, carried on each vehicle or close coupled together (hull to hull). A bridge across the Weser could be completed within an hour of the first rig entering the water while a 3-rig raft, capable of ferrying a 70-ton tank, would take 20 minutes to build. We used to bridge at night, providing crossings for units and formations from company groups up to brigades and sometimes a division. The rigs would carefully drive down to river sites at last light and, once the bridges and ferries plus the trackway approaches to and from the sites were ready, the different units would be called forward by military policemen and marshalled over the crossings in the dark by our NCOs. The traffic synchronisation and convoy discipline had to be especially tight because we operated on radio silence to minimise any electronic messages prejudicing security at the crossings. Once all the vehicles were across the river the rigs would move back into a hide area, either a wood, large farm, or factory complex, before first light, ready to provide more crossings on the next and subsequent nights. Sometimes we would have to 'break bridge' by decoupling a bridge in the middle and swinging both ends to opposite banks, in order to allow a barge or a boat to pass by and we always posted lookouts to detect any approaching vessels to give enough time for this. The bridging operations appeared deceptively simple but every single one required detailed planning and coordination. The river widths, profiles of the river-bed, speed of the current (sometimes up to 8 knots on the Weser), launching sites plus vehicle approaches and exits, routes to the sites, assembly areas and forward RVs all had to be recced and confirmed (usually the night before) and the rigs plus trackway stores well prepared in the hide areas. The timings, routes and call forward procedures for the units crossing the bridges and ferries had to be understood and briefed. Close liaison between our tactical headquarters and the formation controlling its units using the crossings was crucial.

In September 1984, 1 (British) Corps conducted the largest training exercise in Germany since the Second World War. Exercise Lionheart involved over 130,000 UK soldiers and over 13,000 German, Dutch, American and Commonwealth soldiers who provided the main opposing force. It rehearsed the move of the whole Corps from its peacetime barracks, including reinforcements from the regular and reserve units in the UK to designated deployment areas in West Germany before the Corps carried out manoeuvre training, involving three British divisions, to practice plans for defeating a possible Soviet attack in our sector. 28 Regiment provided a number of river crossings during the exercise, but we were not as busy as we expected, because the sheer scale of the numbers inevitably slowed down events. An unusual task for the Regiment was the recovery of a large fuel tanker full of diesel that rolled into the River Weser overnight when an RCT driver from another unit failed to secure the handbrake properly after parking on a ramp at Upnor. The vehicle was swept away by the current and was eventually found completely submerged the next day some distance downstream – fortunately still upright with its wheels on the riverbed. Our divers secured towlines to the vehicle and one of our REME recovery trucks slowly winched it out of the river via a gap and a ramp in the bank constructed by one of our combat engineer tractors. No fuel was spilt, and a major breakdown of Anglo–German relations was thankfully avoided!

Our senior commanders and political masters judged Lionheart a success. None of us then imagined the collapse of the Berlin Wall just over five years later in November 1989; the Soviet threat was still taken very seriously throughout the 1980s.

After 18 months in Hameln, the family moved again, this time to Maidstone in Kent where I took command of 36 Engineer Regiment. Mary and I had both enjoyed Hameln, but we were delighted to be returning to England. We would see much more of David and Anna who were now both at boarding schools in Oxford and I was excited about my new appointment. The Regiment supported 5 Airborne Brigade and had four squadrons; 9 Parachute Squadron (in Aldershot) plus 20 Field Squadron, 50 Field Squadron (Construction) and 61 Field Support Squadron in Maidstone. 50 Squadron also provided the Airfield Damage Repair capability for RAF Laarbruch in Germany in case of a Soviet attack against NATO. We comprised over 800 all ranks and could tackle many different tasks, but we focused on the more likely 'Out of Area' (OOA) operations rather than our General War role. The principles were straightforward, but the logistics were always challenging. A typical OOA scenario might start with a breakdown of law and order in an overseas country that threatened British people who would need rescuing as soon as possible. A UK military force, based on 5 Airborne Brigade but possibly also including 3 Commando Brigade would be flown to the nearest secure airfield which would become the Forward Mounting Base (FMB). Pathfinders from 5 Brigade would free-fall parachute covertly and by night into the troubled area to recce a suitable landing site or DZ for the main assault force. Where feasible the spearhead of the main assault group would land directly on to the landing site (known as the airhead) in a Tactical Air Landing Operation (TALO), secure it and then call forward the remainder of the force. If a TALO insertion was considered too risky the assault force would parachute on to one or more nearby DZs and subsequently mount a more conventional attack to seize an airhead. As soon as the airhead was secure the rest of the force would be flown in, including the logistic support. Troops would neutralise any rebel forces, rescue the hostages and then fly them out to the FMB for further evacuation to the UK. Intelligence, especially locating the hostages and finding out about the rebel forces (both their intention and capabilities), speed and surprise were absolutely crucial. The entry point could be a beachhead (secured by 3 Commando Brigade) rather than the airhead – and on exercises involving both the Commando and Airborne Brigades the beachhead provided the entry point for additional logistic tail to support operations at the airhead.

I deployed on many different OOA exercises on Salisbury Plain, Dartmoor, Scotland, Northumberland and further afield in Oman and Cyprus. The Sapper tasks included: repair and maintenance of the airhead and improvements to the beachhead, Explosive Ordnance Disposal (EOD) support, demolitions, mine clearance, booby traps, water supply, bridging, field defences, helicopter and aircraft support, provision of fuel pipelines, fuel storage and electrical power. 9 Squadron would normally be in direct support of the forward parachute battalions while 61 Squadron would be close to the Brigade Echelon area and crucial for providing engineer stores and construction material. I was double hatted, acting both as the Commander Royal Engineer (CRE) for the Joint Force Headquarters and as CO 36 Engineer Regiment. The Joint Force Commander was not a permanent appointment but would be drawn from who was available and best matched to the particular scenario being exercised. An ad hoc Permanent Planning Group (PPG) provided a nucleus for planning joint force exercises and operations. One of the lessons from the Falklands Campaign was the lack of a joint planning capability to coordinate joint (RN, Army and RAF) assets. The PPG was a stopgap until a dedicated Joint Force HQ (JFHQ) was established later. I was 'on call' to the PPG on an as required basis throughout the year but became CRE of the Joint Force on major exercises – while at the same time remaining CO of 36 Regiment. Fortunately, I had a very capable 2IC who commanded the Regiment whenever I was with the JFHQ.

These exercises were all quite testing because they involved trying out procedures not previously rehearsed and working with different groups who might not know each other. On the Scottish exercise in 1987, known as Purple Warrior, 9 Squadron parachuted in with the leading battalions on an assault on West Freugh Airfield, which became the Airhead, once secured. Meanwhile an amphibious force was approaching the shore on the Dumfries and Galloway coast. I was on an aircraft carrier with Admiral Julian Oswald's JFHQ until command of the Joint Force switched to Major General Nick Vaux, a Royal Marine. I then moved ashore to join my Regiment. 9 Squadron's main task for this particular exercise was to build the protective bunds for the fuel storage tanks at West Freugh and construct a ship to shore pipeline from the beachhead on Luce Bay to the airhead (a distance of about 3 miles), with expert assistance from an RE Specialist Team. Fuel was discharged from tankers anchored offshore into dracones (very large rubber inflatable tanks – in the shape of a cigar) which were towed by an RCT work boat to a small floating pump station about 50 yards from the beach and which was connected to the pipeline. Fuel was then pumped from the dracones through the pipeline into the storage tanks at the airhead. RCT fuel operators had been tasked to man the pumping station but became seasick because it oscillated up and down (and sideways) with the movement of the waves on the beach. They were unable to cope so our divers had to take over, ensuring a steady supply of aviation fuel for the Harriers, Jaguars and Helicopters, plus diesel and petrol for the logistic vehicles. There were no fuel leaks or spillages and no fuel contamination – vital for aircraft safety. I was reminded, yet again, of the remarkable sapper versatility.

An earlier exercise in Oman in 1986 (Saif Sareea) provided an insight into mounting an OOA operation thousands of miles away in a very different environment. Participation from 36 Regiment was limited to 9 Squadron supporting 5 Airborne Brigade while I was the CRE in the Joint Force Headquarters. We flew to Masirah (some 80 miles off the east coast of Oman) and RAF Masirah became the FMB for the air insertion. Amphibious shipping with 3 Commando Brigade embarked was poised off-shore. During the few days before the insertion was launched there were a series of planning meetings and briefings. One evening I escaped the briefings for a chance to witness large sea turtles lumbering ashore on a nearby beach to dig holes in which to lay their eggs. They slowly dragged themselves some 50 or 60 yards from the sea before laboriously digging holes in the sand with their front flippers, disgorging their eggs into the hole and carefully covering them up with sand. They then dragged themselves back into the sea, exhausted by their efforts and leaving the eggs to hatch some fifty-five days later. Their primeval determination to lay the eggs and protect them as best they could, despite the huge physical effort, was very poignant – especially when hordes of baby turtles, just hatched from eggs laid previously by other turtles, were scurrying for the sea to avoid being eaten by hundreds of crabs scurrying to intercept them. It was a remarkable, rather brutal, scene. The crabs were everywhere and only a small percentage of turtles managed to elude them, reach the water and swim away.

A successful combined parachute and commando assault was eventually mounted in the exercise area close to Ras al Hadd, in the northeast corner of Oman to rescue the hostages, after sufficient intelligence had been gleaned on the insurgents and on suitable landing sites and beach entry points by Pathfinders and Special Forces. The exercise was well supported by Omani Forces who were very hospitable and there were a lot of VIP observers, especially for the parachute drop. I was fortunate to spend a few days with the Omani Sappers providing the engineer infrastructure support for the exercise and was struck by their friendly pride in their British links. The Omani Sapper who was my driver looked after me extraordinarily well, concocting so many curry meals every time we paused for a break that I was hard-pressed to eat anything for days afterwards!

Throughout my time in Maidstone, one or more of the squadrons in the Regiment were often away on various projects in the UK and overseas, in addition to their sapper support for 5 Brigade. My visits to these projects were always interesting; both for the chance of seeing different parts of the world and getting to know my soldiers better. 9 Squadron built a road and two extensive accommodation blocks for the Canadian Army at Gagetown in New Brunswick, as well as supporting 2 PARA on a Kenya exercise. 20 Squadron deployed to Northern Ireland to provide increased protection for security force bases against mortar attack and, soon afterwards, to the Falkland Islands to provide the sapper support for the RAF on the airfield and for garrison troops elsewhere on the islands and later, to Belize. 50 Squadron supported the troops in Belize for 6 months, the RAF at Laarbruch, Germany and in the Falkland Islands. 61 Squadron undertook some smaller projects in Gibraltar, plus a couple of projects at Otterburn, Northumberland, and Tregantle,

Cornwall. Smaller detachments from the Regiment supported the UN in Cyprus and a section deployed to Zimbabwe for 6 months to extend some rudimentary barrack accommodation. Additionally, 9 Squadron spent a month on public duties guarding Buckingham Palace, St James's Palace and the Tower of London, much enjoying the experience. Pretty girls would sometimes leave their phone number on a slip of paper that they would place in a sapper's pocket!

The long periods of separation from home and the demanding military commitments on the soldiers had an impact on many of the families. There was a strong community spirit in the Regiment and a thriving Wives' Club led jointly by Mary and the RSM's wife with welcome assistance from the Families Officer and other wives. Nearly everyone was friendly and there was a lot of mutual support. I counted myself lucky to have very decent officers, warrant officers, NCOs and soldiers. The two RSMs I served with (Martin Grimshaw and Steve Smith) were both outstanding. Steve Smith overcame testicular cancer, showing remarkable fortitude and humour. Once he started to lose his hair as a result of the chemotherapy treatment, he had his head shaved. The next day he announced to the whole Regiment that, if any soldiers also decided to become skinheads, he would jail them! Some 30 years later he was sadly defeated by another form of cancer and died in his mid-sixties, but he remained resolutely optimistic throughout his life. I was also fortunate to work for two very supportive brigade commanders in 5 Brigade; Brigadier Robert Corbett, an Irish Guardsman, and Brigadier David Chaundler, who had taken command of 2 PARA in the Falklands after H Jones had been killed. They and the Brigade Staff were always fun to work with. The time passed all too soon. As with 9 Squadron, I was sad to leave 36 Regiment because I knew that I could never return to regimental soldiering. Roddy Macdonald, whom I knew well and who had very successfully led 59 Squadron in the Falklands campaign – and who had also served in 9 Squadron earlier – took over from me. He had some innovative, thoughtful ideas and lived in the fast lane, enjoying hang-gliding, free-fall parachuting and riding motorbikes very quickly! The soldiers would enjoy his leadership.

I was posted to the Army Staff College in Camberley as one of the Directing Staff (DS) and Mary and I decided to buy our second house there, having sold our first one when we moved to Maidstone from Germany. Mary, as always, coped calmly with the turbulence of the move, including furnishing the house. We were now much closer to David's and Anna's schools in Oxford and she found a good job as a school secretary. Within 4 days of leaving Maidstone I started at the Staff College in the Tactics and Training Team as the Team Leader. The team members included David Richards (who later became Chief of the Defence Staff) and Freddie Viggers (later the Adjutant General – and Black Rod in the House of Lords). Term 2, the term for which my team was responsible, was just starting and there was a huge amount I needed to learn about the British Army and Soviet Forces. As well as Term 2, I taught on Terms, 3, 4, 5 and on the short TA Staff Course before a break the following year to have time to prepare for the next Term 2. I managed to keep abreast of the subject matter (just!) and found it stimulating to work with helpful, professional officers amongst the DS and the students. In contrast to my time as a student, the Staff College had become more vibrant, inquisitive, and more fun under new leadership, especially from Brigadier Rupert Smith, the Deputy Commandant and Director of Studies. He later commanded the 1st (British) Division in the first Gulf War and subsequently became GOC in Northern Ireland, Commander of the UN Forces in Bosnia and Deputy SACEUR, retiring as a 4-star General decorated with a KCB, DSO (and bar) OBE and QGM. There was less emphasis on the 'DS Solution' and more encouragement to think laterally. My 15 months as an instructor were an eye-opener for me. Most of the students were very quick and I soon realised that my role was to guide them, not to teach them. Within syndicates of ten they learned a great deal from each other (as did I) and I much enjoyed my time at work, on the cricket field and socially with some very interesting people.

The Normandy Battlefield Tour was no longer in the syllabus, because a previous Commandant had considered that the veterans were becoming too old. Instead, the students visited the US Army in Europe, a British Division in Germany and Berlin. Many of the overseas students did not have the required security clearance to visit the American Army so spent 2 days in Arnhem before joining up with the others in Germany. I was privileged to coordinate the Arnhem tour and found the accounts of those who fought there incredibly moving and inspiring. They included: Colonels John Waddy OBE (wounded and taken prisoner at Arnhem) and Geoffrey Powell MC who both commanded parachute companies there; Major Ian Toler DFC, a glider pilot; Captain Jim Flavell, a platoon commander on the bridge; Brigadier Eddie Myers CBE DSO, CRE 1 AB Division at Arnhem; Colonel Carel Wilhelm who had been in the Dutch Resistance. As with the Normandy stories heard 10 years earlier, the Arnhem accounts were a poignant reminder of war's human costs.

On promotion to Colonel I spent a torrid year in the Ministry of Defence working for the Director of Military Operations, a rather formal and serious brigadier, tasked with devising a means of assessing the operational effectiveness of formations within the Field Army in order that resources could be better allocated to provide the most effective return. It was the only period throughout my entire military career when I worked in the MOD and I was thankful never to return there! Commuting to London each day was a bore. I bought another motorbike; a BMW 800cc Boxer Twin, which was great fun although tiring in the London rush-hour traffic. I did not ride it every day but only when I knew I would be working late.

I then became Colonel Tactical Doctrine in the autumn of 1990 working with a small team on rewriting and updating the Army's doctrine publications. I would have preferred something more practical, especially since Saddam Hussein had recently invaded Kuwait and I expected that the British would soon assemble a joint force to support an American–led coalition against Iraq. With my experience of OOA exercises I felt that I had something to offer but, instead, was selected for the Higher Command and Staff Course (HCSC), run from the Staff College at Camberley. I was asked by the Commander Engineer at HQ UK Land Forces, whether I was available to go as the CRE at the Headquarters of the British Forces Middle East (HQ BFME) in Riyadh. I confirmed I very much wanted to go but was then informed that the HCSC course took priority and this would rule me out from deploying to Saudi Arabia.

Shortly after Christmas my mother died. She had been widowed for almost 20 years and had not found life easy in England, having only spent 6 years as a school girl in the country until, some 50 years later moving from Rhodesia to Fleet, Hampshire to find somewhere to settle Richard. She later moved to Topsham in Devon to be near Julia. Almost all her life had been spent in Kashmir, India and Rhodesia and she hankered after Kashmir especially. She could not have done more for Richard and had battled hard for him all her life. She was proud of Julia and me and especially fond of her grandchildren but, she was not easy company and I sensed that she was very ready to die towards her end of life (she had cancer). She had a strong Christian faith, a firm belief in heaven and was convinced she would rejoin my father and her parents (and all the dogs we had known on our farm!) in the afterlife. She was very relieved to know, before she died, that her ashes would be interred in the churchyard of St Bartholomew's Church at Holton. This was the church close to the home at Holton Park where her father had lived as a boy and where many of her Tyndale-Biscoe family relatives were buried.

Soon afterwards, Mary and I received an unexpected telephone call from Calcutta, to be told that our son David was very ill and needed to return to England. While on a gap year in India between leaving school and starting at Oxford University he had contracted both amoebic dysentery and salmonella poisoning from some food he had eaten in Calcutta. We urgently arranged a flight and were very relieved to have him home, but he remained frail for some time and was still struggling with his health when he started at university in September 1991. He did eventually recover, although his stomach remained sensitive for many years afterwards.

The HCSC 3-month course was designed to prepare selected officers for higher command of field formations and senior operational staff appointments. Eighteen of us were on the course, including a RN Captain, an RAF Group Captain and an American and French Colonel. It was most interesting, but I could not help being distracted by events in Saudi Arabia and Kuwait. Indeed, just as the war in the Gulf finished, I was suddenly posted to Riyadh. I missed the last part of HCSC, including the Staff Ride of European Battlefields, and was soon on an RAF flight from Brize Norton.

M2 rigs from 28 Amphibious Engineer Regiment about to form a floating bridge on the River Weser at dusk, in preparation for an armoured brigade crossing.

M2 rigs rafting tanks across the Weser on a daylight training exercise.

36 Engineer Regiment with the HQ is in the foreground and the Officers Mess at the top of the hill.

20 Squadron demonstrating its capability to repair craters at Mount Pleasant Airfield, in the event of an Argentinian air attack. The craters (for such training) were on one of the apron areas and not on the main runway.

An offshore Coastel provided accommodation for units in the Falklands after the war.

An abandoned Argentinian recoilless gun near Mount Longdon.

An accommodation block being built in Belize by 50 Squadron in 1985.

A river patrol in Belize from 20 Squadron in 1988.

A ferry crossing in Belize.

New accommodation on the Gagetown Training Area in Canada, built by 9 Squadron.

Practising parachute exit drills off a jetty in Cyprus with 5 Airborne Brigade Staff Officers!

Barney, our very playful golden retriever.

11

KUWAIT

For some time before the Gulf Campaign in 1990/91, Iraq had disputed Kuwait's extraction of oil from its northern oil fields close to the Iraq border. Saddam Hussein claimed that some of the oil was being drawn from Iraqi reservoirs deep underground by Kuwaiti drilling procedures and claimed substantial compensation payments. Kuwait refused and the dispute escalated. In August 1990 Hussein ordered his Army to invade and occupy Kuwait. He subsequently ignored UN resolutions ordering his withdrawal and it soon became obvious that he would only be ejected by force. A very large Coalition Force, comprising over 700,000 soldiers, sailors and airmen from 35 nations was rapidly assembled in Saudi Arabia and on naval ships offshore. The Americans provided by far the most (over 500,000) and the British contributed a sizeable number of over 30,000. Hussein meanwhile continued to build up his forces and was reckoned to have deployed over 300,000 troops.

The Gulf Campaign (codenamed Operation Granby by the UK MOD) was also known as Operation Desert Shield, during the build-up, and Desert Storm once the war started. The American–led coalition concentrated forces in Saudi Arabia and off-shore from

September 1990 until General Schwarzkopf (the US Commander of the Coalition) was ready to launch Operation Desert Storm in mid-January 1991. An intense 6 week-long air campaign substantially degraded the Iraqi Army dug in along Kuwait's border with Saudi Arabia. The ground assault, which started on 24th February, lasted only 100 hours and liberated Kuwait in a decisive victory.

I arrived in Riyadh shortly after 3am on the morning of 14th March. British Forces Middle East (BFME) was still commanded by General Peter de la Billière but he was due to return home shortly, along with much of the staff at HQ BFME and nearly all the British units in Saudi Arabia and Kuwait. John Major, the Prime Minister, had recently visited to congratulate everyone on the successful campaign and had promised that they would all be home by Easter. The next day I visited Kuwait City, flying up in the General's Jet (an HS 125) with Alasdair Wilson who was handing over the appointment as Chief Engineer to me. We passed through a lot of smog and smoke between Riyadh and Kuwait from the burning oil wells but the sky over Kuwait City was clear. We met Mike Brooke at the airport in Kuwait City, still closed to civil aircraft but open for military flights. Mike briefed us about the work he was coordinating with the Americans, French and British on Battle Area Clearance before we drove to the British Embassy to talk to the British Ambassador, Michael Weston. Kuwait City was in a mess; the Iraqis had wrecked many of the buildings, laid mines everywhere and set fire to more than 500 oil wells. In one spot alone we counted 37 burning oil wells and the air was black. The MOD wanted to bring all the soldiers back as soon as possible but there was pressure from the Kuwaitis for a military force to stay behind.

Back in Riyadh, it soon became obvious that the sappers would not become involved in any reconstruction tasks but would leave for home as soon as possible along with the rest of the British military units. Meanwhile two fresh squadrons from 36 Engineer Regiment and a small regimental headquarters would fly out from the UK to backload a huge quantity of engineer equipment and stores through the port of Al Jubayl in Saudi Arabia. Clearing up and tying up loose ends was a frustrating business. We were back on peace-time accounting and bureaucracy was digging in. The main effort was now the return of equipment and peoples' attention was focused very definitely on going home. However, the MOD also agreed to provide an EOD squadron for a limited period to assist a civilian company (Royal Ordnance) secure a contract for Battle Area Clearance in Kuwait, until the company could recruit enough workers to deliver the contract themselves.

Plans were changing frequently. I was tasked to hand over my (now limited) sapper responsibilities to Chris Guthkelch, the commanding officer of 36 Engineer Regiment, and drove to Kuwait on 1st April to a deserted factory complex at Doha, on a small peninsula some 25 kilometres north west of Kuwait City centre. I had no directive but had to write my own, once in my new appointment, and then have it approved by Air Vice-Marshal Ian MacFadyen, who had taken over as Commander BFME in Riyadh. I was not sure that he ever really understood what I was supposed to do but Brigadier Rob McAfee the Chief of Staff in HQ BFME was always helpful. Essentially, I was to command all assigned UK forces in Kuwait and act as the single point of contact for all UK military involvement there. I soon found that the job comprised plenty of variety with all sorts of unexpected matters cropping up.

The force in Kuwait was somewhat of a compromise in typical British fashion to demonstrate a presence in Kuwait at minimum cost to the British Government. The MOD had hoped to withdraw all fighting troops within 6 weeks of the war's end, but a decision was taken at the last minute to leave a battlegroup behind, to provide reassurance for the Kuwaitis, along with whatever larger force the Americans also left behind. A fresh battlegroup based on the 2nd Battalion The Royal Anglian (known as the Poachers and commanded by Alan Deed) was sent out from Germany to take over from the 3rd Battalion, The Royal Regiment of Fusiliers battlegroup who had fought in the war. This new grouping comprised two infantry companies mounted in Warrior armoured fighting vehicles, a fire support company with the Milans, Mortars and the Recce Platoon, an armoured squadron from 5th Inniskilling Dragoon Guards in Challenger tanks and 31 Field Battery with M-109 self-propelled guns. The battalion had only just converted to Warrior, the armoured squadron had yet to convert to Challenger (being equipped with Chieftain in Germany) and the battery had to convert to M-109 as it was from Thorney Island where it had FH-70 (towed artillery). There was no integral close sapper support and the second line logistic slice was pretty thin, provided from a composite company drawn from the Logistic Support Group (LSG) in Al Jubayl some 200 miles south.

Fortunately, Brigadier Noel Muddiman who commanded the LSG, generously went the extra mile to help when he could. My small HQ was co-located with the battlegroup in a factory complex close by the Doha power station some 15 miles north west of Kuwait City centre. The HQ was initially provided by some officers in HQ 4 Armoured Brigade who volunteered to remain behind to oversee the handover between the outgoing and incoming battlegroups before returning to Germany for their overdue leave. I then had a skeleton staff until replacements arrived from the UK and Germany. It was all very ad hoc, but the new battlegroup was keen and could not wait to move out to the desert to start training.

We had strong medical back up which included a medical support team with a surgeon, based at a local hospital by the Ahmadi oilfields and had our own support helicopter detachment of 3 Sea Kings, flown by a robust bunch of RN pilots from 845 Naval Air Squadron. A fresh signal squadron from 11 Armoured Brigade in Germany arrived to sort out the communications. On the sapper side we had a small composite troop drawn from a number of units in the UK and Germany and, for a short period, we had the welcome assistance of another troop from 36 Engineer Regiment based in Al Jubayl who set up our initial living accommodation with power, field showers and ablutions and secured the camp perimeter. There was also a company from the King's Own Scottish Borderers (KOSB) with us for a few days to help guard captured Iraqi equipment and a nearby base for the British Reconstruction Implementation Team (BRIT), which provided support for British firms trying to win business in Kuwait after the war. The total size of the force was about 1200. I liaised regularly with the Americans (with help from a very pleasant US Liaison Officer), the French and the Kuwaitis, as well as with the British Embassy. I also had an attached RN Liaison Officer (an Australian on an exchange posting with the RN) who kept me informed of the Navy's activities.

The small Battle Area Clearance (BAC) Team coordinating the Coalition Forces' clear up and marking of the minefields and huge quantities of unexploded munitions lying all over the place was initially based at the airport. This team was commanded by Mike Brooke and we provided him with some administrative support. Within a few weeks 21 (EOD) Squadron deployed from the UK to take on clearance of munitions (but not minefields) after a slightly unsavoury series of negotiations. Essentially the MOD would only deploy the EOD Squadron if Royal Ordnance paid for the squadron to assist them with clearing key areas, such as the port, access to oilfields, etc. But Royal Ordnance, in turn, needed assurance that they would be awarded a contract by the Kuwaitis to conduct larger clearance operations and needed the squadron until they had recruited enough workers of their own. The deal struck me as being too mercenary – perhaps an indication of things to come with an ex-Chancellor of the Exchequer as the PM! I became involved in a number of discussions with Mike Brooke, the Ambassador and with Royal Ordnance who seemed to think that because they were paying for use of the squadron, they could treat them exactly as they wanted without recognising the limitations imposed in order to ensure that the risks to the sappers were minimised. Although the Royal Ordnance managers negotiated the commercial contract, they had to accept that the squadron would be under Mike Brooke's military command and that the soldiers could not be tasked in the same manner as their civilian workers.

My first few weeks were challenging but always interesting. The scale of the logistic effort still in theatre, especially with the Americans, was staggering; vast logistic bases, massive non-stop convoys and huge parking lots of every type of military vehicle. It certainly emphasised the importance of detailed staff planning in moving and maintaining a force of any size. I was impressed by the patience and tolerance of the British, American, and French soldiers. The conditions were not anything to write home about; no relaxation and nowhere to enjoy a bit of scenery, a meal out or a beer. The place was like a rubbish dump and too many soldiers were killed or injured after the war finished in traffic accidents or by exploding munitions that they had either picked up or trodden on.

Kuwait itself had suffered devastation on a massive scale with the burning oil wells, the sea pollution, and the mindless vandalism of the Iraqi Army. Much of the country resembled an untidy garbage tip with a random scattering of looted vehicles all missing their wheels (taken by the Iraqis), burnt out military hulks, civilian cars and lorries alongside most roads; rubbish mixed up with abandoned children's toys, women's shoes, pieces of furniture, pictures, clothing and belongings. Nearly every building inhabited by Iraqis had broken doors, smashed windows, no light switches, door handles, wall sockets (all looted) and rubbish strewn everywhere. They broke everything! When the wind blew in the wrong direction (blowing smoke from the oil fires) the sun and much of the daylight was obliterated; at 10am it could be as dark as a gloomy winter evening at nightfall. It was even worse flying through the actual smoke plume. Dust and soot accumulated everywhere; the smell, feel and taste of oil was all pervasive. Yet, despite the damage, the Kuwaitis themselves appeared to do little to sort it out and improvement was very gradual. Vehicle hulks slowly disappeared from the edges of the major roads; power and water were spasmodically restored; shops and hotels in Kuwait City began reopening again. Local Kuwait Army roadblocks often fired randomly into the air, especially at night – just for the hell of it. A sinister development was the victimisation of the remaining Palestinians by Kuwaitis yet, ironically, it was the Palestinians and other non-Kuwaitis who had done most of the work to make the country so rich. In every other country that I know the local population would have done more to help themselves sort out such a terrible aftermath, but the Kuwaitis understandably remained traumatised for a long time by the Iraq invasion; one general whom I met had lost 3 of his 5 sons and many people had yet to come to terms with their personal grief.

On Wednesday 24th April, CinC FLEET (Admiral Sir Jock Slater) visited briefly to talk to our RN helicopter pilots and crew who were an outstanding bunch; he was really friendly and I very much enjoyed meeting him. The next evening, I again met the British Ambassador to discuss the Royal Ordnance contract, together with Mike Brooke. I personally reckoned that the whole deal was dicey, but the Kuwaitis had signed the contract with Royal Ordnance and we awaited their MOD contract to be confirmed. On Friday evening I had supper with Peter Grant-Peterkin who was the Chief of Staff of the UN Kuwait Observer Monitoring Force (UNIKOM, which included a 20-man British contingent). Their headquarters was in a temporary base at the Scandinavian Air Services (SAS) Hotel by a beach just south of the city centre. He moved later to Umm Qasr, just over the Iraq/Kuwait border. I did not envy him his job – everything in the UN seemed chaotic and it took them longer than expected to establish a presence along the proposed Demilitarised Zone (DMZ) between Iraq and Kuwait. On 27th April we had yet another of Air Vice Marshal MacFadyen's frequent visits; he was over an hour late so I had to cancel his lunch with the Kuwaiti Chief of Staff (General Jaber) and reschedule his programme so that he could visit the battlegroup and enjoy firing the Rarden Cannon and Chain Gun on a Warrior armoured vehicle and witness a Milan anti-tank missile firing. Every time he visited he was on a 'swan'.

That evening the battlegroup had a temporary break in their training and the officers arranged an open-air mess dinner in the desert to which they had invited a number of Americans from 3 (US) Armoured Division (to whom they were loosely affiliated), including the Commanding General. It was a first class dinner (typically British) except no alcohol and no silver. The drums and pipes played the odd piece now and again (the band came out as medics during the war and had all returned home so we only had the drums, who were in the machine gun platoon). We toasted the President of the United States and the Queen with orange juice. The meal was excellent and at the end the Adjutant recounted a gripping story about a burning bomb, which had been rushed out from the Mess of one of the earlier Royal Anglian regiments before it exploded and thus saving the Mess. While he was speaking, a simulated stick of plastic explosive was passed around the tables with a length of burning safety fuse hissing quietly. No one knew whether the stick was genuine or not (certainly not the Americans!) The Mess Sergeant retrieved the 'bomb' just before the safety fuse burnt out, rushed away with it and we heard a loud bang! It made a fitting climax to the evening.

The final British and American withdrawal was dependent on the ability of UNIKOM to take over both the DMZ and the safe custody of refugees in southern Iraq from the US forces. 3 (US) Armoured Division worked very hard to sort out the DMZ and assist the UN force as much as possible; additionally by late May the division had moved all the refugees out of Safwan in Iraq to Rafha in Saudi Arabia and all seemed set for a withdrawal. Suddenly the Kuwaitis expressed alarm at us going and, at the last minute, 1 (US) Armoured Brigade (from 3 (US) Armoured Division) was tasked to remain in Kuwait and we were also ordered to stay. A number of Americans even had to be pulled back from aircraft in Saudi Arabia as they were already on their way home. The American brigade moved into the factory complex next door to us and parked up most of its vehicles on the enormous parking areas in our camp. Their move was impressive (very quick), their logistic back up excellent, they were friendly, and we enjoyed getting to know them.

11 Air Cavalry Regiment from Fulda in Germany would replace them the following month.

The French, having done a great deal of mine clearance, had pulled out their 800 odd soldiers (nearly all sappers) but were bringing in a small force of EOD specialists to work for their military attaché and retain the goodwill of the Kuwaitis. The Royal Ordnance contract with 21 (EOD) Squadron had at last been agreed and signed by all parties; the Squadron was now in Al Jubayl sorting out kit, with its recce and advance parties planning the tasks. HQ BFME at Riyadh was soon to close, and we would then be commanded directly from the Joint Force Headquarters in High Wycombe.

Meanwhile the battlegroup had completed some first class training in the desert, firing more ammunition in their first 3 weeks than they would normally have fired in 4 years in Germany. The area used for training was full of old Iraqi positions and contained an a lot of unexploded ordnance, some of it very dangerous, including MLRS bomblets, cluster bomblets, the odd anti-personnel mine, grenades and tons and tons of ammunition of all kinds (mortar bombs, artillery shells and charges, tank ammunition, cannon shells, anti-aircraft shells, anti-air missiles, anti-tank missiles and all sorts of small arms ammo). It was only safe to move about on roads and existing tracks in wheeled vehicles but, was relatively safe to move across country in tracked vehicles as they had armoured protection, provided anti-tank mines were avoided. Fortunately, these were not encountered away from the Iraq/Kuwait border or away from the coast. But, since the end of the war just less than 3 months earlier, the Coalition Forces had lost 40 soldiers killed and over 200 injured in accidents involving munitions of all kinds; a terrible waste. We had one soldier injured in a freak incident when tracer from a GPMG SF set fire to some ammo in an Iraqi bunker that then

ignited an anti-air missile which, in turn, flew straight into the side
of a Warrior vehicle. The driver's right eye was badly damaged, and
he was evacuated to the Woolwich hospital in the UK. We also had
a lucky escape when a Land Rover was struck by a Kuwaiti vehicle
failing to stop at the lights of an intersection; the Land Rover
overturned and it was a miracle that no one inside was killed or
seriously injured. Our helicopters were redeployed to Bangladesh on
a disaster relief operation after a cyclone cased catastrophic flooding
and enormous loss of life there, so we rearranged helicopter support
for casevac and range clearance through the Americans for the next
couple of weeks, but could not expect to rely on their generosity
forever.

The UN certainly had an interesting start to their tour. The
Kuwaiti Army were using immigrant labour to help clear unexploded
munitions from a stretch of beach, but they seldom briefed or
supervised them properly. One day, the immigrants gradually filled
a 20-ton truck with an assorted mixture of grenades, mortar bombs,
RPG7 rockets, ammo etc., and backed the truck along a narrow
road beside the SAS hotel close to the beach – and the temporary
HQ for the UN. A Kuwaiti Army roadblock had allowed the truck
through. As it was backing down, someone noticed that smoke was
pouring from the truck (perhaps caused by a leaking phosphorous
grenade) and shouted a warning to the driver who promptly jumped
out of the cab and ran away, without first stopping the truck, which
proceeded to move ever closer to the hotel and some UN vehicles.
Suddenly there were a series of explosions; grenades, rockets and
bullets started striking the side of the hotel. Inside there was
pandemonium; the UN in the building thought they were under
attack! After some 25 minutes the truck eventually burnt out and
a number of UN vehicles were also destroyed. Miraculously there

were no casualties, but the UN thereafter guarded themselves! There were other incidents and the UN being top heavy with officers and officials did not have enough transport and logistic assets. Without support from the Americans they would have foundered and were finding their mission very difficult. It must have been a nightmare trying to organise 37 nationalities and very awkward for individuals sharing an OP duty with 3 or 4 other strangers from different countries in the middle of nowhere. One of the observer parties on the DMZ forgot to take a mallet with them so could not bang in the pegs to erect their tent and had no shade for 4 days until relieved. Their faces were burnt bright red like prunes. A Hungarian observer quit early and left for home. Another OP contingent tried to rescue an Iraqi who stepped on a mine in the DMZ, losing both legs. By the time he reached the Norwegian Field Hospital he was dead, and they were surprised when the hospital arranged for the helicopter to return the body to them – a new twist on medical procedure!

Kuwait's recovery accelerated slowly as more people and equipment entered the country. The city regained power and mains water more or less everywhere, but the water supply could not be guaranteed. In our camp we still trucked in most of the water we used. Shops were starting up again and Kuwait Airlines ran about 10 or 11 flights a day in and out of the airport. The locals were using the beaches for fishing, but I would not allow our soldiers to either fish or swim in the sea. Although the mines and ammo had been cleared from much of the city coastline by the French and the Saudis, there could be no guarantee that they cleared all of them and the sea swell could well have moved a number of mines. The sea was also full of sewage and contained traces of oil. The attitude of the Kuwaitis to the Palestinians still remaining and to the immigrant workers was a concern. The trials of those who collaborated with the Iraqis before and during the war had just started and did not appear to be impartial; one youth was sentenced to 15 years imprisonment for supposedly wearing a Saddam Hussein T-shirt.

We had a whole series of senior visitors during May, culminating in Tom King's visit on the 20th. The Kuwaitis were still very nervous about their security and had specifically asked the Americans and us to stay on. Indeed, the Crown Prince was very insistent with Tom King that we did! Although somewhat disillusioned by the lack of clear direction, I found it interesting to observe the political/military interface at first hand and to experience the real problems of extracting from the aftermath of the war. Our continued deployment in Kuwait was now firmly tied to the eventual withdrawal of the Logistic Support Group (LSG) from Al Jubayl; we were to remain until the end of July but would leave 21 (EOD) Squadron and Mike Brooke's BAC Cell behind to continue supporting Royal Ordnance until the end of September. The battlegroup reorganised, leaving one company behind in Kuwait in the armoured infantry role, and moved to Al Jubayl in early June to relieve 1 KOSB as the guard force for the LSG. The Armoured Squadron and 31 Field Battery returned home. The infantry company in Kuwait was rotated every 10 days to 2 weeks to give each company the chance to carry out low level infantry training in the desert and to vary the routine for the soldiers. Knowing that we were to remain for at least 2 more months in our base, called St George's Lines, portacabins and an extra-large generator were sent up from Al Jubayl to provide air-conditioned accommodation for those remaining, some 400 in total. HQ BFME in Riyadh had been disbanded and we were now commanded directly from the Joint Headquarters at High Wycombe, which was also RAF Strike Command.

Mains power and water had been restored and the sapper troop quickly improved the camp's facilities by plumbing in better ablutions, wiring up the portacabins and even erecting 2 small portable swimming tanks sent out from the UK! Daytime temperatures were now regularly nudging 50 degrees centigrade in the shade and the accommodation enhancements were a most welcome relief. The hottest temperature recorded in St George's Lines by the medics was above 50 degrees centigrade; it may have been even slightly hotter in those areas of the desert unaffected by the oil smoke plumes. Life on the whole was pretty slow as the heat was not a great spur to frantic activity. The Kuwait officials seldom admitted to temperatures as high as 50 degrees because they were then supposed to stop all the immigrant workers from working; it invariably stuck at about 47 degrees! Sadly, the mines and munitions still left from the war continued to cause unacceptable casualties.

On 20th June two NCOs from the BAC Cell rescued 2 Kuwaiti boys who had been badly injured when they took a short cut through a minefield close to a beach in order to go fishing. As a result of their prompt actions, they saved the boys' lives and both were later recognised by gallantry awards. Sergeant Rogers RAF was awarded the George Medal and Corporal Winters RE the Queens Commendation for Brave Conduct (QCBC). Sergeant Rogers was experienced in dealing with air-delivered munitions, but he had never dealt with land mines until this incident. An extract from his citation reads:

"Sergeant Rogers is employed as the Senior Non Commissioned Officer (Air) in the UK Explosive Ordnance Disposal (EOD) Cell in Kuwait City. On 20 June at 1040 hours he was summoned by a Kuwait police captain to an incident in an Iraqi laid coastal

minefield nearby. Lying in the middle of scores of densely laid anti-personnel mines were two Kuwait boys, both very seriously injured from at least two mine detonations. Both were conscious but had each lost a leg and had multiple lacerations and other injuries. Sergeant Rogers immediately ordered all onlookers behind cover and then entered the minefield secured by a secure line back to Corporal Winter. With complete disregard for his own safety he crawled towards the first casualty and recovered him along the approach route to safety.

Without hesitation he entered the minefield again. Now dehydrated in temperatures in excess of 45 degrees centigrade, he breached through more mines past the first position to reach the second casualty. Thinking only of the boy's safety Sergeant Rogers painstakingly retrieved the boy back along the breached route, between many mines, eventually delivering him to a medical team. In the opinion of the military medical officer on the scene he acted just in time to save the boys' lives…"

Royal Ordnance had their first major casualty in early June when one of their employees (an ex-sapper officer) detonated 2 or more PMN mines in a mines dump and suffered appalling injuries, losing a leg and being blinded. He was brought back to our medical team in the Kuwait Ahmadi hospital and was nursed around the clock by a dedicated team, led by Sergeant Darke, who saved his life and was later awarded a BEM for her nursing and leadership of the intensive care ward at the Ahmadi hospital throughout the deployment. She cared for all patients in difficult circumstances and had to cope with the smoke, darkness and oil pollution caused by oil-well fires around the hospital, combined with frequent power cuts and lack of water and was an inspiration to her team and her patients.

21 (EOD) Squadron had started work with Royal Ordnance on 1st June but we kept the Squadron tasking totally separate from the Royal Ordnance works parties to minimise the risk of our soldiers picking up any slack habits. The Independent Newspaper years later reported in 1996 that of the 110 Royal Ordnance people employed in clearing mines in Kuwait, 8 were killed and at least 13 seriously injured. We were clearly justified in being critical of their operating procedures. Towards the end of June, 6 Egyptian soldiers were killed and a further 5 injured by a box of grenades that exploded.

The Americans rotated their last remaining formation (1 Armoured Brigade) with 11 Air Cavalry Regiment (11 ACR) from Fulda in Germany who were always friendly and generously invited us to their 4th July celebration. They all seemed pretty tired but perhaps not surprising as they started every day with early morning runs at 0430 hours! The Egyptians and Syrians indicated that they would each be leaving about 3,000 troops in Kuwait to reinforce the eventual Gulf Cooperation Council (GCC) Force, comprising mainly Saudis and Kuwaitis but this was by no means definite and GCC intentions were generally more impressive than real! The Kuwaitis were taking an awfully long time to make up their minds about anything; the situation was not helped by many of the most senior officers leaving when the Iraqis invaded.

I had an interesting visit up to the DMZ between Iraq and Kuwait in the UN southern sector. There was very little happening and it must have been soul destroying for the UN observers. The major hub of activity appeared to centre on a market in the middle of nowhere right on the border where a number of trucks turned up from time to time every day, parked haphazardly and the drivers and passengers then tried to sell arms and whisky! The UN observers were trying to move the market on because it was a potential flashpoint.

God knows who purchased the stuff but there were always people
around. One memorable sight (for me) was a Ghanaian soldier near
one of the UN bases providing the infantry guard force for the OPs
in the heat of the day wearing a face mask to keep out dust, a jersey
and a woolly hat. It was boiling hot! As we passed, he removed his
face mask, threw a casual salute, gave an enormous grin, and put his
mask on again!

On 11th July, a week after participating in 11 ACR's American
Independence Day celebrations, which began with a battery firing
a 50-round salute at 0500 hours, we had a series of more serious
explosions to contend with. Over 50 American vehicles fully
loaded with war stocks of combat supplies and parked close to
my headquarters, were all destroyed in a chain reaction of massive
blasts initiated by a fire starting in a field artillery support vehicle
(FASV) that was loaded with 90 rounds of 155mm ammunition.
The estimated losses included 8xM109 self-propelled guns,
8xFASV, 5 or 6 M1 Abrahams tanks, some M2 Bradley Armoured
Fighting Vehicles, 3 bridge layers and a large number of logistic
vehicles that included fuel bowsers. More vehicles were damaged
but not totally destroyed, and a number of warehouses and buildings
were also badly damaged. We were first warned about the fire in
the FASV around 1030 hours, but the Americans felt they could
control it. Some 30 minutes later we were warned to evacuate the
camp area immediately. As I left my headquarters with my staff an
enormous blast occurred within 150 metres (fortunately shielded by
the building) and a small piece of shrapnel flew through the rear
windscreen of my Range Rover and ended up on the dashboard as
I was getting in. We evacuated the camp as quickly as possible and
set up a Command Post by the main gate some 800 metres from
the vehicle park containing 11 ACR vehicles which were now

all in danger of exploding. This Command Post then became the focal point for keeping track of our soldiers and the incident; we decided to concentrate everyone at Doha Port, about a mile north of the camp until we could arrange something better. I placed St George's Lines out of bounds until it could be cleared and made safe by 21 (EOD) Squadron, stationed elsewhere working with Royal Ordnance. In the confusion of the random series of explosions, as the fire spread and while evacuating the camp, casualties were miraculously light with only 2 British soldiers taken to hospital with minor injuries; 13 American soldiers ended up in hospital, one with serious head injuries. Damage was extensive with shrapnel, pieces of vehicles, unexploded shells, mines and bomblets spread over a one-kilometre radius (not surprising with over 1,000 rounds of 155mm calibre shells having exploded!) and it soon became apparent that we would have to move from the camp permanently, due to the devastation and the threat from unexploded munitions, especially M42 bomblets. Captain Peter Shields and Lance Corporal Plant were both later awarded Queen's Gallantry Medals and Company Sergeant Major Rimmer was awarded a Queen's Commendation for Brave Conduct for their actions in the aftermath of the explosions. The RSM had a lucky escape while moving an 8-tonne lorry down to Doha Port when he drove over a bomblet 100 metres outside the main gate by the side of the road. The bomblet destroyed the diesel fuel tank and two tyres but nothing else, fortunately.

While my Chief of Staff, Alistair Sheppard, was arranging alternative accommodation with the RFA Sir Galahad, moored in Shuaiba Port, and a camp on the other side of the city run by the civilian British Reconstruction Implementation Team (BRIT) who both went out of their way to welcome us, we went ahead with a CSE show that had been previously arranged in the camp. The hastily rearranged performance on an improvised stage in Doha Port on a very warm evening was a memorable event, thoroughly enjoyed by all. We had invited the Americans, but they were too busy coming to terms with the effects of the explosions. The entertainment proved a tonic for the soldiers, some of whom had been badly shaken by the incident and provided a useful interlude to allow time to sort out where and how they would live for the next few days. During the clearance operation in the camp, which started early the next morning, 21 (EOD) Squadron found well over 100 bomblets within our accommodation and vehicle hangars which they destroyed. Sadly, Sergeant Wright was injured in a leg and a foot by an M42 bomblet. Once we had recovered all our vehicles and equipment and tidied up our portion of the camp we handed over the whole of St George's Lines to 11 ACR so that they could finish their clear up. Colonel Skip Bacevich, commanding 11 ACR, dropped me a friendly note to thank me and my soldiers for helping his Regiment during and in the aftermath of the explosions. His last sentence stated that "… We owe you a great debt of gratitude and will never forget what you have done for our soldiers." Twelve days after the original accident, 3 American soldiers were tragically killed by an explosion, while moving munitions to be destroyed outside the base.

Sir Galahad had to move south on 23rd July, which brought forward our final withdrawal by a few days. We completed our departure through Al Jubayl 2 days later leaving a small rear party under Alistair Sheppard in Kuwait right up until 31st July in order to fulfil the commitment to the Kuwaitis that there would be a UK presence until the end of the month.

After returning home I had a few days to reflect on my time in Kuwait and ponder on some lessons. Perhaps the key lesson was that the post conflict phase is part of the overall campaign and needs to be tied into the campaign from the beginning. Another was that uncertainty abounds in any operation, even after the fighting is over; as my American LO often remarked "Stay fluid 'cos flexible is too damn rigid!" To witness at first hand the after effects resulting from the mindless devastation wreaked on Kuwait by Iraq was very sobering, but we were fortunate to have had an opportunity to contribute something to the country, to experience a new, challenging environment, to become familiar with some of the new equipment sent to the Gulf and to learn more about some of our allies. The battlegroup enjoyed excellent training; the sappers, signallers, medics and logisticians had the satisfaction of doing a real job. For me it was a privilege to command officers and soldiers who tackled anything thrown at them with humour and tolerance.

Twenty years later Tom King (now Lord King) wrote an article for the Guardian in January 2011 that provides an interesting perspective between the first and second Gulf wars – and highlights (again) the importance of post-conflict planning before the fighting even starts.

"The 20th anniversary of the first Gulf war inevitably invites comparisons with the second. The first conflict was for the liberation of Kuwait – the second the much more challenging undertaking of the invasion of Iraq and the overthrow of Saddam Hussein. The first comparison is the much clearer objective in 1990. Kuwait had been illegally invaded and Saddam had either to withdraw peacefully or be forced out. To achieve this, clear UN resolutions were agreed. A coalition of more than 30 countries came together, and very substantial forces were assembled. The second, more revealing comparison, in that for the much more limited task of expelling Saddam from a country he should have not been in, a force of no

less than 750,000 – land, sea and air – was deployed. The effect of that overwhelming force, with a six-week air campaign, was to achieve total victory for the land campaign in less than a week, with minimum casualties. For the much more testing challenge of invading and occupying Iraq, a force barely a fifth of that number was employed. The one disappointment in the 1ˢᵗ Gulf War was that the very speed of the success caught the allies somewhat unprepared for establishing the right ceasefire and peace terms. There was no question of continuing the advance to Baghdad, for which we had no UN authority. What is certainly arguable is that we stopped 24 hours too soon and lost the chance to capture two Republican Guard divisions. Their loss to Saddam could well have tipped the balance in the subsequent Shia uprising, which he only narrowly survived."

Abandoned Iraqi tank.

Oil discharged from
damaged wells.

Series of burning oil wells in the background.

Iraqi beach obstacle of wire and A/P mines.

Another burning oil well.

Iraqi trench, behind wire and mines.

Minefield south of Kuwait City, 50 km long.

Destroyed Iraqi tank.

Entrance to Ali Al Salem Air Base.

Aftermath of air strike at Muttla Pass.

Welcome to Kuwait City!

Little traffic but road
space for sheep.

The battlegroup spent as much time as possible training in the desert. The photographs on this page are from the Poachers' magazine. Above is a Warrior vehicle.

Two M-109 guns ready for action.

Vehicle maintenance.

With Tom King, Secretary of State for Defence. Alan Deed, CO 2 R Anglian, is on his far left.

With General Peter de La Billière, who accompanied Tom King during his visit.

The UN Monitoring Force sent to Kuwait (UNIKOM) established a number of observation posts in the Demilitarized Zone (DMZ) along the border with Iraq.

Weapon smuggling in the DMZ.

Discarded ammunition left everywhere.

Discarded ammunition being destroyed.

Some of the captured Iraqi tanks, guarded by a company from 1 KOSB.

View of some of the vehicle and equipment belonging to 11 Air Cavalry Regiment (US Army) co-located with us in Doha.

Exploding ammunition in US Army vehicles parked close to our base.

A towed ammunition vehicle belonging to 11 ACR caught fire on 11 July 2001. This soon spread, resulting in a series of explosions, extensive damage and destruction of many buildings and US vehicles in the base. We had to abandon the base due to the threat of unexploded ordnance, which included many M42 bomblets. Our area was subsequently cleared by 21 Squadron (EOD) but the Americans lost 3 soldiers killed while clearing their area.

12

WIDER HORIZONS

A few months after returning from Kuwait Mary and I spent a nostalgic three weeks in Zimbabwe; our first visit there for nearly twenty years. The climate and scenery were as stunning as ever – and the people, black and white, just as welcoming as before. We spent some idyllic days on Lake Kariba, at Victoria Falls and in the Inyanga mountains and it was wonderful to catch up with Richard, Jill and Anna Fleming (Mary's uncle, aunt and cousin) plus a number of old friends. It was only ten years since Mugabe had swept to power and our friends were cautiously optimistic about their future in the country. The land seizures by the 'so-called war vets' were still a few years away. Nevertheless we could sense an unease and restlessness amongst some whites, who would have liked to leave but felt trapped financially as they could not sell their businesses or farms for a fair return, and amongst many Africans whose standard of living and job security had diminished under black rule.

We spent a morning at Swallowfield to find the farm in terminal decline. The African owner had pulled down many of the farm buildings to sell the bricks and roofing, but had not cleared up the remaining rubble; he had cut down most of the trees my father planted to sell or burn the wood, but had not planted new ones; the farmhouse was looking very shabby and the garden was dying; there were no crops planted save for a few acres of scruffy mealies spread in a random manner close to the house. However, Thornbury (my father's other farm), had been bought by a white farmer, who at that time was serving as a minister in Mugabe's government. He had developed a most beautiful home and garden and had also sunk three boreholes in order to provide a guaranteed water supply for his maize fields. The two farms reflected, in miniature, the fortunes of much of Africa. We also went to look for my father's memorial and ashes in the Warren Hills Cemetery, close to Harare but without success until the cemetery's manager, a very friendly African, asked if he could help us. When I told him my father's name and said we could find no sign of his memorial on a wall where it had been mounted soon after his cremation, he explained, "Ah yes, I know exactly what you are looking for and have it in my office behind my desk" and kindly showed us to his office where he gave me the box containing the ashes and the inscribed stone with my father's details. When we asked why it was no longer on the wall he explained, "It fell off about three years ago and I haven't got a screw to put it back securely." I decided immediately to bring back his ashes to England. They were buried next to my mother's ashes in St Bartholomew's Churchyard, Holton Village, near Oxford, in a small family ceremony on a beautiful, cold winter's day in December 1992.

Back in England I returned to my job running a small team updating the Army's tactical doctrine and rewriting a number of Army manuals to take account of the end of the Cold War, resulting in more emphasis on expeditionary operations and peacekeeping. One interesting assignment was a short-notice task to produce a tactical aide-memoire for British soldiers deploying to Bosnia on Op Grapple in support of the United Nations Protection Force (UNPROFOR). In April 1992, The British Army had earlier sent a Field Ambulance, with limited logistic support, to provide some medical assistance to the UN on Op Hanwood. This small group was based at a defunct Yugoslav Air force location on a Croatian Airfield. Additionally, a Sapper field troop had deployed to provide military engineering support to the Field Ambulance Group and to the UN Headquarters and UN Observation Posts (OPs) in Sarajevo. Op Hanwood lasted until October 1993 by when the British focus shifted to a 2,400 strong Op Grapple Force that comprised a Brigade HQ plus 1 CHESHIRE battlegroup, 35 Engineer Regiment, a number of logistic elements and helicopter support.

When the former Yugoslav republics of Slovenia and Croatia declared their independence from Belgrade in June 1991 the Federal Government of Yugoslavia took military action to prevent this. It soon abandoned its struggle against Slovenia but intensified its actions against Croatia, which suffered some very bitter fighting losing part of its territory to the Serbs by the end of 1991. The Serbian leader, Slobodan Milosović, accepted UN mediation that resulted in a ceasefire. Much worse was to follow in Bosnia-Herzegovina when it seceded from Yugoslavia and the Bosnian Serbs, aided by the Federal Republic of Yugoslavia forces, attacked both Croat and Muslim communities and laid siege to a large part of Sarajevo. By mid-1992 Bosnia was in a critical condition with Bosnian Serbs, Croats and Muslims fighting each other and where law and order had broken down completely. The hatred and distrust between the different communities was intense and there were some appalling acts of brutality, especially by the Bosnian Serbs – but also by Muslims and Croats. Relief to protect lives was urgently needed and the UN expanded UNPROFOR to provide assistance for the population. In contrast to Croatia, the UNPROFOR mandate for Bosnia and Herzegovina was not to monitor a pre-existing cease-fire, but to keep the population alive until the war ended. UNPROFOR was an international force of over 20,000 troops with contributions from twelve nations: Belgium, Canada, Denmark, Egypt, France, the Netherlands, Norway, Portugal, Spain, the UK, Ukraine and USA.

I flew to Zagreb, spending a couple of days with a Canadian unit, 3rd Battalion Princess Patricia's Light Infantry (PPCLI) in Croatia, and a short visit to Colonel Ian Johnson, the Chief of Staff of the European Commission Monitoring Mission (ECMM). I had worked closely with him on the same team at the Staff College a couple of years earlier and found his honest appraisal of the situation in the Balkans most illuminating. It was sobering to witness the random destruction of large swathes of Croatia with burned out houses and destroyed villages, set amongst seemingly peaceful, scenic countryside. The Canadian soldiers I met were deployed in section and platoon strength in a variety of locations within the local communities, providing reassurance with courteous tolerance but, as with all UN missions, they had limited military capability to prevent any serious breaches of the Serbian/Croat agreement. Their patience and sympathy for the local population was impressive. I was refused permission to visit Sarajevo or any area controlled by Serbs and so could only gain a fleeting impression from the Canadian unit's perspective. The resulting small aide-memoire, compiled with the aid of my team back in Wilton with some hurried research of Yugoslavian history and geography and a dig through other documents, was printed just in time to be issued to the Op Grapple units before they deployed in October 1992.

The former Federal Republic of Yugoslavia showing: Slovenia, Croatia, Vojvodina, Bosnia and Herzegovina, Serbia, Montenegro, Kosovo and Macedonia.

A couple of months after returning from my short visit to Croatia, I was appointed as the Commander Engineer UK Land Forces, based at Wilton near Salisbury, and promoted to Brigadier. I soon found myself focusing on the military engineer support for Op Grapple.

Within a few weeks in my new appointment I visited Bosnia. I was under considerable pressure from HQ UK Land Forces, initiated by the bean counters in the MOD, to reduce the size of the Sapper effort on Op Grapple. Virtually every single sapper post had to be justified, line-by-line, and the MOD seemed paranoid about minimising existing military commitments while also engaged on reducing the size of Britain's Forces now that the Cold War had ended.

35 Engineer Regiment were spread from Split, on the Croatian coast, to Tomislavgrad just over the border with Bosnia, to Vitez further north (1 Cheshire Regiment's main base) and a number of other sites in Bosnia. It was late January and very cold with quite a bit of snow in the hills, but much warmer in Split where the Brigade HQ was located, along with the logistic units. 35 Regiment had already completed a number of herculean tasks and was still working flat out. They had constructed bases to accommodate the Op Grapple units, built roads and tracks to enable supplies to reach Vitez, repaired and built bridges on the main supply routes, carried out EOD clearance (and some limited mine clearance) for the safe passage for troops, provided water supply and purification, constructed bulk fuel installations and provided general combat engineer support for the force. Their most critical task was the building and maintenance of the supply route over the hills from Tomislavgrad to Prozor and on to Vitez, a distance of over 200 kilometres. The existing main road through Mostar (further east) could not be used because the Serbs frequently shelled it. Before starting, the Commanding Officer (Lieutenant Colonel John Field) had somehow negotiated clearance to work on part of the route in the mountains, where local groups had many vested interests, by offering to buy a 25-mile stretch for 10 dinars (approximately 10 pence) from the local council. The offer was surprisingly accepted! Paddy Ashdown, while visiting the UK contingent in December 1992 had travelled up the (then) very bumpy route to Vitez and wrote an article for the Independent Newspaper on his return which included the comment: "... The soldiers clearing this vicious little track through the snowy woods are performing a job to be proud of ..."

I was most impressed by 35 Engineer Regiment and all that they had achieved. Their main base in Tomislavgrad had been shelled by the Serbs a few weeks before my arrival, fortunately with no casualties, and they had successfully overcome numerous other challenges throughout their tour. John Field had recently been posted as an instructor at the Zimbabwe Staff College, but his officers and soldiers clearly had fond memories of him. I reached Tomislavgrad late one evening, just in time for a Burns Night Dinner in the soldier's mess hall where an NCO I knew well from 9 Squadron days addressed the Haggis in fine style! The next morning, feeling slightly the worse for wear, accompanied by the new CO, John Durance, and with the RSM WO1 Graham Ferguson driving, we travelled via the mountain route to Vitez and I had the chance to talk to many of the plant operators who had built the road and the plant mechanics and fitters who had valiantly kept the machines serviceable, despite the bitter winter conditions. At Vitez I met Bob Stewart, CO of the Cheshire's, who later became an MP on leaving the Army. Our return the next day via a slightly different route took longer as we had to negotiate with a heavy snowfall and parties of drunken Croats at a number of roadblocks, before they would allow us to pass. At one roadblock, the road was barred by some anti-tank mines placed on the road, which were casually kicked away by the militia once they decided to let us through. Back at Split I briefly met the Force Commander, Brigadier Andrew Cummings, before flying back to the UK.

This short visit brought home to me the almost tribal nature of the Bosnian conflict, with deep mutual suspicion and fear between the separate communities. People in one valley may not have known neighbours in the next valley. I did not come into contact with the Bosnian Serb Army (BSA) but saw groups from the Bosnian Croat

Army (HVO) strutting around some of the villages and manning some of the roadblocks. They had no respect for the UN, and it was galling to be interrogated by drunken militiamen about where we were going while pointing their rifles (and sometimes an RPG 7) at our Land Rover. They (and the Bosnian Serbs) took full advantage of the limited rules of engagement under which UNPROFOR was operating and knew there was little the UN could do to prevent their victimisation of the Muslims. I wondered how it was all going to end but it was very evident that the British Army's efforts were saving lives and that we could not walk away from our commitments.

Back at Wilton, I argued that the scale of military engineer support for Op Grapple should not be reduced below regimental level, although there could be some reduction in the total number of sappers now that the main bases had been built. The long lines of communication from Split up into central and northern Bosnia, plus the variety and complexity of engineer tasks definitely needed a regimental level of command. I was overruled and the next two units to replace 35 Regiment were large squadrons (over 250 strong). Although they performed well it became obvious that one squadron was not enough and by early 1994 it was agreed that the Grapple commitment needed a regiment of two field squadrons, a field support squadron, an EOD troop from 33 Engineer Regiment and a Specialist Team RE. The Regiment became the British Engineer Battalion (BRITENGBAT) with the CO and his small RHQ plus one field squadron in Gorni Vakuf, one field squadron in Vitez, a detachment at Bugojno and the support squadron at Tomislavgrad.

The forces on succeeding Op Grapple deployments were all drawn together in an ad hoc fashion and many of the constituent parts had not trained together before hand. Any UN operation would always lack funds, an ideal balance of troops, a clear chain of command, clear political direction, and a clear mission. The factors leading to military effectiveness are often incompatible with political agendas and funding arrangements; the UN is not designed to be a war-fighting organisation. Although UNPROFOR was not engaged in any combat actions, 2 Royal Engineers were tragically killed in 1994 in EOD and mine related incidents; Corporal Warburton and Lance Corporal Nicholas.

Military engineer support to Bosnia remained my top priority throughout my two and a half years at Land Command and I visited nearly all the Op Grapple sapper units while they were there. Sappers were better able to contribute towards an eventual solution than much of the rest of the Army because of our all-round utility and wide range of expertise. As the situation continued to escalate, 24 Airmobile Brigade, with its affiliated 51 Field Squadron (Airmobile) was deployed during the summer of 1995 to substantially enhance the Op Grapple Force. Additionally, an armoured engineer troop from 31 Armoured Engineer Squadron was sent to provide the necessary capability to break into any fortified positions, if required. 35 Engineer Regiment built the substantial infrastructure (hard-standing, fuel facilities, accommodation, storage for ammunition and explosives, etc) for 24 Brigade and its logistic support units at Ploče, near the coast in the south-east corner of Croatia, just before the Dayton Agreement was signed. Dayton dramatically altered the situation and a strong NATO led Implementation Force (IFOR) soon deployed to Bosnia to enforce compliance from the different warring factions. Neither 24 Brigade nor the armoured engineer troop were actually needed. Their deployment might have helped convince the Serbs that the British were fully in support of US resolve to break the Serb stranglehold in Bosnia but some considered it more of a gesture rather than

After the Dayton Accord, Bosnia became an independent state with two separate entities: the Federation of Bosnia and Herzegovina (BH) (joint Bosniac–Croat) and the Republika Srpska (RS) (predominantly Bosnian Serb). Each had its own president, government, parliament, police and other bodies. Above these entities was the central Bosnian Government and rotating Presidency. The Office of the High Representative was established to oversee its governance. Later a third small district (Brčko) was established.

a realistic option, especially as the Serbs anti-air missile defences would have severely limited 24 Brigade's operations. I will return to Bosnia later in the chapter.

In addition to Bosnia, Royal Engineer units in Land Command deployed on other operations; most regularly to Northern Ireland to reinforce the sapper regiment there but also to other parts of the world, including Rwanda and Angola. In 1994, 9 Parachute

Squadron plus a Military Works Force and EOD team, under Major Iain James, deployed to Rwanda two years after the awful genocide there to provide military engineer support for 5 Airborne Brigade's Logistic Battalion and 23 Parachute Field Ambulance. The first task for the Squadron was to establish the British contingent's self-sufficiency for water supply, sanitation and basic infrastructure. Soon afterwards the sappers were helping to construct accommodation, provide water supply and sanitation for the medical centres. Other tasks were the reopening of the Kanzenze Bridge (a 260-foot-four-span Bailey Bridge) on the main road some 20 kilometres south of Kigali and building another small bridge to improve the main road into Uganda from Gatuna. Regrettably, Sapper Copsey from 9 Squadron lost the lower part of one leg when he stepped on an anti-personnel mine while helping to build the Kanzenze Bailey Bridge. The small EOD team from 33 Engineer Regiment, in conjunction with UNICEF, UNESCO and Save the Children, helped in a mine-awareness programme as well as clearing some unexploded ordnance. In 1995, 20 Field Squadron, led by Major Chris Rose, deployed to Angola in support of a UK logistic regiment that was helping a UN peacekeeping mission. The Squadron tasks included establishing camps, providing water, restoring essential services, field defences and security lighting, repair of road surfaces in the port, limited mine clearance, diving (in support of the Royal Fleet Auxiliary Sir Galahad) and a number of humanitarian aid tasks. 20 Squadron, along with the other British units in Angola, was jointly awarded the Wilkinson Sword of Peace.

The drawdown of the British Army gathered pace and command of all units in Germany passed from HQ British Army on the Rhine (BAOR) at Rheindahlen, to HQ Land Command at Wilton. As Commander Engineer, I had direct command of two EOD and four Air Support Regiments. I also provided technical direction and set the Royal Engineer special to arm collective training standards for all sapper units in the Field Army, which included the sapper regiments in 1 Armoured Division in Germany and 3 UK Division in the UK. My small HQ coordinated the engineer manning of the various rolling commitments to Northern Ireland, the Falkland Islands, Belize, Canada, Cyprus and Kenya and the supervision of the engineer projects, less those in Northern Ireland. We were also committed to organising a number of projects to enhance the training facilities in UK. The units tackled all their different challenges very professionally, despite the disruption and long absences from home but I was becoming increasingly concerned about their very-short tour intervals (periods between deployments) that had reduced to 11 months. There were too many commitments for the numbers of Sappers.

The projects that struck a special chord with me were those where a sapper troop or a squadron built something in Kenya for a number of charities. The soldiers enjoyed them also because they built something tangible for local communities in isolated areas and gave them an opportunity to experience a bit of Africa. I had the enviable task of visiting the Kenya projects once a year and choosing the projects for the next year. The criteria were that the work had to offer challenging, worthwhile training and that the charity had to contribute the funding for the materials for each project. Royal Engineers would do the recce and planning, provide the construction plant and fuel, provide the manpower and complete each task to the agreed specification. These projects offered excellent training and helped officers, NCOs and soldiers cope better with unexpected future challenges when on actual operations in Bosnia, Northern Ireland, or elsewhere. One memorable project was for a charity helping Masai tribespeople in a remote part of the country that involved building a small dam, a training centre, a bush airstrip and a small medical station. The Masai had agreed (during the recce and initial planning the year before) to provide the funding for the bricks, cement and timber. When the Squadron arrived to start work there was no money, but the tribesmen had instead gathered together 20 bags of cement that had gone off and around 100 goats! By chance a Gurkha Infantry Battalion from the British Army was training nearby and so the goats were sold to the Gurkhas to supplement their rations, which provided enough money for the construction materials and work started. Once built, the Masai used the training centre to house some of their precious cattle, rather than for its original purpose! I visited that project as it was nearing completion and my warm welcome included sharing a meal from a goat that was cooked over an open fire within minutes of it being slaughtered.

Another of my responsibilities was to act as the Senior Military Commander on joint training exercises with the Police and the Scientists from both Aldermaston and Porton Down to prepare a capability to tackle possible future terrorist attacks that might involve nuclear, chemical or biological material. These exercises were taken very seriously and involved a great deal of detailed planning and preparation. During my tenure we exercised with 8 different police forces in the UK on a variety of testing scenarios which challenged the expertise and operating procedures of the scientists, the units from 33 Engineer Regiment (EOD) and 11 (EOD) Regiment RLC, plus the police. Although it was (then) considered improbable that such a sophisticated attack would be mounted, the threat could not be ignored, and we maintained a capable response ready to deploy at short notice. Either I or my Chief of Staff (Colonel Mike Gill), together with selected teams of experts, was at a few hours notice to move every day of the year with some others at even shorter notice; for example, 2 search teams at 2 hour's notice. It was a demanding call on limited numbers. Fortunately, we were never tasked for real, but I could not help worrying about the catastrophic consequences that would result should we ever fail.

I was due to handover the appointment of Commander Engineer around mid-1995, with no guarantee of another job in the Army, which was becoming smaller with the inevitable squeeze on brigadiers' appointments. I had no desire to work in the MOD and so opted for redundancy, hoping to try my luck in Civvy Street. My redundancy papers were duly forwarded but soon afterwards I received a phone call from the Deputy Military Secretary (Brigadier John Sutherell) asking me to think again because I had been in the running to take over as the Engineer-in-Chief (EinC) once the current EinC (Major General John Drewienkiewicz, known as DZ) moved on. The post was about to be downgraded to one star (a Brigadier's job) in line with the other Arms Directors. I had never imagined that I would ever hold that position so of course retracted my request to leave the Army and felt enormously privileged when I was later selected.

During my farewell interview with the Commander in Chief at Land Command (General Sir John Wilsey) he asked me to highlight any concerns I might have about the Sappers in his command. I mentioned that, although I was worried about overstretch with some 2,000 Sappers on operations over the past 12 months, the officers' and soldiers' morale and resilience was surprisingly high despite the changes in force structures and the intensity of the tasking. I was confident that the Royal Engineer units would continue to deliver if they were given enough time to recover and regroup between their many operational tours. However, I was more concerned about the capability of the MOD and Army Board to cope with the changes facing the Army than I was about the Royal Engineers. He was slightly taken aback (as an Army Board Member) but generously allowed me to clarify my statement. I told him that the top level jobs in the MOD were clearly becoming increasingly complex and that, ideally, the Army Board members should remain in post longer in order that that they could better influence and deliver the policies they initiated rather than passing the baton on to their successors when their stint was not finished properly. I felt that the Army needed more strategic continuity, especially with diminishing resources. For comparison I mentioned that any large civilian organisation that changed directors on its board every two years and (worse still) changed them in their last years of service would soon go bankrupt. General John courteously listened to me, smiled, and agreed to differ!

Mary and I were now well settled in Salisbury, close to Wilton, and had bought a thatched cottage (named Old Sarum View) in the small village of Stratford Sub Castle, 2 miles north of Salisbury Cathedral and between the ancient Hill Fort of Old Sarum and the River Avon. It was a lovely location. We moved into the cottage once I finished in Land Command and have stayed put ever since. I commuted to HQ EinC in Minley, near Camberley and my new job entailed a lot of travelling both in the UK and overseas, so it made sense to stay in the Salisbury area that we both liked. Mary had qualified as a Blue Badge Tourist Guide showing tourists around the Cathedral and the City and she had a part-time job working for Age Concern. She was keen to continue with both commitments. David had recently finished at Oxford with a first-class history degree and was off travelling again, this time to Australia. Anna had started her second year at Oxford, reading English, but had unfortunately been diagnosed with Cancer (Hodgkin's) and needed to take a year out while being treated at the John Radcliffe Hospital. She came home for a few days after each treatment to gather her strength before returning to Oxford where she ran a social events club part-time, organising a number of large parties that all broke even financially and gave her useful experience in event management. Once her treatment was over and she had recovered, she returned to her studies at Oxford, graduating successfully 2 years later. Old Sarum View became a haven for her – and David when he returned from his travelling – and an ideal family home for us all with welcoming neighbours in the village.

Once in my new post in September 1995 after a friendly handover from John DZ, I reckoned that my role was to provide both the focus and direction for the Corps of Royal Engineers. We had to learn to live with change, adapt to it and prosper from it. We were busier than at any time since I joined the Royal Engineers 28 years earlier, apart from the Gulf War, and needed a strategy for our future direction. Our reputation was very high as a result of current and recent operations and I was keen to stress that Royal Engineers were first and foremost soldiers who are military engineers; they were not simply engineers in the military. Successful sappers have always balanced the demands of the technical engineer, the combat engineer, and the soldier. My first (self-imposed) priority was to produce a Development Strategy to help keep me focused on the main issues throughout my time in the job. I found this to be a very useful mind-clearing exercise and the resulting strategy helped steer me throughout my tenure in the job. The budgetary arrangements in the Army were changing, resources were tighter and the Royal School of Military Engineering (as with the other Arms schools) was placed under the direct command of the Director of the Army Recruiting and Training Agency (ATRA), rather than remaining under my command. I now had only a small budget but still retained a lot of influence over all aspects of military engineering. My role encompassed trying to maintain the Royal Engineers' overall capability by achieving the right balance of skills for both war fighting and nation building, by recruiting and training high quality officers and soldiers, by influencing what new sapper equipment was developed and by reducing the cumulative load on our soldiers so that they did not burn out. The sequence of operational tours followed by formation training, construction projects, career upgrading and qualification courses was taking a toll even on the most committed individuals and we needed somehow to reconcile the Army's requirements against individuals' aspirations if we were to retain those whom we wished to keep. The nation was no longer able to afford a large Army so the Royal Engineers had to ensure that we continued to nurture talent and innovation to make up for what we might lack in size and resources. Sappers had numbered 280,000 after the Second World War, and we now numbered almost 9,000 regulars and some 5,500 TA (part-time volunteers); only 5% of our size 50 years earlier. Yet we still maintained (just) the same combat capabilities in our armoured, mechanised, amphibious, EOD, parachute, commando, plant, wheeled field and field support units to help the Army fight and move – and nearly all the trade and specialist skills to help the Army (and the other Services) to live. But we had very little depth and were below critical mass in some areas, such as amphibious bridging. We had lost our capability for heavy logistic engineering, such as ports and railways, sometime ago and needed to reinforce our links with industry. Here the Engineer and Logistic Staff Corps (more widely known as the Staff Corps), a high-powered group of Captains of Industry in the engineering and logistic field, was always helpful. The Staff Corps is made up of chief executives, directors and senior managers of engineering, transport and logistic companies who were invariably willing to give freely of their time to provide advice and expertise when asked.

Much of my time was taken up with managing the changes but I was heartened by the high reputation of the Royal Engineers and the attitude of the many units and individuals I met and worked with. There were one or two critical comments, mainly from those who thought that our soldiers did not need to be trained as both combat engineers and in a trade (such as electrician, bricklayer, design draughtsman, etc) and that we could save money by curtailing much of our individual training. The CGS (General Sir Charles Guthrie) questioned me about this when he called me for an interview shortly after I had become EinC. I explained that of course we could simply train only combat engineers or only tradesmen but then the Army would need more Royal Engineers because our current system enabled our sappers to be employed either as a soldier, or combat engineer, or a tradesman (or specialist). The Army was effectively gaining three capabilities from one individual and so needed less sappers in total than if they were trained for only one role. He reluctantly concurred. But, unsurprisingly, he did not accept my follow-up suggestion that perhaps the infantry should train all its soldiers to be HGV drivers to provide them with greater flexibility (for example in case they were needed on future firemen strikes) and also to encourage more soldiers to remain instead of leaving. The retention in the Infantry was then much lower than in the Sappers, so the increased cost of driver training might well be covered by the consequent reduced recruiting and training costs. As I left his office he remarked "Bloody sappers – always have an answer for everything!" His successor, General Sir Roger Wheeler was much friendlier.

The squeeze on resources was relentless and a major issue affecting the Royal Engineers was an attempt to close either the Chatham or Minley locations where all individual Military Engineering was delivered. Most of the retired members of the Corps, including many retired Generals and also the Chief Royal Engineer (General Sir John Stibbon) were in favour of retaining Brompton Barracks in Chatham, where all our trade and specialist training was taught. Nearly all the serving members were keen to retain Gibraltar Barracks at Minley, where our combat engineer training was delivered. Chatham had long been the spiritual home of the Corps with the Royal Engineer Museum and the Headquarter Mess. Should Chatham close then we would have to build new facilities at Minley for trade training; should Minley close then all combat engineer training would have to be delivered at Chatham with new facilities required there too. In the end (thankfully) the decision was made to retain both Brompton and Gibraltar Barracks under a Public and Private Partnership (PPP) contract. The negotiations, arguments and meetings leading to the eventual decision were very time-consuming and often heated. Because I was only a Brigadier and not a Major General, the Chief Royal Engineer (a distinguished 4-star retired officer and Head of the Corps) would ring me at home in the evenings to offer his friendly advice. If Mary picked up the phone General John would loudly enquire, "Where's the boy? I need to speak to him!" To his credit, he did accept (albeit reluctantly!) that I represented the serving Corps while he was responsible for overseeing the traditions and customs of the Corps and for the continuity of Corps 'Regimental Policy'. He had no responsibility for operations, training, manpower or equipment, but was extraordinarily proud of the Sappers and took an enormous interest in everything connected with the Royal Engineers. Although we fundamentally disagreed about the Chatham/Minley option he was always courteous, and it never affected our personal relationship or my respect for him. After one particularly heated disagreement about an issue he loudly announced that he would demand to go and tell the CGS what he thought. I replied (as tactfully as I could) that I would follow him into CGS's office after he had finished and asked him, "whom do you think the CGS would listen to most – someone retired or someone still serving?" General John smiled broadly and simply replied, "Well, I hope you know what you're doing!" He was a generous man and also a talented artist; he kindly gave me one of his paintings (of a scene in Bosnia) when I finished as EinC, when I went to his home to say goodbye – and to thank him for his whole-hearted support.

NATO's Allied Rapid Reaction Corps (ARRC) spearheaded the IFOR Force in Bosnia with the British Lieutenant General Sir Mike Walker as the Commander. The codename for the British deployment in support of IFOR (and later SFOR) was Operation Resolute. This superseded Op Grapple. There was an American led multinational division in the north, a British led multinational division in west and central Bosnia and a French led multinational division in the south. 3 (UK) Division provided most of the effort in the west with the Sapper support from its own engineers, now commanded by Colonel John Field who had returned from Zimbabwe and was now back in familiar territory. The ARRC's Chief Engineer, Brigadier John Moore-Bick, had a huge challenge to kick-start vital repairs at Corps level to Bosnia's shattered infrastructure, especially bridges, railway line and roads. He had very few sappers to call on so, he set about finding some and soon formed a remarkably capable international grouping of Hungarian, Romanian and Italian engineers. A major effort was aimed at returning the country to normal life, which, while not a military task per se, involved the military, and more specifically the sappers, attempting to 'build the peace'.

As part of a 'building the peace' initiative I invited Walter Hogbin, then Chief Executive of Taylor Woodrow and the Commanding Officer of the Staff Corps, to accompany me on a visit to Bosnia in 1996, kindly hosted by John Moore-Bick, to see for himself what sappers were achieving there but also to provide us all with ideas about how and when civilian engineering firms might best be able to provide the more permanent infrastructure improvements when military forces withdrew. Sappers should start 'building the peace' as the situation on the ground stabilised, but once it was safe then civilian firms were better suited to take the process forward while also providing jobs and developing skills for local people.

Both John Moore-Bick and I subsequently put in a lot of thought and effort about how to develop a strategy for building the peace but could not generate enough interest within the MOD and other relevant organisations such as the Foreign and Commonwealth Office and the Department of Trade and Industry to take it further. However, one success was the establishment of a small Mines Information and Training Centre that was strongly endorsed by George Robertson, Secretary of State for Defence, on a visit to Minley in November 1997.

I also tried, but failed, to persuade the MOD that soldiers who were injured on operations in Bosnia or elsewhere should be eligible for compensation (as they were in Northern Ireland). Some 25 years earlier, when Froth Beer had suffered serious injuries from an IRA explosive device while serving with 9 Squadron in Northern Ireland, he had eventually received a substantial compensation payment under the Criminal Injuries Compensation (CIC) scheme, which had enabled him to buy a house after his medical discharge from the Army and get on with a new life as a civilian. However, those injured in Bosnia or Rwanda received nothing (nor did their families) apart from small payments from military charities such as the Royal Engineers Association or the Royal British Legion. Sadly, 26 British service personnel had been killed and 79 seriously injured in Bosnia by 1997. These numbers included casualties from road traffic accidents and other accidents, as well as those caused by shootings, mines and EOD incidents, and are quoted from an article in the Sunday Times dated 27th April 1997.

Sergeant Walker lost a leg in Bosnia after a Bosnian Serb tank fired on a UN observation post where he was working, Corporal Warburton and Lance Corporal Nicholas were killed by mines and Corporal Onions lost an eye in a mine explosion. Spr Copsey had lost a leg in Rwanda. When I took up Sergeant Walker's case, the MOD sent a letter to his solicitors stating that he was not entitled to compensation because his injuries were the result of "war operations or military activity by warring factions" despite the fact that he was on peacekeeping duties! The situation was irrational and unfair. For example, if a soldier was injured in a fight when off-duty in Split (a coastal town in Croatia) he would be entitled to compensation under a CIC (Overseas) scheme whereas if he was shot or blown up on a mine in Bosnia he would get nothing. Sergeant Walker would eventually receive some form of war pension, but he really needed a lump sum (in addition) to help him to make the transition to civilian life. This was not forthcoming. I felt that the MOD was isolated from reality and I have never understood the byzantine Whitehall culture.

Aside from Bosnia, the Corps was still heavily committed on operations in Northern Ireland. The varied tasks included high-risk search, constructing hilltop fortified Observation Posts (Ops) in South Armagh, rebuilding RUC stations and blast and ballistic protection enhancements at many Security Force bases. Although circumstances were not as murderous as they had been in the 1970s and 1980s, the threats posed by the IRA Mark 15 Mortar and the Barrett Sniper Rifle were deadly. 25 Engineer Regiment, based in Antrim had the challenging role of responding to terrorist violence and also helping to deal with very severe rioting in the marching season, especially at Dumcree, near Portadown. The Regiment became expert at creating portable obstacles, mounted on DROPS racks that could be deployed quickly to block off routes and prevent face-to-face confrontation. It also developed a new modular concrete and steel composite blast protection panel to withstand the increased threat from the Mark 15 mortar bombs and vehicle borne IEDs. This system (called Redline) was tested and validated in live tests on a range in Scotland before being installed at some particularly vulnerable bases and vehicle check points. The Redline panels took up less space than the thicker reinforced concrete barriers and were easier to place. Soon afterwards the Good Friday Agreement of 10th April 1998 heralded a change of political direction throughout Ireland and 25 Regiment began dismantling the hilltop OPs in 1999. The Peace Process initiated a gradual return to normality, but the situation remained tense.

General Sir Rupert Smith, who was GOC Northern Ireland from 1996–1998, commented on Sappers:

"When I was a cadet at the Royal Military Academy Sandhurst I was told that, 'on operations you could never have enough Sappers'. Since I was told this by a Royal Engineer, I doubted this piece of advice. But with experience I came to believe it. I have learnt to

value not so much the quantity of Sappers in my command but their quality: the product of their qualities of versatility, adaptability and ingenuity. It is their versatility, the ability to do a range of things; their adaptability, the ability to adapt what they do to the circumstances; and their ingenuity, the ability to find a solution to a problem using the materials to hand, that I have learnt to value highly."

We had sappers committed or on training in many other countries, most regularly in Germany, the Falklands, Canada, Belize and Kenya but also elsewhere in many other countries. I could not visit all of the locations but greatly enjoyed meeting American Military Engineers and South African Sappers – and a visit to a Queen's Gurkha Engineer Squadron in Nepal. The American Army's huge size and massive resources gave me a perspective on the British Army's limited overall capability, in comparison, and reinforced how vital it was to attract and retain high quality individuals in order to remain effective. The South African Sappers were extraordinarily hospitable, despite undergoing a huge transformation since withdrawing from Namibia. They were very proud of their links with the Royal Engineers, but I could not help wondering how they would cope with the changes facing them. I was particularly impressed by their mine clearance expertise; their Meercat vehicle with its sloping, raised chassis and its wheels well away from the chassis was very effective in reducing casualties from mines and IEDs. We needed something similar in Bosnia for proving routes that had not been cleared.

My visit to Nepal was a rare opportunity to see both 67 Gurkha Independent Field Squadron (based in Hong Kong) and some Royal Nepalese Army (RNA) Engineers who were building a road from Katari to Okhaldhunga in the north east of Nepal, not far from

Everest. 67 Squadron only had 10 weeks on site, having first had to build their own camp so took on a relatively small discrete package of culverts, heads walls, gabion walls, a small concrete causeway and some 4 kilometres of road surfacing. The total length of the road, when finished, would be around 100 kilometres. The RNA Engineer Battalion had started it 2 years earlier and expected to finish it in another 6. Working ahead of 67 Squadron they were forcing the road through very steep country with the route becoming narrower by the kilometre; the head of the pilot track was just about navigable by a Land Rover (or a Nepalese bus!) with huge drops in places to the valley 3,000 feet below. Nine Nepalese sappers had been killed in accidents on the project, usually by falling off the edge of the road while operating bulldozers or other pieces of plant. It was dangerous work and they had a very different approach to 'Health and Safety' than the British. The Queens Gurkha Engineers were extraordinarily keen and clearly very proud to be helping their own country in support of the RNA. In addition to the 120 men from the Squadron some 100 local Nepalese labourers were also employed at the going rate (then) of only 85p a day (unskilled) to £1.50 a day (skilled). For this they worked all day filling gabion baskets with rocks, laying stones inside the drainage ditches, mixing and pouring concrete, hand digging culverts and some of the drains. It was very difficult country with precipitous drops, many gullies and streams, thick woods and unstable slopes and the people/machine ratio was much larger than on similar projects in the West.

Alastair Sheppard was commanding 67 Squadron and we both enjoyed catching up, having served together in Kuwait 6 years earlier. As well as visiting his squadron he had also arranged for me to spend 2 days on a short trek in the area of the Sun Kosi River with Dal Sahib, one of his Queens Gurkha Officers (QGOs), accompanied by no less than a cook and 3 porters – just to look after 2 of us! We walked along the side of a river that ran into the Sun Kosi for much of the first day, passing by a steady stream of porters on their way to or from Katari and Okhaldhunga, all carrying enormous loads in baskets strapped to their backs, supported by headbands. I saw baskets with heavy bags of rice, baskets with roof trusses somehow secured to them (for a village school somewhere), baskets with everything but the kitchen sink – and more. Many of the porters were only 14 years old; some were younger, but these were usually part of a family group. Everyone (except very tiny tots) carried something, even the grandmothers. It appeared that their age determined their load. Ten year-olds carried 10 dharnis (55 pounds – one dharni equated to 2.5 kilograms), while 14 year-olds carried 14 dharnis (77 pounds), etc. They were nearly all in flip-flops; a few were barefoot. They all carried a T shaped stick that doubled up as a walking stick and a seat stick (rather like a shooting stick) when they stopped. Not one of them could physically lift their loads on to their backs; if they stopped for lunch or a longish break they would balance the load on a rock or a bank so that it was possible for them to lift them up later by kneeling down and pulling the baskets to their backs with help from another porter. I could not help feeling embarrassed that, in comparison, I was only carrying a day sack but every person I passed by invariably smiled a friendly greeting. Some would even often offer to help me negotiate any difficult sections of the path, despite their own huge burdens! I was amazed and humbled by their endurance, humour and patience.

The second day we walked back amongst some beautiful country. We saw an old man with a retinue of wife and daughters who was immaculately dressed in slacks, blazer, tennis shoes and a fez-type hat, at the top of a very steep pass in the middle of nowhere, on his way back to Kathmandu from Okhaldhunga. Dal Sahib reckoned he was probably an ex-Gurkha officer from the Indian Army. The villages we passed through were as basic as anything I had seen in Africa and the people really had to grind out their existence. Always, they were friendly and ready for a smile. We arrived back at the Squadron's camp just in time to shower and change for a farewell dinner with all the officers, warrant officers and Senior NCOs (British and Gurkha). Also invited were the CO and 2IC of the local RNA Kaliprasad Engineer Battalion. The CO (Lieutenant Colonel Deepack Gurung) was a most affable chap who had been trained at both Sandhurst and the Staff College at Camberley. The next morning it was time to say goodbye and head back to Kathmandu. After a squadron parade where I was asked to present a trophy (a mounted Kukri) named after a previous Commandant of the Queens Gurkha Engineers (Major General Bowring who knew both my father and Uncle Jerry and was a previous EinC) to the best Lance Corporal in the Squadron, I was seen off with garlands and flowers. My few days with 67 Squadron and the short trek in Nepal had been a most memorable experience. On the flight back to Gatwick from Kathmandu the following morning I sat next to a Royal Nepalese Airline pilot on his way to Denver, USA, to do his mandatory refresher training and the King's Secretary (of Nepal) who was travelling to do some more research at Cambridge university. They were both a million miles away from the villagers I had seen only 2 days earlier.

There was an amusing encounter when I visited some units at the Royal Engineer Training Camp at Wyke Regis, Weymouth in the summer of 1997. Lance Corporal Bickel, my driver, was playing cricket for the Corps that day and I had arranged to drive myself in the staff car, but his car broke down the day before so I suggested that he use the staff car instead; he was a talented cricketer and we wanted to win the game. I then rode down on my motorbike on a rather dismal, wet morning to meet some students in the Queen's University Officer Training Corps (UOTC), affiliated to the Royal Engineers, before then going on to see another squadron also training at Weymouth. The gate at Wyke Regis was open and, as I halted my bike alongside the CO of the UOTC who greeted me, the RSM (attached from one of the Guards Regiments) came storming towards me, ramrod stiff, and bellowed at me "Move this bloody machine out of the way because the EinC will be driving through this gate at any minute." I removed my helmet, said good morning, and explained that I was the EinC. "Officers don't ride motorbikes!" he expostulated. "This officer does RSM," I replied. "I thought you'd be arriving in your staff car?" "My driver needed the car to go and play in a cricket match for the Corps." "Your driver, using your car to play cricket! That would never happen in my regiment!" A section from the UOTC waiting by the gate to meet me all doubled up in laughter, thoroughly enjoying this little cameo.

My time as EinC finished in May 1998 when I was posted to Sarajevo to work in the multinational Stabilisation Force (SFOR) Headquarters for 6 months. Before departing for Bosnia, the Corps RSM and the Warrant Officers and Senior NCOs of the Corps afforded Mary and me the rare honour of dining both of us out of the Corps in their mess at Chatham; we were both very touched. At the dinner they generously presented us with 2 engraved silver candelabra with both of our names inscribed on the bases and a set of silver napkin rings, each listed with the names of different regiments in the Royal Engineers and mounted in a beautiful wooden box; very treasured possessions. I could not help feeling regret on leaving the Corps while having more time left to serve in the Army; I realised how fortunate I had been to have had a unique overview of the Royal Engineers, both as EinC and Commander Engineers at Land Command for a period of more than 5 years. For a soldier there can be no greater honour than having a position of trust or leadership for others. Being a Sapper is hard work; it is part and parcel of wearing the cap badge but it is also a privilege. I felt very proud of what our units and individual soldiers had achieved and what they had put up with; they had most certainly earned their pay and I often took heart from Rudyard Kipling's poem about the Royal Engineers (the first and last verses copied below) which always struck a chord! I owed much to those who worked for and with me throughout this time and especially valued the wise counsel of my Chiefs of Staff, Mike Gill, John Hoskinson and Steve Sherry. I was also blessed that Mary had always stood by me, ready to offer support to anyone in the Corps and their families. Albert Whitley, an old friend who had taken over from me as 3 Troop Commander in 59 Independent Commando Squadron 24 years earlier, was to be the new EinC and I knew that the Corps would be in safe hands.

"When the Waters were dried an' the Earth did appear,
('It's all one' says the Sapper),
The Lord he created the Engineer.
Her Majesty's Royal Engineer,
With the rank and pay of a Sapper!
I have stated it plain, an' my argument's thus,
('It's all one' says the Sapper),
There's only one Corps which is perfect – that's us;
An' they call us Her Majesty's Engineers,
Her Majesty's Royal Engineers.
With the rank and pay of a Sapper!"

A return to Zimbabwe in 1992: Mary on the Zambezi.

Elephants on the shore at Lake Kariba.

A Kariba sunset.

Old Sarum View, our home near Salisbury.

Lydia, trained as a guide dog, joined us before we moved into the cottage and became a much-loved member of the family.

Bosnia – a view of Lake Prozor from Fort Resort.

Engineer plant, based at Fort Redoubt, for building Route Triangle.

The Serbs often shelled the main road north of Mostar so 35 Engineer Regiment built Route Triangle across the mountains in order that the British Force had a secure supply route.

Corrimec hutted accommodation was used in many of the British bases in Bosnia.

A dining area built from prefabricated units nearing completion.

Destroyed bridge at Visoko replaced by a Mabey-Johnson bridge built by German
Sappers after IFOR deployed.

The mine threat was ever present. Photo shows
a PMR AP mine.

Visiting a road being built in Nepal by 67 Gurkha Independent Field Squadron in partnership with Nepali Sappers. The country desperately needs more roads and other infrastructure.

Despite their very heavy loads, these child porters only had flip-flops on their feet.

Meeting Lieutenant General Williams, Chief of the US Corps of Engineers, during a visit to the US Army Engineers.

With Admiral Sir Michael Boyce, 2nd Sea Lord (later Chief of the Defence Staff) at the opening of the Defence Diving School where RN and RE divers are trained.

13

SARAJEVO

I flew to Split on the Croatian coast on 28th May 1998 arriving late afternoon to find an American Blackhawk Helicopter waiting for me on a nearby helipad to fly me to Sarajevo. It was a beautiful day with clear visibility and wonderful scenic views of jagged limestone peaks, deep valleys, a mixture of dense woods and bare stark landscapes, deep blue lakes and stunning rivers, but with occasional glimpses of burnt-out houses and destroyed barns in some of the villages. I landed in the early evening dusk on the helipad at HQ SFOR, quartered in the Ilidza Hotel in the southwest edge of Sarajevo.

SFOR, the Stabilisation Force that had replaced IFOR (the Implementation Force) was a diverse organisation numbering over 30,000 servicemen and women from 40 different nations. The Commander was General Shinseki, who was also commanding all US forces in Europe at the same time; a very busy man. While serving in Vietnam he had lost part of a foot after stepping on a mine but his injury never held him back and he kept himself fit with early morning workouts in the gym with his personal staff every day. The French Deputy Commander was Lieutenant General Elie, ex-Foreign Legion; tough with a quiet sense of humour, he would tease me by starting a conversation in French until I had to admit I could not understand him, before switching to English. The British Deputy Commander Operations was Lieutenant General Sir Hew Pike whom I knew well having served with him in Airborne Forces and who had won a DSO in the Falklands commanding 3 PARA; well respected and always helpful. The German Chief of Staff was Major General Gosch and the Assistant Chief of Staff (Military Operations) was an American Major General, JB Burns; my boss. There was also an Italian and a Spanish Major General. We had a surfeit of Generals, a complex chain of command and scope for mixed messages! With all the different nationalities in the headquarters it was a miracle that it functioned at all. Nevertheless, I found a lot of dedicated individuals working pretty hard to help Bosnia to develop into a better country. There were a few idle folk around but they were very much in the minority. The headquarters did not really 'run' the show although some were deluded that it did, but it did take much of the complex coordination away from the three multinational divisions led by the Americans, the British and the French who delivered results on the ground. There were all sorts of fingers in the pie ranging from SFOR, agencies such as OHR, OSCE, ICTY, UNHCR, ICRC and a myriad of Non-Government Organisations – not to mention the higher level direction from SHAPE, National Governments and National Defence Ministries.[1]

---

1. SFOR – Stabilisation Force. OHR – Office of the High Representative. The High Representative and the OHR oversaw the civilian implementation of the Dayton agreement and represented the countries involved in the implementation of the Agreement. OSCE – Organisation for Security and Cooperation in Europe. ICTY – International Criminal Tribunal for the Former Yugoslavia. UNHCR – UN Refugee Agency. ICRC – International Committee of the Red Cross. SHAPE – Supreme Headquarters Allied Powers Europe.

My appointment in HQ SFOR was Chief CJ-3; a challenging job running the joint operations branch of the headquarters. I also had a direct link with the Combined Air Operations Cell in Vicenza, Italy. My daily routine was pretty gruelling with long days (averaging from 0600 to 2300, sometimes longer) but the time passed surprisingly quickly. I had 80 people working directly for me from 18 different nationalities with less than a dozen whose native language was English (the Americans, Canadians and British). All of them tried hard but I often ended up having to redraft written work that would include contingency plans, operation orders, situation reports, recce reports and presentations. Our staff work was inevitably slow, but a bunch of Brits would have coped no better if we had been forced to operate entirely in another language. An incident concerning a shooting near Rogatica, within the Portuguese Battalion's area of responsibility, was just one example of the language glitches. The Portuguese reported it (in English) to the Italian Brigade who, in turn, relayed the message (again in English) to the French Division based near Mostar who relayed it to the Duty Watchkeeper in my Ops Room, who was Turkish. He could not understand the message so checked with the Shift Director (a Norwegian) who was none the wiser but who clearly realised it could be important and let me know that something had happened near Rogatica but he was not sure what. Fortunately, I had a Portuguese Captain working for me in the Air Operations Cell so asked him to phone the Portuguese Battalion directly and we at last had an accurate report! Something that would have taken a few minutes if we had all been the same nationality took much longer. My American boss was impatient and found it difficult to cope with such frustrating delays.

SFOR ensured that The Dayton Peace Accord was not breached by any of the Entity Armed Factions (Bosnian Serb, Bosnian Croat or Bosniac) but our focus was forever being drawn towards enabling Bosnia to stand on its own feet. We spent a lot of time on issues for which we had not trained as soldiers, such as elections, weapon certification in designated storage sites, monitoring the return of displaced persons and refugees, retraining Specialist Police (with assistance from the International Police Task Force), assisting the ICTY and OHR with mass grave exhumations, assisting with security during the import of new Bosnian currency in convertible marks and its safe deposit to the Central Bank in Sarajevo, enforcing compliance with regulations such as new licence plates, etc. In addition there were of course the military tasks of patrolling, identifying and marking minefields, coordinating the lifting of mines with organisations such as the Mines Action Group, security, intelligence gathering, communicating, searching for war criminals, monitoring the frontier with the Former Republic of Yugoslavia, liaising with local mayors and police chiefs, crowd control, etc. A major effort over the coming months would be the elections in mid-September; if they went well the prospects for a better Bosnia would be much improved. The OSCE were in the lead here but required security support from SFOR. We also became increasingly involved in contingency planning for Kosovo. We tried to monitor progress by assessing trends in a number of key areas which included the return of displaced persons and refugees, reform of the media, public security and law enforcement, democratic governance, economic development, military stability, organised crime and corruption, the arrest of prisoners indicted for war crimes, the stability of Brcko in the northeast corner of Bosnia. Benchmark indicators linked to these areas would be analysed periodically to provide evidence whether or not the situation in Bosnia was improving step by step, before SFOR could further reduce force levels.

SFOR could call on support from three NATO commands; AIRSOUTH (for air support), STRIKE FORCES SOUTH (with combined amphibious landing forces and other forces) and NAVSOUTH (for maritime surveillance and presence). There was nearly always an American Carrier Group (sometimes two) off the Adriatic coast and the Air Operations Cell in CJ3 (led by an American Air Force Colonel) helped coordinate the many daily air sorties flying from the aircraft carriers as well as those flying from NATO air bases in the region, while also monitoring SFOR flights within Bosnia and civilian flights in and out of Sarajevo airport. Within Bosnia, the American led multinational division near Tusla in the north was the largest and contained the most combat power, including more than 50 tanks and a battalion of Apache attack helicopters. In addition to an American brigade it included a Russian brigade, a Turkish brigade and a multinational brigade with battalions from Denmark, Poland, Sweden, Norway and Finland. The French led a multinational division near Mostar in the southeast with a joint French/German brigade that included a Ukrainian battalion, a Spanish brigade and an Italian brigade that included a Portuguese battalion; the division also contained Egyptians and Moroccans. The British led a multinational division in the northwest near Banja Luka with battalions from the UK, the Netherlands, Canada, Czechoslovakia and Belgium.

Although we never had to use the Apache helicopters in their attack role, they were very useful as an observation and recce aid with their advanced optical sights. Predator drones, controlled by US operators based in Hungary, were also very useful in helping to monitor the border, weapon sites, demonstrations and any significant event, especially where the presence of troops might escalate a situation.

Two days into my appointment I visited an exhumation site of a mass war grave near Zvornick in Eastern Bosnia by the Cancari Road. The ICTY had firm evidence that this grave was one of a number of secondary graves where the bodies had been dug up from an earlier grave and reburied in an attempt to conceal the earlier killings. It was horrific; the Bosnian Serbs had dug up the earlier grave (or graves) by mechanical earth-moving machines, loaded the mangled corpses into tipper trucks, moved them to this site (and others), reburied them and compacted them with heavy machinery. This particular grave was subsequently found to contain 309 bodies, or mangled human remains. It was weirdly incredible that such gruesome acts were enacted in such beautiful countryside and ignored by local people living nearby, who must have known what was happening. I wondered whether it would ever be possible for the Serb and Muslim communities to co-exist peacefully again. There were another 12 such graves along the Cancari Road. Not all of them would be exhumed during my time in Bosnia; only some of them in order to find forensic evidence linking the killers to the bodies so that they could be hunted down, detained and prosecuted for war crimes. The civilian specialists undertaking the exhumations had to be guarded on site and escorted to and from Tusla where the bodies and body bits were taken to a morgue for examination and identification. The site also needed guarding 24 hours a day in order to maintain continuity of evidence and refute any claims of interference with it.

On Thursday 11th June 1998 the first return visit of Muslim women to Sebrenica was organised in order that they could visit the local graveyard in the town. They were all widows and mothers of husbands and sons who had been massacred by Bosnian Serbs 3 years earlier, it was an emotional, highly charged event. Two busloads (about

110 women) made the visit and fortunately it went well, helping to set the tone for future visits. Predator surveillance of this occasion helped keep it relatively low-key and enabled local SFOR troops to maintain a presence from a discrete distance, available if required. A few days later SFOR Forces in Eastern Republika Srpska arrested Milorad Krnojelac, a 64 year-old Bosnian Serb who was indicted for war crimes committed while he was commanding the Popravni Dom prison centre from April 1992 to August 1993. He was charged with permitting prolonged torture and beatings, countless killings and forced labour practices, with providing inhumane conditions and with the exportation/deportation of Muslim and non-Serb males from Foca on the River Drina. He had been the school principal for the past couple of years, since the war ended. As a result of his arrest, the school children held a demonstration that afternoon. The next afternoon there was a bigger demonstration that turned into a small riot and caused some minor damage to buildings and property, mainly belonging to the IPTF and the OSCE. The Multinational Division in the South East, headed by a French General, soon sorted the problem out but there was intense interest from SHAPE, including SACEUR, in what was a pretty minor disturbance and the sort of incident which was almost routine in Belfast not so long ago. The Division were pretty smart by mixing up joint French and German patrols and tri-national French/German/Ukrainian patrols in order to try and calm down the local Serbian hatred of Germans (a long-standing hangover from the Second World War). The next day all was quiet but every time one of these former war criminals was arrested, there was always the chance of a backlash and events in Foca could have been far worse.

Later that week I attended two long meetings that dealt with different issues. The first concerned the security that SFOR provided the ICTY finding the evidence at mass graves that could subsequently be used in evidence against the perpetrators. The Americans in the Northern Multinational Division in Bosnia were very reluctant to take on anything that they perceived as non-military. Understandably, there was a risk that SFOR could have ended up doing more than necessary with the various civilian organisations using the military as a crutch in too many situations, instead of the agencies and the local population becoming more self-reliant. Unfortunately, the ICTY had stopped work at one particular set of mass graves, previously guarded by American soldiers, until they could be persuaded that SFOR was providing sufficient security. The issue needed to be resolved quickly otherwise the continuity chain of evidence might be lost and ICTY would not be able to convict those who had carried out such dreadful mass slaughter. Fortunately, two Special Force officers, one American and the other German, later offered to help with security in the American sector at subsequent grave excavations and the work resumed.

The next meeting was much better and helped resolve the retraining and certification of the former Bosnian Serb Specialist Police who had all been 'grounded' for the past year. A new training programme was agreed with an optimistic intention to provide a force to assist the local police in keeping order during the forthcoming elections in Bosnian Serb areas. The problem was that many of them had a very dubious history and we did not want the IPTF to train them if their loyalties were suspect. We reckoned that we could minimise the risk, but it was an interesting dilemma. If we did not allow them to return as policemen there was a greater danger that they could become more disaffected and form a 'break-away' nucleus for creating unrest and instability. Regrettably, the training subsequently organised by the IPTF was not as rigorous as expected and instilling principles of 'Law and Order' to underpin policing operations proved challenging because of the variable caliber amongst the different nationalities within the IPTF.

Soon after this I found myself in an awkward situation where I had to confront my American boss (Major General JB Burns) over his obsessive demands and intolerance. In order to keep everyone in the headquarters informed there were 3 daily briefings in the conference room next to the operations room. I ran a short morning briefing at 0800, General JB led a longer briefing at 1700 and either General Hew Pike or JB would run the evening briefing (which included a video link to the multinational divisions – and sometimes SHAPE near Mons in Belgium and/or AFSOUTH in Naples). My first introduction to JB was at one these briefings just after my arrival; he shook my hand and announced to everyone present (about 50) "I'd like to welcome the new CJ3, Brigadier General McGill. Welcome to SFOR McGill – and make sure you don't screw up!"

During one of the evening video conferences a month or so later, he bawled out one of my officers in public very aggressively. Immediately afterwards I followed JB to his office. The door was shut and his MA (military assistant) politely told me "Sir, the General does not want to be disturbed." "Please let him know that I need to talk to him now," I replied. The MA got up, knocked on JB's door, went in, relayed my request and came back shaking his head saying, "Sorry Sir, you'll have to wait." I thanked him but went ahead and opened JB's door to find him working on his computer while also speaking on the phone and lifting up a barbell exercising one of his biceps. A 'Meals Ready to Eat' ration pack was open on his desk, which indicated he would miss the evening meal and eat in his office. "General, I need to speak to you" I began. "I'm too busy just now" he interjected. I continued "General, I'm your CJ3 and a key member of your team. If you refuse to listen, someone is likely to get a flat nose and someone will probably be sacked." JB looked up in amazement and remarked, "No one has ever spoken to me like that! I can't believe what I've just heard!" I replied "I'm not comfortable talking like this to a senior officer. My CJ3 team in the Ops Room don't understand you, are frightened of you and tell you what they think you want to hear. In over 30 years of military service I've never worked for anyone like you. If you can't change the way you treat me and my staff, then I will keep challenging you until you do, or you'll have to fire me." JB looked up me intently for a few seconds before saying, "Ian, I'm sorry; I guess I'm just too wound up. You don't realise just how many issues I'm dealing with, but I take note of what you've said. I will try to be more considerate but make no promises". He then shook my hand and, to my astonishment, remarked, "Reckon you and I make a good team".

Thereafter, JB and I understood each other better. It was never easy working for him, but he made an effort to be more reasonable, although he often reminded me that "reasonable men do not effect change!" He had a number of amusing phrases such as: "This is getting ugly, damned coyote ugly!" (when in awkward situations) "Just take care around that lady; she's hard – so damned hard that her lips are harder than a woodpecker's beak!" (when describing someone due to visit during the Bosnian elections in September) "You can dress like a cowboy and wear a cowboy's hat and you can talk like a cowboy – but if you ain't got no cows you ain't a cowboy!" (when commenting on the feasibility of HQ EUROCORPS replacing HQ SFOR). JB was confident that he could change Bosnia for the better, convinced that the best way was the US way and that the other nations in SFOR lacked commitment and focus. He had a genuine desire to improve Bosnia by setting goals and driving forwards with a "Go, get 'em" approach but he distrusted any non-Americans and was determined not to allow other nationalities to 'screw-up'. When JB finally left his post in mid-September, handing over to Major General John Sylvester while I still had 2 months left in Sarajevo, he kindly gave me a book Portrait of an Army' with paintings from the American Army's Art Collection. It was a generous gesture and I should have welcomed his offer to sign the book, but I requested that he did not, simply remarking that I had seen more than enough of him and his signature. Years later I regretted my lack of grace; no one was more dedicated or hard-working than JB.

By mid-July there was no serious military aggression between the Bosnian Serbs, Croats and Muslims but there were a number of serious confrontations between the different communities which could escalate into riots and violence. Few of the units within SFOR had any experience of riot control, except for the British, French and Canadian troops, and so a decision was made to form a Multinational Specialised Unit (MSU) to deal with riots and disorder and bridge the gap between SFOR military forces and the civilian police. The MSU deployed to Bosnia in early August 1998 in time for the elections the following month. It comprised a small battalion-sized force drawn mainly from the Italian Carabinieri with reinforcements from an Argentinian company plus Romanian and Slovenian platoons. Before its deployment, the MSU had to be certified as competent to carry out its role and I spent an interesting day near Trieste watching a Carabinieri demonstration of their range of skills and capabilities, along with others from HQ SFOR and General Clark (SACEUR) before the Carabinieri MSU contingent were formally invited to join SFOR. Their 'modus operandi' and rules of engagement then had to be agreed during a series of protracted meetings in HQ SFOR. The Carabinieri wanted the freedom to operate throughout Bosnia in a similar fashion to how they operated in Italy and certainly did not want to be placed under any local commander on the ground if tasked for assistance. They expected autonomy of action and their Chief of Staff, Colonel Coppola, made his feelings abundantly clear when he exclaimed in exasperation towards the end of a very long meeting in HQ SFOR, chaired by JB, "General, with the Carabinieri you have a Ferrari. Why do you insist on wanting to drive us like a Fiat?" Unfortunately, when the MSU were first deployed in October 1998 on an operation near Caplijina near Mostar, the situation was badly handled. Croatian demonstrators, who had been evicted from Central Bosnia during the conflict a few years earlier and been resettled further south not far from Mostar, formed a roadblock to protest against the return of some Bosniac (Muslim) families to their village. Although the MSU proposed negotiating with the demonstrators rather than confronting them, they were overruled by a Spanish officer and ordered to clear the roadblock by force. The MSU then mounted a baton charge against the group of mainly women and children that was filmed by a local TV station and resulted in some very negative publicity. The return of displaced persons and refugees was often emotional for those returning. Their homes (if still standing) may have been occupied by others, who would refuse to leave, or their houses may have been destroyed and they would struggle to rebuild them. Many of their family, friends and neighbours might have been killed. Rebuilding their lives was a challenge for them all.

I was the main point of contact for the MSU within HQ SFOR and spent quite a bit of time getting to know them. The more I saw of the Carabinieri the more I liked them. They had been carefully selected, were experienced policemen with additional military skills and many spoke good English. They were always courteous, with a sense of humour and a warm humility. Their Commander, Colonel Leso, had a strategic vision for improved policing in Bosnia but the IPTF and the local police forces, along with SFOR, were perhaps too busy with the immediate present issues rather than looking further ahead. One area where the MSU might have been effective was tackling the criminality and smuggling in the Mostar area, especially in Stolac, where the Croats were terrorising Muslims and preventing them from returning after driving them out during the war; a concerted joint MSU/military effort may well have stopped the thuggery and crime.

The Bosnia elections were a complicated process, with over 60 political parties plus additional independent candidates and coalitions providing some bewildering choices for the voters! The voter ballot form was also difficult to fill in, needing 4 separate bits to be completed. During the elections we had a flood of visitors including Madelaine Albright (US Secretary of State), the German Foreign Minister, the Chairman of the US Joint Chiefs of Staff and SACEUR. The election weekend on the 12th/13th September 1998 turned out to be quiet but the voting disappointingly resulted in a swing towards extremism amongst all the communities. No matter how honourable our intentions, all of us involved in trying to build a peace in Bosnia needed to accept that our influence was limited. We could only set the conditions for the people to choose what they wanted. Depressingly, it seemed that they were motivated more by hatred, fear and revenge than anything else.

My last few weeks passed very quickly, and I managed to get out of the Headquarters a bit more and meet some of the staff in the three multinational divisions after JB had left. Lieutenant General Jack Deverell (friendly as always) took over from Hew Pike and General Meigs replaced General Shinseki who moved on to become the Vice Chief of the US Army Staff. I handed over my appointment on 22nd November after an evening enlivened with Beaujolais Nouveau, procured by one of the French officers. I was sorry to say goodbye to the team in CJ3. They had been remarkably tolerant and had cheerfully put up with the long hours, the turbulence and, at times, hectic routine. I was touched that they and others that I had worked with in the headquarters had written some farewell comments in a book that they gave me as I left. The book, 'Sarajevo – The Wounded City' had been published in 1992 as a testament to the suffering of the people of Sarajevo during the siege by the Bosnian Serbs. The photographs and script vividly portray the terror and destruction they endured then. Lieutenant Colonel Norbert Zorn, my French XO, wrote in the book: "…Sometimes it's difficult to write something down. It was a hard time, I learned a lot. I very appreciated how well you were always able to keep things 'low' and your ability to manage the different people. Sometimes I had difficulties to understand your language and writing but at least I understand you. I wish you all the best, Your XO." Despite the intervention of IFOR and SFOR, the Balkans will always remain volatile and it will take many more years before Bosnia is able stand on its own without international help. En route for the flight home I called in to visit 9 Parachute Squadron at Gorni Vakuf and caught up briefly with 50 and 61 Squadrons in Split; it was a tonic to meet up with old friends whom I had served with previously.

With Lieutenant Colonel Norbert Zorn, my very helpful French XO, on the road to Mostar.

Exhumation of a mass grave by the Cancari Road, near Zvornick in eastern Bosnia. Thirteen mass grave-sites along the road had been identified, but not all were exhumed.

A Joint Military Commission Meeting in Travnik. To the right of the interpreter in the white dress are the Entity Armed Forces Commanders: Generals Delić (Bosniac), Talić (Bosnian Serb wearing the peaked cap) and Budimir (Bosnian Croat). Between Delić and Talić is Major General Gosch (SFOR Chief of Staff). On the far right in the maroon beret is Lieutenant General Sir Hew Pike (SFOR Deputy Commander Operations) who normally chaired the JMC meetings.

The Dutch Battalion Base at Sisava in the mountains above Travnik in central Bosnia. It was, perhaps, the most pleasant location of any of the SFOR camps.

14

CLOSING THE LOOP

I was now 52 and knew that I would have to leave the Army after my next appointment as Commander of the Initial Training Group, responsible for training all recruits. My predecessor in the post was not due to leave for a few months so, in the interim, I was tasked by the Adjutant General with a project to identify the Spiritual Needs of the Army and how best they should be delivered, in order to help promote the ethos of the Army. I hardly knew where to start and had been given the task because I was available, not because of any religious conviction. My report would not promote religion but would be focused on how spiritual values might help develop individuals and improve the Army's effectiveness. My priority was the Army and not Chaplaincy. I was keen that the Army retained an ethos founded on Christian traditions and standards but believed that no individual or single faith had a monopoly of virtue.

The report was completed after 4 months with nearly all its recommendations being endorsed. Although mentally stretched by the project, I found it valuable preparation for my next job. Two key principles in the report were:

"The relationship between society, government and the military requires mutual respect, if armed forces are to remain effective. The Army's priority remains military effectiveness, in its widest sense, and the unlimited liability of soldiering demands both a selflessness and a sound ethical foundation which soldiers believe, understand and accept. The Army needs to instil values which underlie its military ethos in its officers and soldiers during training and nurture these values throughout their service.

The British Army's values, standards and ethos are founded on our Christian history, culture and civilisation. The chain of command has the ultimate responsibility for delivering the Army's motivation and standards within a trinity of endeavour encompassing command, training and chaplaincy. Military service is far better suited to a covenant, founded on trust, rather than a contract which implies self-interest and coercion. Character is more fundamental than rules and the human element is a key component of military capability. Selflessness, commitment and trust are mutually dependent on the covenant between the Army and its soldiers and dependants."

The Initial Training Group (ITG) comprised 5 widely dispersed Army Training Regiments (ATRs) for adult recruits, plus an Army Technical Foundation College (ATFC) and an Army Foundation College (AFC) for junior entrants. The ATRs were located at Glencorse, near Edinburgh, Bassingbourne near Cambridge, Lichfield, Pirbright and Winchester. The ATFC was at Arborfield near Reading and the AFC was at Harrogate, North Yorkshire. My small headquarters was at Upavon, co-located with the headquarters of the Army Training and Recruiting Agency commanded by my new boss. The ITG's role was to turn civilians into soldiers and prepare them for the next phase of their 'special to arm' training (Armoured, Infantry, Gunner, Sapper, Signals, Logistics, Medic, Royal Electrical and Mechanical Engineers, Army Air Corps, Adjutant General's Corps) that would be delivered elsewhere. The ATRA was a huge, complex organisation with an annual budget in excess of £700M; the ITG was its largest group with an operating budget of £80M, some 1400 military instructors plus 550 civilian staff and we trained around 15,000 recruits each year.

The adult recruits were all trained according to a common military syllabus that involved one week's induction plus 2 or more weeks further preparation before the 11-week course. This concentrated mostly on Skill at Arms, Fieldcraft, PT and Drill, but also covered Nuclear, Biological and Chemical Training, Map Reading, First Aid, Adventurous Training, Health and Hygiene, Military Education, Character Training, Financial Matters, Security, Military Law and Welfare. Before their arrival at one of the training regiments the recruits had all successfully passed a short one-day selection at a Recruit Selection Centre and so (in theory) should all have the potential to complete their training. However, there were wide variations in ability and aptitude and some recruits struggled, especially with basic fitness, and either gave up or became injured. The wastage rate, approaching 30%, was far too high. I was then given command of the 4 Recruit Selection Centres so we lengthened the selection process to 2 days, increased the tempo of selection and made it more fun. This helped enthuse the recruits, demonstrated that Army life was very much a team effort and gave them a sense of achievement that they brought with them when they later arrived at one of the training regiments. It also helped the selection staff identify more accurately those who were not ready for training; these were encouraged to try again once they had worked on their particular shortfall. We also raised the entry standard slightly in an attempt to achieve an optimum throughput during training, not simply a maximum input.

Another initiative, started by my predecessor, was setting up an Instructor Course for all military instructors in order that they understood the young recruits better. I made it mandatory for everyone and we all spent a few days at the Army Training Regiment at Lichfield undergoing some of the recruit basic tests and training, living just as recruits did in a barrack room and eating in the cookhouse. It was salutary for us to queue for meals, queue for a shower and have no control over one's own time, but it reminded us why many recruits found it a difficult adjustment and why it was important for instructors not to overrun a lesson (otherwise their section or platoon might then miss lunch), nor to add extra training to an already full programme. This induction was not just about living as a recruit but also included briefings on the delivery of lessons, employment legislation, drug abuse, bullying and discrimination. I and all the ITG officers and warrant officers attended, in addition to the senior and junior NCO instructors. The platoon commanders, platoon sergeants and section corporals then went on to complete a 2-week adventurous training course in Wales so that they would be qualified to lead basic adventurous training with their recruits. Most instructors appreciated the need for this induction training, but some resented it, because they assumed that they already knew all they needed to train soldiers. After all (in their eyes) they had been recruits themselves and so knew the form. Those individuals failed to understand that their young recruits did not suddenly become soldiers, they needed encouragement and time to make the mental adjustment from 'civilian to soldier'.

The Instructor Course and changes in recruit selection resulted in better pass rates but it was a never-ending challenge to minimise injury. There were some recruits who might walk further during their first week of training than perhaps they had during their whole previous year and it took time to build up their physical robustness. All recruits wore training shoes instead of boots for the first 5 weeks, which helped prevent knee and lower leg injuries. I inherited a raft of targets against which our performance was judged but many of these were meaningless 'box ticking' and so just 4 performance targets were then agreed with the ATRA which we monitored monthly: maintaining instructor staff fully qualified for their role; reducing wastage to the targets set by each regiment or corps; the percentage of students completing the course; the training injury rate. We did not always meet these targets, but they were relevant and kept us focused on the key issues.

Some years earlier the Army had disbanded the Junior Leader Regiments that had trained and educated younger recruits aged 16 plus, who then subsequently attended special to arm training before joining their units. Only one junior training unit had survived; the Army Apprentice College at Arborfield (subsequently retitled the Army Technical Foundation College), which trained young soldiers for specific trades in the Royal Engineers, the Royal Signals and the Royal and Electrical Mechanical Engineers. But the Army soon realised that it also needed a junior entry for the Infantry, Armoured Corps and the Gunners and so established a new Army Foundation College at Harrogate. It was an ambitious project funded through a Private Finance Initiative that involved lengthy and complex negotiations with the contractor (Jarvis). The approach to training of the younger recruits at Arborfield and Harrogate, compared to the adults in the 5 ATRs, was subtly different because they were not mature, but they very keen.

I was always impressed by my many visits to the five Training Regiments and two Foundation Colleges. The recruits were motivated; the instructors professional and well led by dedicated commanding officers and their officers, warrant officers and NCOs. The supporting staff played their part too, taking pride in their contribution and I felt fortunate with my small headquarters team, especially my Chief of Staff, Colonel John Ibbotson from the Parachute Regiment. Attending numerous pass-off parades, it was heart-warming to see how proud the respective families were of their sons, daughters, brothers, sisters and cousins who had completed their training and were moving on to their next stage of training. At one of the pass-offs, no less than 50 members of one family came to the parade! In my talk as the Inspecting Officer at these parades I often included a quote from Sir Arthur Bryant who wrote an article called '*The Fate of the Regiment*' in the Sunday Times soon after the Second World War. He wrote:

> "*The safety and honour of Britain depend on the character of her people. This is in turn depends on the institutions which form character. In war, it depends in particular on the military institutions which create the martial habits of discipline, courage, loyalty, pride and endurance.*" I would congratulate those passing off and add, "*By serving your Regiment or Corps and by developing your own individual skills and characters, you will be serving your country, your families and yourselves.*"

Ideally, the initial selection should have been more stringent, which would have cut wastage, and the training could have been more flexible to allow for injured recruits to take a little longer without having to drop out and start again. But there was always pressure on my budget; what was ideal was never affordable. I could not convince my boss to raise the entry standards because he was anxious about sufficient numbers (especially infantry recruits) entering training whereas I was only too well aware of the training drag caused by those individuals who were not ready and who invariably dropped out. Nevertheless, those who successfully completed the course were as good as their predecessors; in some cases better, because they were less deferential and so were less afraid to question issues that they did not understand, rather than blindly accepting everything they were told. Many of them went on to serve with great courage and distinction in Iraq, Afghanistan and elsewhere. The same fundamental training principles were as relevant to the treatment of recruits as to seasoned soldiers – and these were instilled into the officers and NCOs:

- *Teamwork. You have a team (your NCOs) and they will help you.*
- *Lead, don't follow; you set the example; expect and demand high standards.*
- *Treat recruits as you would wish to be treated.*
- *Decency, courtesy and manners are vital.*
- *"Talk to" rather than "talk at" your recruits.*
- *Listen!*
- *Your recruits will judge you just as critically as you judge them.*

On Friday 6th April 2001 I handed over the ITG, proud to have led a dedicated group who had worked hard to ensure that our recruits were as ready as possible for the next phase of their training. But it was concerning that the Infantry were planning to train their recruits separately from the rest of the Army, which might result in standards falling for some non-infantry recruits. I was worried about the other arms and services who were dependent on the 'infantry glue' to ensure that their basic military skills remained up to standard. In the event, when the changes took place a year after I had left, my fears proved unfounded.

Before searching for a civilian job, I went walking in the Pyrenees, where all I would have to think about for a few weeks was simply how to climb the next hill! Looking back on my time in the Army I realised how fortunate I had been to share such a variety of experiences with committed soldiers at many different levels. Military service is all about teamwork and the Sandhurst Motto 'Serve to Lead' rings very true.

My Chief of Staff and Commanding Officers in the Initial Training Group Back row (L to R) Lt Cols Paul Farrar, Jim Mitchell, David Greenwood, Jonathan Garnett Front row (L to R) Lt Col Huw Morgan, Col John Ibbotson, Me, Lt Cols Ian Condie, Richard Watson.

15

CHANGING STEP

I found a job in the early autumn of 2001 working for an Amey/ Bovis Lend Lease consortium (called Abraxis) who were bidding for a major Private and Public Partnership project to improve many of the Army's barracks in the south of England. The working and living accommodation in most of the different barracks was a disgrace, having had minimal investment for too long. Much of it needed to be demolished and rebuilt; some could be refurbished; additional buildings and infrastructure were required for units returning from Germany. I liked the Abraxis team who all had a genuine desire to improve soldiers' lives, but was not impressed with how the MOD organised the bidding process; it certainly was not a partnership but more a case of the MOD dictating events with ever-changing timelines and their contracts team were struggling with the scale of the project, valued at £4Bn over 30 years. There were, indeed, short-term benefits for the Army because the funding for the new buildings was being raised by industry, but the Army would then pay for the service charges throughout the contract's lifetime: catering, cleaning, security, maintenance, etc, and I was puzzled how such a deal would provide military cost-savings overall.

Any variations to the contract would incur extra charges and these were bound to happen over such a long-time scale. Abraxis were very professional, had a talented team and conceived a visionary plan, but the contract was eventually awarded as a Public Finance Initiative deal to our competing consortium in 2006, Aspire Defence Ltd (a joint venture between Carrillion and KBR), by which time its cost had apparently more than doubled! In 2018, Carillion was forced into compulsory liquidation and KBR assumed operational control of the Aspire Defence joint venture.

While working for Abraxis, I was approached to see if I would be interested in becoming the General Secretary of the Army and Combined Cadet Force Associations (ACFA and CCFA). I felt slightly guilty leaving the bid team after being with them for just a year; they had treated me well, but I knew I could offer more to the Cadet Movement. There were almost 45,000 cadets and over 8,000 adult volunteers in the 61 Army Cadet Force (ACF) units, with over 1700 detachments and just over 42,000 Combined Cadet Force (CCF) cadets and 2,100 CCF adults spread through 251 CCF Contingents. My role was to promote and represent both the ACF and CCF for the benefit of cadets and their adult volunteer instructors, but I first needed to overhaul the governance of both Associations. The role was very much 'Secretary' and not 'General'! I met many wonderful volunteers who were dedicated towards helping their cadets and became more and more impressed by the cadets' achievements. Both associations focused on non-military activities that included adventurous training, first aid, sport, music, vocational qualifications, the Duke of Edinburgh's award and competition shooting. Military activities were overseen by military instructors, not by us, and the MOD (especially the Army) provided nearly all the funding and overall supervision for the cadets.

We also ran an Outreach programme in the ACF where cadets acted as role models to youngsters who had been in a bit of trouble. The programme challenged and encouraged these youngsters and helped turn their lives around; they developed more confidence and self-esteem. Many of them had never before spent any time in the countryside, climbing a mountain, cooking their own meals, being part of a team or away from home for more than a day. The improvement in their behaviour and attitude after just a week on an Outreach course was remarkable and some of them ended up joining their local cadet force.

The office was in London, near Liverpool Street Station, and the commuting time from my home by train from Salisbury and then by tube from Waterloo was around two and a half-hours each way, which entailed leaving my house before 6am and returning around 9pm. I also attended cadet events on the odd evening, at weekends and a selection of cadet camps on the Army's training areas each summer, so was working long hours throughout the year. My daughter Anna was in London with the BBC and helped me find a small flat in Notting Hill, close to Hyde Park, which I bought with a substantial mortgage, but it saved me many hours of weekly travel and enabled me to treat Anna to supper each week in a friendly pub opposite the flat called the Mall Tavern. It was lovely to have a chance to keep in such close touch after all the years when we had seen little of each other while I had been away from home in the Army.

After working with the Cadet Movement for nearly 4 years and approaching 60 I felt that someone younger should take over. Lieutenant General John McColl who had ultimate responsibility for the ACF as Commander Regional Forces in Land Command, wrote: "I know from many that I've spoken to that the Cadet

Movement will be very sorry to see you go, as will I. You've given tremendous service – thank you." This was generous of him but the key influence on cadets has to be the quality of their volunteer adult instructors and realistic funding.

There was now more time to maintain a balance between family, work and interests. Determined to work only part-time from home and not commute anymore, I leased the London flat for a while before eventually selling it. Mary and I shared some delightful holidays together and she kept busy with her tourist guiding in and around Salisbury and being closely involved with village activities in Stratford Sub Castle. Very sadly she was later diagnosed with Parkinson's, which inevitably has an impact, but she determinedly remains positive and as active as possible. She follows a sensible fitness regime with walking, Pilates and a weekly exercise class run from Salisbury Hospital and is still the same cheerful, loving person she has always been. David is teaching History at Abingdon School and married to Liz with two lively daughters (Isla and Tess) who enjoy life to the full and are great fun. Anna moved to Bristol to join the BBC Natural History unit and has recently met Alex. They are happily living together and Anna's dog clearly also approves of Alex!

Having always been interested in leadership and team development I enrolled on two courses with the Coaching Academy, qualified as a Personal and Executive Coach and subsequently set up a small, part-time coaching business 'Aim and Achieve' for a few years. Most individuals who approached me for coaching only required some simple mental tools and procedures that they could use themselves and it was enjoyable helping them to find out how they could match their aspirations with their talents. I was also involved for a time as a trustee of the Institution of Royal Engineers and the Airborne Forces Museum, and on a panel at the Institution of Civil Engineers connected with the professional development of engineers. I became an independent member of the Wiltshire Council Standards Committee, but was frustrated by bureaucratic council procedures and resigned after only two years during a meeting where I said that we would be more effective with far less members. Needless to say, no one else followed me out of the door!

Supporting Help for Heroes, both by acting as a mentor for an ex-soldier and on a number of cycle rides with Team Sapper in aid of the charity has been humbling and also heart-warming. Our longest ride was from Berlin to London and the ex-9 Squadron officers in the team are referred to as 'The Crazy Gang'! I have also enjoyed cycling with David on some local sportive rides, although the hills became steeper as the years passed! Regrettably, a fall from a rope during the Commando Course that later resulted in arthritis in my back has curtailed running, but I have become keen on golf and thank Denis Aitken (Anna's godfather and a friend since Sandhurst) for sparking my interest in the game; I just wish I had taken it up earlier.

Trekking in the Alps, the Pyrenees and Ladakh, sometimes with David, has been an added bonus. The Lakadh trek, with Paddy Hughes, followed a trip to Kashmir in order to visit the Tyndale-Biscoe school, which my grandfather ran for over 50 years until 1947. There are now over 2,500 children at the school and his legacy is venerated. The School Principal, Parwez Kaul, mentioned that my grandparents lost a young son (called Donald) aged only two, soon after my mother was born, and we visited his grave. My mother had never mentioned Donald and I never knew about him until that day, but it explains why my second name is Donald – rather nostalgic. Before our return to the UK, Paddy and I spent a morning with the 4th Battalion of the 8th Gorkha Rifles

(4th/8th GR), stationed near Delhi airport and a sister battalion of the 2nd/8th GR, commanded by my father during the Second World War. 4th/8th GR is very proud of its heritage and we were warmly welcomed because of my father's connection. The letters in my book, "Four Brothers in Arms" written by my father, his three brothers and his parents about their experiences before, during and after the Second World War have touched many readers, portraying an unselfish fortitude typical of that generation. Mary and I have visited Italy to follow in the footsteps of my father and Uncle Jerry who were both in the Italian Campaign and it was moving to see where they fought and imagine what they must have endured. Even more poignant was my later visit to Burma (now Myanmar) to honour Uncle Malcolm who was killed near Imphal on 26th June 1944 and who is remembered on the Rangoon Memorial at the Commonwealth War Graves Cemetery at Taukkyan. The achievements of the 'Forgotten 14th Army' during the Second World War were extraordinary.

It is a blessing to have an active life, good friends and a loving family. Above all, I thank Mary for her unstinting support and her gentleness, understanding and love. Her constant encouragement for me and for the families of those who have served with me has always been treasured. She also played the major role in looking after David and Anna during my frequent absences from home and we value our precious bonds with them and our grandchildren.

David and Liz on their wedding day. With respective parents.

Just married!

Liz and Isla with Mary and Anna.

David and Anna enjoying some surfing in north Devon.

Mary on a coast walk in Dorset.

David and Liz with Isla and Tess on a beach in France.

With David in the Pyrenees at Breche de Roland.

Above the Ordessa Canyon with Ray Faull.

With John Ashcroft near the start of a trek in the Alps en route to the Aletsch Glacier.

On the Petersgat Ridge later in the trek.

Before setting off on a battlefield tour to Ypres with David.

Team Sapper at Dunkirk, after completing a cycle ride in aid of Help for Heroes.

The Tyndale-Biscoe School in Srinagar, Kashmir – Morning Assembly.

Pangong Lake, Ladakh – altitude 14,000 feet.

With Paddy Hughes at a mountain pass in the Sham Valley, Ladakh.

Above Temisgam Village with a view of the Zanskar mountains in the background.

View of Monte Cassino
Abbey from the Polish
War Cemetery.

The Gurkha War Cemetery
near Rimini. One hundred
and two soldiers from
2/8 Gurkha Rifles
(my father's battalion)
are buried there.

A plaque commemorating the Gaiana River Crossing in Italy in WW2; my
father's last battle.

The Rangoon Memorial at Taukkyan and Commonwealth War Graves Cemetery.

I'm pointing to my uncle Malcolm's name in the bottom picture.

Proud grandparents with Isla and Tess – Stonehenge in the background.

Celebration of our Golden Wedding on 5th September 2020. From left: Alex, Anna, Mary, Ian, Isla, Liz, Tess, David.